The
IRISH
BOARDING
HOUSE

BOOKS BY SANDY TAYLOR

The Runaway Children
The Little Orphan Girl
The Orphan's Daughter
The Irish Nanny

BRIGHTON GIRLS TRILOGY
When We Danced at the End of the Pier
The Girls from See Saw Lane
Counting Chimneys

SANDY TAYLOR

The
IRISH
BOARDING
HOUSE

Bookouture

Published by Bookouture in 2022

An imprint of Storyfire Ltd.
Carmelite House
50 Victoria Embankment
London EC4Y 0DZ

www.bookouture.com

ISBN: 978-1-80314-083-4
eBook ISBN: 978-1-80314-082-7

This book is a work of fiction. Names, characters, businesses, organisations,
places and events other than those clearly in the public domain, are either the
product of the author's imagination or are used fictitiously. Any resemblance
to actual persons, living or dead, events or locales is entirely coincidental.

To my keeper of dreams, my partner in crime. My minder, my nurse, my rock.
My very dearest friend, my Louie.

PART ONE

CHAPTER 1

Mary Kate Ryan knew all about being abandoned. Her own mother had given birth to her and immediately disappeared off the face of the earth, never to be seen or heard from again, leaving her in the care of her beloved grandparents, whom she had adored. They had been in their fifties when they had taken her in and they had cared for her as if she had been their own.

The small cottage in Tanners Row where Mary Kate had grown up had no luxuries like running water, this was collected from the pump at the end of the lane. But what the cottage lacked in comfort, it made up for in love and laughter. Mary Kate's mother, Agnes, had been her grandparents' only living child and it must have broken their hearts when she ran away. Yet they never had a bad word to say about her leaving, they spoke only of how beautiful and clever she had been and when they spoke of her, their eyes would fill with tears.

Her mother had left a note, saying only that she was sorry and asking them to think of her sometimes, as she would always think of them. 'Keep me in your prayers,' the note had said. 'And light a candle for me now and again.' There was no mention of Mary Kate, the baby she had left behind.

A faded black-and-white photograph of her mother as a child had stood on the mantlepiece, and beside it was the letter, yellowing as the years passed.

As her grandparents' health failed, Mary Kate took care of them and felt it was a privilege. Leaving school at twelve hadn't bothered her one bit – she hadn't made any close friends, she'd had no desire to be running the hills and lanes like the other girls. No, Mary Kate had responsibilities, she had neither the time nor the inclination to try to fit in.

She was thirty when they died, first her grandmother and then, shortly afterwards, her beloved grandfather, who had no desire to live in a world without the woman he loved by his side. Mary Kate had envied them, their complete and utter devotion to one another.

The night before he died, he'd taken her hands in his and asked her to promise him two things.

'Anything,' she'd said as the tears ran down her cheeks.

'When you leave here, I want you to go to the post office and set up a box number, where you can collect your letters.'

'But I've never had a letter in all my life,' she'd said. 'Who would be writing to me?'

'Well, that's not for us to know, but you'll never get one if no one has a clue where you are. Do you want people to be tearing around the whole of Ireland trying to locate you?'

Mary Kate hadn't been able to think of anyone who would be tearing around Ireland on her account but as he'd seemed to be so set on the idea, she had agreed.

'And secondly,' he'd continued, 'at the beginning of each New Year, I want you to buy yourself a diary.'

She'd been beginning to think that, being so close to death, he was losing his mind, but she'd gone along with it. She'd stroked his hand; it was bony and gnarled with age, the hand of a man who had laboured hard all his life. 'Why would I have the need of a diary, Grandad?'

'To keep account of your life, Mary Kate, to mark your red-letter days, to gain wisdom from your failures and take pride in your successes. Never throw them away, but read them now and again, for they will remind you of how far you have come.'

She'd nodded but she had known there would be nothing ahead of her that would be worth setting down in a diary. She had neither her mother's beauty, nor her grandfather's wisdom. Her life had already passed her by, there would be no red-letter days for her.

The cottage on Tanners Row had been rented and when her grandfather died, Mary Kate had been turned out of the only home she had ever known. But her grandfather had always said that no good ever came of living in the past, best to cut all ties with it and move on.

The day she left, Mary Kate looked around the cottage where she had been so happy. There was little of any value in it. The table was scratched and burned from the hot pans of stew that her grandmother would place in front of them. Her grandfather's chair by the fire had seen better days, the arms were shiny with age and the material was ripped and torn. She closed her eyes and imagined him sitting there, puffing away on his pipe and rattling the peat in the hearth with his stick. How could she leave this place that held so many happy memories? What would become of her?

She took down the picture of the Sacred Heart, where it had hung for so many years, smiling down at her, leaving behind the outline of the frame on the whitewashed wall. Mary Kate carried it next door to her neighbour.

Mrs Finn answered the door and shook her head when she saw Mary Kate standing on the doorstep. 'This is a sad day,' she said. 'For you will be sorely missed and may God forgive me but I hope that landlord, sitting in his fine house in England, rots in Hell for turning you out into the street. He's a boil on the arse of life, so he is.'

A boil on the arse of life? Oh, that was funny, it was. She hadn't expected to be smiling this day.

'And it could happen to any one of us, Mary Kate, for he owns every cottage in the lane and the man has a swinging brick in the place of a heart.'

'Then we should feel sorry for him, Mrs Finn. For all his wealth, he will never know the love of God or the company of true friendship.'

'Indeed he won't. Now, what is it you have there?'

'It's my grandmother's picture of the Sacred Heart and I can't bear to leave it hanging on the wall. It would give me great pleasure, Mrs Finn, if you would take it.'

'That's awful kind of you, girl, but I can't take it from you.'

'Oh.'

'But what I will do is mind it until you have your own wall to hang it on.'

The tears that Mary Kate had been holding back all morning burst out of her and she could hardly breathe. Mrs Finn took her into her arms and Mary Kate sobbed into her ample bosom.

'You're a strong girl, Mary Kate, and a kind one, and I will pray every night that life will be good to you. I don't have much but I want you to know that you will always have a home here.'

'Oh, Mrs Finn, I will miss you.'

'Let me have your address when you are settled.'

'I will, goodbye.'

'Goodbye, love, and may God go with you.'

Mary Kate returned to the cottage, picked up her case and looked around one last time at the little room that held so many memories. The only thing she took with her was the photograph of her mother and the letter. She tucked them into her coat pocket, closed the door and walked away, without a backward glance.

CHAPTER 2

DUBLIN, NEW YEAR'S EVE, 1951

Fifteen years had passed since Mary Kate had left Tanners Row. She had moved from boarding house to boarding house, each one worse than the last, with their lists of rules pinned up behind the bedroom door and not a scrap of comfort to be had. Hard-faced landlords and landladies, with their hands out every Friday for the rent and sour-faced girls serving up barely edible food. Every move held a tiny bit of hope, that the next house would offer some comfort, might even feel like a home, but it was never to be.

She kept the promise she had made to her grandfather and set up a box number at the post office. Once a month, she called in to check for the letter she knew would never come and at the start of each new year, she bought a diary that was never even opened.

It was New Year's Eve and Mary Kate stood in Merrion Square, staring across at a tall Georgian house with a 'for sale' sign stuck in one of the downstairs windows. The square was beautiful and this house must have been beautiful once too, but now it looked abandoned and unloved, its glory days lost in the passing of time. It was made of red brick and was four storeys high. Stone steps, bordered by rusty and broken railings, led up to the wide front door with paint so peeled and scratched it was hard to tell what colour it might have originally been. The elegant stone pillars that surrounded the door had turned black with age and neglect.

She'd spent Christmas day alone in her room, thinking of Christmases long ago, spent with her beloved grandparents. There had been very little money for gifts but herself and her grandfather would walk out to the woods and collect holly, laden with big, fat red berries to decorate their little cottage. They'd go to midnight Mass and sing the age-old carols, then light a candle at the foot of the nativity scene. As a child she had loved walking home in the dark, under a sky filled with stars, for that was how she remembered it, that was how she would always remember it, a sky full of stars.

She had never felt more alone in her life, for the year ahead held nothing for her except misery. What was the point of this life of hers? Was this it? Was there never to be any hope? She could think of no reason to be here at all. Wouldn't it be better all-round to just jump off O'Connell Bridge and be done with it? There would be no one to mourn her passing and not a single soul to light a candle in her memory.

Once this thought had come into Mary Kate's head, a feeling of peace came over her. No more horrible boarding houses, no more rotten jobs, she could put an end to this whole sorry mess that was masquerading as a life. This was a way out and she wondered why she had never thought of it before. She could be with her grandparents; someone would love her again.

That night she slept better than she had in a long time and when she woke it was with hope in her heart. The only thing she was taking with her was the photograph of her mother and the letter. She certainly wasn't going to leave them behind for her landlady Mrs Gibb to get her dirty hands on.

Mary Kate left the house and started hurrying towards the bridge. As she passed the post office, she heard someone calling her name. She turned around to see the owner running towards her. He had a big grin on his face and he was waving a letter.

She had been visiting his shop every month for the past fifteen years and for the past fifteen years the answer had always been the same. 'Sorry, Miss Ryan, nothing this time, maybe next month with the help of God.'

Well, God hadn't been much help over the years, had He? Why did He have to start now, when she had a plan?

She felt cross. It was too late for a letter. What good would a letter do her now? It would only end up floating away down the Liffey, with her following in its wake.

'Do you want to come into the shop and read it?' said the shopkeeper.

He looked terribly excited for her, so she smiled at him.

'I'll read it at home, but thank you.'

'I hope it's the news you've been waiting for, Miss Ryan.'

Had she been waiting for news? She didn't think so. She'd just felt she owed it to her grandfather to fulfil his dying wishes.

She walked slowly back to the boarding house in Ginnetts Row, ran up the stairs and sat on the hard bed. She didn't take off her coat, as it was freezing in the room. She stared for a long time at the letter in her hand. The writing was beautiful, the i's topped with complete circles. Above the address was written, 'Renson and Renson, Esquires, Solicitors'. Her hand was shaking as she opened the envelope and started to read. This was the moment her life changed; when her mother had remembered the baby she had left behind. This was Mary Kate Ryan's red-letter day.

CHAPTER 3

The next morning, Mary Kate was standing outside the solicitors' office. There was a brass plate beside the front door that read, 'Renson and Renson'. She wished she was better dressed but she only had the one coat, so it would have to do. She took a deep breath, smoothed down her hair and walked up the steps and through the ornate doors.

She could feel her shoes sinking into the beautiful gold carpet as she walked towards the desk. She felt out of place; she knew she didn't belong there and wouldn't have been surprised if at any minute the Garda grabbed her by the collar and dragged her out into the street. But the young girl in front of her smiled, and it was such a sweet smile it brought a lump to her throat – she wasn't used to such sweetness.

'Do you have an appointment?' the girl asked.

Mary Kate could feel her face going red. 'I didn't know I needed one, I'm sorry.'

The girl smiled again. 'It's no problem. Were you wanting to see one of our solicitors?'

Mary Kate nodded and handed her the letter.

The girl looked at the letter and beamed. 'Oh, Miss Ryan,' she said. 'We have been expecting you.'

'You have?'

'Oh yes. Young Mr Renson said that when you came in, I was to spoil you rotten.'

'He did?'

'Yes, Miss Ryan, he did.'

Mary Kate could feel her eyes filling with tears, this was almost too much.

The young girl came around the desk and put her arms around her. 'Oh, Miss Ryan, you'll start me off. Here, take my hankie.'

The hankie she gave her was pure white, with the letter 'J' embroidered in the corner.

'Oh, I can't take this,' she said.

'Of course you can. I was told to spoil you and I can make a start by giving you my hankie.'

'It's awful good of you. What does the "J" stand for?'

'Jenny, well, Jennifer, but that's a bit of a mouthful, don't you think?'

Just then a woman came into the hallway. She was no more than five feet high and as wide as she was long. She smiled. 'I just heard you talking, Jenny, is this herself?'

Jenny nodded. 'Duffy, it is my absolute pleasure to introduce you to Miss Mary Kate Ryan.'

The woman grabbed Mary Kate's hand and shook it so hard she thought she was going to pull it clean out of its socket. 'I'm that pleased to meet you, Miss Ryan, I am that. We've been waiting for you, 'aven't we, Jenny? Thought you'd never get 'ere.'

Mary Kate smiled at her. 'Does everyone know about my visit? I only found out myself yesterday.'

'Well, news travels fast in this place. Now don't get me wrong, we're not nosey.'

'Oh no, we're not nosey,' said Jenny. 'In fact, outside these doors, we are sworn to secrecy but inside...'

'We take an interest,' said Duffy, grinning.

'Yes, I think that just about sums it up,' said Jenny. 'We take an interest.'

'But only in the special ones,' added Duffy.

'And you, Miss Ryan, are special,' said Jenny.

Mary Kate couldn't understand why she was suddenly so special; she'd never been special in all her life.

'Shall I get you some water?' said Duffy. 'For the shock.'

'She hasn't had a shock,' said Jenny. 'She hasn't seen Mr Renson yet.'

'Oh, there I go,' said Duffy. 'My mouth has a habit of running away with me.'

Mary Kate laughed. 'You're not Irish, are you?'

'I'm from the Black Country, Miss Ryan. That's in England.'

'And what brought you to Dublin?'

'My husband, Frankie. He swept me off me feet at the Palais ballroom in Birmingham and whisked me off to Ireland, like a knight in shining armour.'

Mary Kate smiled. 'That's desperate romantic.'

'The armour's a bit on the rusty side now, but he's still got a twinkle in his eye. Oh, I do wish my late husband could meet you, Miss Ryan.'

'I'm sorry for your loss,' she said.

Duffy laughed, till the tears were rolling down her cheeks. 'Bless you, no, he's not dead, he's *late* and you'll probably be gone by the time he gets here. Well, I'd best get on and oh, it's been lovely meeting you.'

'It's been lovely meeting you too.'

'Now, sit yourself down,' said Jenny. 'I'll let Mr Renson know you are here.' As she walked away, she looked back. 'He is going to be delighted.'

Mary Kate sank into the green velvet chair. She felt like laughing; she could feel it bubbling up inside her and it was such an unusual feeling that it caught her off guard. She tried to work out what the feeling was and the word that came to her was *hope*.

It was only yesterday that she'd been dead set on jumping off the bridge and floating away down the Liffey and now here she was, sitting in this beautiful velvet chair, holding a white hankie with the letter 'J' embroidered in the corner and, what's more, she'd been expected – more than expected, she'd been welcomed.

She stood up as a tall gentleman came striding into the lobby, his hand outstretched as he approached her.

'James Renson,' he said, smiling. 'This is indeed a pleasure, an absolute pleasure, wouldn't you say, Jenny?'

'Oh, I would, Mr Renson.'

'And have you been looked after by our girl here?'

'I have, she gave me her hankie, which I have every intention of washing and returning.'

'There's no need for that, Miss Ryan, please keep it.'

Mary Kate put the hankie in her coat pocket. 'Thank you, Jenny.'

'You are very welcome, Miss Ryan.'

Mr Renson smiled at Mary Kate; he had a lovely smile. 'Come into my office, Miss Ryan. You and I have a lot to talk about.'

CHAPTER 4

The room they entered was large. One wall was completely taken up with bookshelves that stretched almost to the ceiling. Mary Kate had never seen so many books in her life. She was surprised that they weren't in tidy rows but instead sat higgledy-piggledy on the shelves, leaning into each other as if they were old friends, tall ones were next to small ones, fat ones next to thin ones – somehow it made her feel less nervous, although she couldn't say exactly why. There was a lovely wooden desk covered in papers and the long windows were framed with beautiful grey velvet curtains. It was the nicest room she had ever seen.

Mr Renson motioned for her to sit down and he took the chair facing her. She placed her hands in her lap and waited.

He shuffled some papers and then looked up at her. 'Where to start,' he said, smiling. 'Where to start...'

'You said in your letter that it concerned my mother,' she said. 'Does she want to see me?'

Mr Renson paused. 'I'm sorry to have to tell you, Miss Ryan, that your mother has passed away.'

Mary Kate's eyes filled with tears. 'When?'

Mr Renson shook his head. 'I'm afraid that I don't know. I haven't been given much information about your mother at all. I wish I could tell you more.'

Mary Kate didn't know how to feel; it was hard to mourn someone she had never met but she felt a pain in her heart for the mother she had never known and, now, never would. 'Is that why you wanted to see me? To tell me that my mother is dead?'

'And a lot more besides.'

'Did she have children? Have I any brothers or sisters?'

'As far as I can tell she never married, the only child she gave birth to was yourself.'

Mary Kate felt sad. It would have been nice to have had a brother or sister, someone to call her own.

'That is why, Miss Ryan, she left her entire estate to you. You are her only living blood relative and therefore everything she owned comes to you.'

'She remembered me?'

He looked down at the papers in front of him, and hesitated. 'She did,' he said.

'That's nice, isn't it?'

'It is indeed, Miss Ryan, it is indeed.'

'And you say that she left me something?' It would be lovely if she had perhaps left her a ring, or maybe a necklace; it would be something to remember her by.

'Your mother had a very impressive portfolio, Miss Ryan.'

Mary Kate could feel sweat breaking out under her armpits. 'What in God's name is a portfolio?'

'Property. She owned a large number of houses, Miss Ryan, in some of London's most prestigious locations.'

'My mother lived in London?'

'She did.'

'And she had houses?'

'She did.'

'But what am I to do with them, Mr Renson? I'm not a busi-

nesswoman. Isn't there someone else she could have left
them to?'

James Renson threw his head back and laughed. 'You are a
breath of fresh air, Miss Ryan. A breath of fresh air. If you give
us instructions to sell them, we can do that for you, but I would
suggest that you keep at least one of them.'

'What would I be wanting with a house in London?'

'You may want to visit the city one day. And wouldn't it be
convenient to have a house there?' He put his head to the side
and smiled. 'Miss Ryan, have you fully understood what I have
been saying?'

She nodded. 'You're telling me that I have a load of houses
in London that I have no need of.'

'What I am telling you, Miss Ryan, is that you are now a
very wealthy woman, and you can buy whatever your heart
desires.'

Mary Kate sat quietly, letting it all sink in. She was rich.
Her life would never be the same again, and wasn't that what
she had wanted? A better life than she had now?

'May I enquire where you are staying at the moment?' said
Mr Renson.

'In Ginnetts Row, down by the docks.'

'Is that Mrs Gibb's place?'

Mary Kate nodded. 'Do you know her?'

'Yes, I have had that unfortunate experience. Just the once,
but that was enough.'

'She's an awful baggage of a woman, Mr Renson.'

He grinned. 'I couldn't have described her better myself.'

'But I suppose she's no better, or worse than the rest of
them.'

'Can I make a suggestion?'

'You can, of course.'

'What I suggest, my dear Miss Ryan, is that you move out
immediately.'

'Immediately?'

'In fact, I would strongly advise that you move out today.'

'And live where? They're all the same.'

'I can highly recommend the Shelbourne hotel; I've stayed there myself and it's a charming place. I think that it would suit you very well. In fact, why don't we go the whole hog and book a suite of rooms?'

Mary Kate started laughing and then, to her horror, the laughter turned to tears and she was sobbing.

'Oh, dear,' said Mr Renson, coming around the desk. 'This has all been too much for you, hasn't it? My wife, Erin, would say I barged in like a bull, when the situation needed a delicate touch. I'm so sorry.'

She couldn't speak, she couldn't stop crying, it was as if all the sadness she had bottled up for the past fifteen years had come flooding out. She was crying for the loss of her grandparents, she was crying for the little cottage, for every lousy boarding house she had stayed in and every rotten job she had been forced to take but, most of all, she was crying for all those lonely years, when she had neither kith nor kin to love her. She was crying for herself, she was crying for Mary Kate Ryan.

Mr Renson rang a bell on the desk. 'I think we need Jenny,' he said.

'Oh, Miss Ryan,' said Jenny, running into the room. 'Has the great man been upsetting you?'

'I think I came on a bit strong, Jenny. I suggested that she moved into the Shelbourne. In fact, I suggested a suite of rooms.'

Jenny knelt in front of Mary Kate and held her hands. 'Well, I agree with Mr Renson, for no one would fit into the Shelbourne more than yourself. Now, I shall make you a grand cup of tea and put a drop of brandy in it, for the shock?'

'Good idea, Jenny,' said Mr Renson.

Mary Kate took a deep breath and dried her eyes on Jenny's lovely hankie. 'You have all been so kind.'

Jenny put a hand on her shoulder and left the room.

'Am I really that rich?' she said.

'You are and I am delighted for you. We are *all* delighted for you. Now, the only thing for you to think about is how you want to spend it.'

As she sat there, she pictured the beautiful old house in Merrion Square and an idea began to form in her mind. An idea that was so ridiculous and so delicious, it made her smile. 'I know exactly how I want to spend it, Mr Renson.'

'You do?'

'Yes. I want to buy a house that is for sale in Merrion Square and I want to turn it into a boarding house for single ladies.'

CHAPTER 5

When Mary Kate woke the next morning, she smiled. It hadn't been a dream; her life really was about to change. She was filled with hope and for the first time in so many years she was looking forward to the day ahead. She snuggled down into the soft quilt that covered the big bed; no more hard, scratchy blankets, no more stained pillows and definitely no more bed bugs.

She felt like crying again, but they would be tears of happiness. She shuddered when she thought about what could have been if the postman hadn't run out with the letter. She liked to think that her beloved grandparents had had a hand in it. She could almost hear her grandfather saying, 'Don't give up, Mary Kate. We will meet again one day but not yet, not today. Today is for living, today is the first day of the rest of your life, today is your red-letter day.'

She pulled herself up in the bed and looked around the beautiful room. The walls were of the palest yellow and the snowy-white curtains drifted into the room, like a ship in full sail.

She was still trying to get her head around all that had happened in such a short time.

She laughed as she remembered her encounter with Mrs Gibb. Oh, she would live on it for years, she would, she would live on it for years.

Mr Renson had insisted he drive her to the boarding house to collect her things. As they'd stopped outside number seven, Ginnetts Row, he'd said, 'Do you want me to come in with you?'

'No thank you, Mr Renson, I think I may enjoy this.'

He'd grinned. 'I have no doubt about that at all, Miss Ryan, but if you do need a little moral support I will be right here.'

She'd taken the key out of her pocket but before she could let herself in, Mrs Gibb was at the door, her mean little eyes out on two stalks, staring at the car. She'd folded her arms over her dirty pinny and glared at her.

'Well, Miss Ryan, and who might you be canoodling with? Swanning about in a grand car for all the world to see. Have you no shame, woman?'

'I don't think that who I canoodle with has anything at all to do with you, Mrs Gibb. In fact, if I have a mind to canoodle, I shall.'

'It has everything to do with me, you brazen huzzy. It's my house that you are residing in and I have a reputation to keep up.'

'You have a reputation all right,' said Mary Kate. 'A reputation for keeping a filthy house that is overrun with bed bugs. A reputation for meanness and idleness. Oh, you have a reputation all right, but not one that I would wish on myself.'

'Well then, I suggest you move out right this minute. In fact, I insist on it. But you won't find anything better in the whole of Dublin.'

'I very much doubt that, Mrs Gibb. And, as it happens, I am already settled.'

Mrs Gibb had sneered at her, her thin lips seeming to disappear into a gaping hole full of blackened and broken teeth. 'And where is Miss High and Mighty lodging this night? Is it with yer fancy feller behind the wheel?'

'Well, as you seem so concerned about where I am going to be laying my head tonight, I am happy to tell you that I shall be staying at the Shelbourne hotel. In fact, I shall have a suite of rooms. I have merely popped by to collect my things.'

Mrs Gibb's face went a kind of ashen colour, and it was clear that she didn't know what to believe. She'd quickly pulled herself together and moved closer to Mary Kate, so close that Mary Kate could smell her fetid breath.

'A liar as well as a fallen woman,' she'd hissed. 'Well, don't think that I am going to let you in to collect your belongings. We have a contract, you and I, or have you conveniently forgotten that little thing? A month's notice to quit.'

'I think the best person to speak to about a contract, Mrs Gibb, would be my solicitor, who is waiting outside in the car. I'm sure he would be very interested to hear that you have been slandering his good name, by calling him my fancy man. Besides, I haven't given notice, it was your good self that told me to get out. Now I might not know much about the law, but I'd say that makes your little contract null and void. Now please step out of my way.'

Mrs Gibb had reluctantly stepped aside, leaving just enough room for Mary Kate to squeeze past. Mary Kate's heart was beating out of her chest as she ran up the two flights of stairs. Had she really stood up to Mrs Gibb like that? Did having a bit of money in your pocket make you so much braver? She'd looked around the drab room with its filthy windows, the green mildew running down the walls and the stained bedding. She didn't take any clothes, just the empty diaries, the photo of her mother and the letter.

She'd run back down the stairs and pushed past Mrs Gibb. Mr Renson was standing by the car and made a great show of opening the rear door and helping her in.

'The Shelbourne, madam?' he'd said, loud enough for Mrs Gibb to hear.

As they pulled away from the kerb, Mary Kate heard the door slam, loud enough to have shaken the house to its timbers.

'I'm sensing that your little meeting with the gruesome Mrs Gibb was to your liking?' said Mr Renson.

'I said everything you told me to say. I couldn't believe the swanky words that came out of my mouth. I sounded like a proper person.'

Mr Renson had stopped the car and turned around. 'Oh, Miss Ryan,' he'd said. 'You are the most proper person I have ever met.'

Oh, he was nice, he was, he was nice. She'd settled back into the leather seat and watched as Ginnetts Row disappeared behind them. What was it she'd said? Oh yes, 'If I have a mind to canoodle, I shall.' She couldn't remember the last time she had had so much fun and had started to giggle.

And now here she was in this beautiful room, as far away from Ginnetts Row as it was possible to be. She got out of bed and her bare feet sank into the soft rug, she wiggled her toes and smiled.

Hanging on the wardrobe door was a white dressing gown and on the floor a pair of matching slippers. She put on the gown and marvelled at the way the soft fabric wrapped around her body like a cloud of silk. She slipped her feet into the slippers and walked across to the long window. The Shelbourne hotel was opposite St Stephen's Green, the beautiful park in the centre of the city. If this was all a dream, she never wanted to wake from it.

Once again, she thanked God for intervening on her behalf, before she'd dived headfirst into the Liffey.

CHAPTER 6

Mary Kate had walked past Clerys department store many times. She loved looking at the beautiful clothes on display in the six long windows that spanned the front of the six-storey building but she had never had the courage to venture through its doors. Clerys wasn't for the likes of her but you didn't have to be rich to admire the fashionable clothes on the models. She had often looked at the beautiful green clock on the wall as she'd hurried past it on her way to work. The clock had two faces, so whichever direction you happened to be coming from, you could see the time.

'Ready?' said Jenny.

Mary Kate took a deep breath. 'As ready as I'll ever be.'

'Aren't you just a tiny bit excited?'

'Are you sure they'll let me in?'

'If there is one thing I've learned since working for Mr Renson, it's that money talks. If you were a tramp off the street and smelled like a dog's dinner but had the money in your hand, they would welcome you with open arms. Besides,' said Jenny, grinning, 'we have an appointment.'

'Does everyone who shops in Clerys have an appointment?'

Jenny slipped her arm through hers and smiled. 'Only the special ones, Miss Ryan.'

'So, money makes you special?'

'I'd say you would be special, with or without the money. Now, straighten those shoulders, we're going in.'

Mary Kate couldn't believe the size of the place as they walked through the wide doors. She stood still and gazed in front of her at the beautiful sweeping staircase that rose upwards to the balcony on the floor above. Women were browsing the goods on sale and fingering the beautiful materials on the shiny glass counters. Others were holding clothes up against them and moving this way and that in front of the mirrors. Assistants in smart clothes stood quietly, ready to help. Mary Kate wanted to dig a large hole and bury herself in it, but Jenny was striding towards the reception desk and she had no option but to follow her.

'We have an appointment,' she said to the young girl. 'Miss Ryan, eleven o'clock.'

The girl opened a large book and ran her finger down the page. 'Ah yes. You will be seeing Miss Pring. Please take a seat and I'll let her know you are here.'

'I'm feeling a bit sick, Jenny. I don't want to be making an eejit of myself.'

Jenny squeezed her arm. 'Don't we all make eejits of ourselves at some time in our lives? I've made an eejit of myself more times than I can say, but I'm still here, aren't I?'

Mary Kate smiled at her. 'And I'm awful glad you are.'

The woman walking towards them was tall. She was wearing a severe black suit and her hair was pulled back into a bun that sat on the top of her head and made her look even taller, as did the spiky heels she was wearing. *God love her, her feet must be hanging off her by the end of the day.*

'Miss Ryan?' she said, holding her hand out towards Jenny and smiling a tight smile that didn't quite reach her eyes.

'No,' said Jenny, gesturing towards Mary Kate, 'this is Miss Ryan.'

You could see the woman's face change, as she looked Mary Kate up and down. Mary Kate could feel herself shrinking under the woman's gaze. This Miss Pring knew that she was an imposter, of course she did. The lovely feeling she had woken up with was gone, she was the same nobody as she had been yesterday and the woman could see it.

'Before we go any further,' said Jenny, 'I would like to see the manager.'

'And may I ask why?' said the woman.

'I would be obliged if you would just fetch the manager,' said Jenny, ignoring her question.

'I shall need to tell him why he is wanted.'

Jenny stared at her. 'We'll wait here while you get him.'

The woman strode away, her spiky high heels tapping on the floor.

Mary Kate looked at Jenny in awe. 'You have a great way with the words.'

'Never let anyone intimidate you, Miss Ryan, or make you feel as if you are not good enough. My mother always says that the problem is theirs, not yours.'

'That woman scares the bejabbers out of me, Jenny.'

'She'd scare the bejabbers out of the Pope himself.'

'I think I'd rather just go home.'

'And let that baggage spoil our day? I think not. There's a rail of clothes over there, Miss Ryan, why don't you have a look through them, get a feel for what you might like, while I have a quiet word with the manager?'

Mary Kate hesitated but walked across to the rail of clothes, wishing she was anywhere but there.

Jenny didn't have to wait long, as a man hurried towards her, followed by Miss Pring, trying to keep up with him in her high heels.

'I believe you were wanting to see me Miss... umm?'

'Conrad, Jennifer Conrad.'

He held out his hand. 'Mr Walsh. Now how can I help you?'

Jenny didn't say anything but stared very pointedly at Miss Pring.

Mr Walsh noticed. 'You can leave us now, Miss Pring,' he said.

A red rash was creeping up Miss Pring's skinny neck. Mary Kate could tell she was only bursting with anger, but she had the good sense to nod and walk away.

'Mr Walsh,' said Jenny, 'I am here with my friend, Miss Ryan. She's over there, looking through the clothes.'

'And what's the problem?'

'Miss Ryan deserves the best treatment that Clerys can offer. She has had a piece of good fortune and she intends to spend a large amount of it in this shop but not, I'm afraid, under the guidance of your Miss Pring. I'm sure she is very efficient but efficiency is not what is needed this day. What is needed is kindness and a bit of fun, someone who can make Miss Ryan feel special, someone who will treat her like the lady she is and, I'm afraid, Mr Walsh, if we can't find that here, we will quite happily go elsewhere. I'm sure there are plenty of other establishments in Dublin who will be only too glad to relieve Miss Ryan of her money.'

The manager shook his head. 'Oh dear, Miss Conrad, I am so sorry that this has been your unfortunate experience in our store and I can only apologise and hopefully make amends.'

'I'd appreciate that.'

He smiled. 'I know just the person for the job.'

'You do?'

'I do. And when you are finished, I would like to offer yourself and Miss Ryan afternoon tea in our restaurant. Eat as much as you like, it's the least that Clerys can do. I wish you an amazing and special morning in our store and if you need anything else, I shall come running.'

Jenny smiled and shook his hand. He was nice, he was, he was nice. 'Miss Ryan and I would be delighted and thank you.'

'Now, ladies, if you would like to follow me. From this moment on I can assure you that yourself and your friend will be treated like royalty.'

Jenny laughed. 'I think that would frighten her even more than Miss Pring already has. Just a bit of kindness, Mr Walsh, and a small slice of humanity.'

'That we can do.'

They followed him up the beautiful staircase and were taken into a private salon.

'Please make yourselves comfortable,' he said, 'while I fetch the lady I have in mind and, again, I can only apologise on behalf of Clerys for your less-than-happy experience with us. I can assure you that is all about to change.'

The salon was lovely, with low lighting that bathed the cosy room in a soft golden light that reflected in the ornate mirrors that hung on the walls. They sat side by side on the pale-yellow sofa and Mary Kate started to giggle, which set Jenny off. They were still giggling when a woman opened the door and came into the room.

She was everything that Miss Pring wasn't. Her face had a softness about it and when she smiled, Jenny knew that Mr Walsh had chosen the right person for the job.

'Well now, isn't that a lovely sound?' she said, smiling. 'I could hear you laughing from halfway up the stairs.'

'I think it's nerves,' said Mary Kate, drying her eyes.

'Well, there is no need for nerves here, Miss Ryan. You and I are about to have the time of our lives, or as my dear departed mammy used to say, we're about to have a ding dong of a morning.' My name is Mrs Catherine Leamy and I am at your service. Shall we make a start?'

'Oh, let's,' said Mary Kate, grinning.

'May I ask what budget you had in mind?'

Mary Kate looked at Jenny.

'There is no budget, Mrs Leamy, the sky's the limit. She is to have whatever her heart desires and more, much, much more.'

Mrs Leamy took a tape out of her pocket and started measuring Mary Kate from head to toe, then began running up and down the stairs, laden with clothes. Blouses and skirts, dresses and cardigans, hats and coats and bags and shoes, all of them in the most beautiful shades of pinks and blues, lemons and greens. By the time they had finished Mary Kate wondered if there were any clothes left in the shop. It had been the most wonderful morning and one that she would never forget.

Jenny had picked up a woollen scarf in a pale mauve and thrown it around her neck, then pranced up and down the room, like a model, making them laugh.

'It suits you,' said Mary Kate.

'Pure cashmere,' said Mrs Leamy. 'Isn't it lovely?'

'Please wrap the scarf separately,' whispered Mary Kate.

Mrs Leamy winked at her.

'Thank you for everything,' said Jenny.

'You have made this day so special,' said Mary Kate.

Mrs Leamy smiled at her. 'No, Miss Ryan, it is you, who have made this day special.'

'Can I give you a hug? Is that allowed?' said Mary Kate.

'Yes, please,' said Mrs Leamy, moving towards her and wrapping her in her arms. She smelled of Devon Violets, the talcum powder Mary Kate's grandmother used to wear.

There were tears in both their eyes as they moved apart.

'I'll not forget this day, Mrs Leamy, and I'll not forget you.'

'And I will not forget you,' said Mrs Leamy, smiling.

Mary Kate and Jenny finished the day eating sandwiches, pastries, and warm scones and jam in the restaurant.

'There is one more thing I need to buy, Jenny,' said Mary Kate.

'Do you want me to get Mrs Leamy back?'

'It's not clothes I'm wanting, I've enough here to last me till the end of my days.'

'What then?'

'A new diary.'

'A diary?' said Jenny.

'Yes, a diary. For if ever there has been a red-letter day, then this is surely it.'

CHAPTER 7

The next morning, boxes and boxes full of the beautiful clothes were delivered to the Shelbourne hotel. By the time Mary Kate had finished her breakfast, they had all been hung up in the vast wardrobe. After going through them all, she settled on a pale-blue woollen dress and beautiful cream coat, then draped a navy scarf around her shoulders, just as Mrs Leamy had suggested. She finished off the outfit with a navy leather handbag and matching shoes.

There was a spring in her step as she made her way to the department store. She couldn't help looking at her reflection in the shop windows as she passed. Was that really her? Was she really that woman who strode along with her head held high, as if she were someone? As if she fitted in with the best of them. Could that really be Mary Kate Ryan from Tanners Row? What would her grandparents have said if they saw her now? What would they have thought? That she'd forgotten her station in life? That she'd forgotten where she came from? No, they'd be laughing their heads off and dancing round the room, that's what they'd be doing. Oh, they'd be happy for her, they would.

She reached Clerys and, with not an ounce of hesitation, walked up the steps and through the doors. People smiled at her, the way they hadn't smiled at her the day before. She was the same person inside, the clothes hadn't changed who she was, but they had changed the way people viewed her – and that made her feel sad. Shouldn't everyone be judged on their kindness? Shouldn't everyone be judged by the qualities that made them good honest people? She supposed not. The world must be full of those who hid their true natures beneath silk and satin. It made her feel better to think it wasn't going to do them much good when they stood in front of Saint Peter at the pearly gates. He would see through all the finery to the sins that lay beneath.

Mary Kate walked across to the reception desk. The young girl recognised her and smiled. 'How lovely to see you again, Miss Ryan.'

'I have an appointment,' said Mary Kate, 'with a stylist. I'm to have my hair cut.'

'Well, you have lovely hair,' said the girl. 'I'd only die for waves like yours. I'm demented trying to get a bit of a curl out of mine.'

Mary Kate looked at the young girl with her shiny straight hair that swung gently against her cheek as she moved her head. 'Well, if I had hair like yours, I'd be down on my knees thanking the good Lord for seeing fit to give it to me.'

'I suppose we all want what we can't have.'

'I suppose we do,' said Mary Kate. 'I suppose we do.'

'Would you like me to show you the way?'

'That's awful good of you.'

'It's my pleasure, Miss Ryan. And can I say how lovely you look.'

'You can and thank you.'

The young girl led her to a lift that took them up to the salon. The room was long and narrow, taking up one side of the

second floor of Clerys. A row of chairs had been placed in front
of large mirrors in fancy frames, hanging on the walls. All but
one of the chairs were occupied by women wearing pink smocks
over their clothes with ribbons that tied at the back of the neck.
Most of them were looking at their reflections in the mirrors.
Hair stylists and colourists, all very glamorous and dressed in
black, were attending to them. Some had trolleys beside them
on which were placed bowls of hair dye, which they were
painting onto the women's heads. Others were primping almost-
finished, shampoo-and-sets with their fingers. Two of the
customers were sitting with their heads inside giant hairdryers,
shaped like upturned eggcups. One young girl, her hair in a
short bob, was sweeping up the cut hair from around the chairs
and collecting it into a dustpan.

The women having their hair dried had their legs crossed
and were reading magazines on their laps, while the others were
chatting to their stylists. There was a smell of good coffee and
hairspray, and a buzz of conversation and happiness as lively as
if the room had been full of small birds. The glamour was
further enhanced by the pictures on the walls: photographs of
models and actresses wearing false eyelashes, with their hair cut
and styled in the most fashionable ways. One of the pictures
showed a model with her hair piled high on her head in a series
of complicated curls. Mary Kate smothered a giggle as she imagined herself walking along Tanners Row, sporting that pile of
delight on top of her head. Jesus, they'd be talking about her for
months.

*I mean what happened when you slept on it? Wouldn't it be
completely flat when you woke up?* No, it wasn't for her. She
wanted something natural-looking, like the young girl at the
reception desk.

A young woman was walking towards her, smiling. 'Miss
Ryan?' she said.

Mary Kate nodded.

'If you'd like to take a seat, we'll talk through what you would like done today. Can I take your coat?'

Mary Kate sat in the empty chair and stared into the mirror. There had been no mirror in her room in Ginnetts Row, which had probably been a blessing, all things considered, for there had been very little to admire.

'So,' said the hair stylist, 'have you thought about what you'd like me to do?'

'The young girl who brought me up here?'

'Carla?'

'Is that her name?'

'Yes.'

'Well, I like her hair.'

'Carla's hair is naturally straight, but yours, Miss Ryan, has a lovely wave to it. I'll give it a really good cut and we can go from there.'

Mary Kate smiled at the girl in the mirror. 'What is your name, dear?'

The young girl screwed up her nose, as if there was a bad smell under it. 'Majella, isn't it an awful mouthful?'

'After Saint Gerrard Majella? I think it's a lovely name, it has always been one of my favourites.'

'I would have preferred a name that didn't belong to a man,' she said, grinning. 'So, Miss Ryan, if you would like to follow me over to the basins, I'll wash your hair.'

Never had hair washing been such a wonderful experience. The shampoo smelled so gorgeous; she'd only ever washed her hair with a bar of soap but from now on, Mary Kate Ryan would treat herself to a bottle of shampoo.

'That's a lovely smell, Majella,' she said. 'If I was thinking of buying a bottle of shampoo, what would I be asking for?'

'Jasmine. It really does smell of flowers, doesn't it?'

'It really does.'

'Shampoo comes in all sorts of scents. We have a great stock

of them here. I'm not trying to persuade you to buy our prod-
ucts, Miss Ryan, please don't think that. But I can vouch for
ours and I know they are lovely.'

'Sure, I didn't think that for one minute. I'm only grateful to
you for pointing it out. Now why would I be going anywhere
else to buy it when you have it right here in Clerys?'

Majella continued gently massaging her head. Mary Kate
closed her eyes; she could easily have fallen asleep, it was so
relaxing.

Her head was then wrapped in a warm towel and she was
led back to the chair. She watched as her hair fell in long
strands around her shoulders and onto the floor. There was so
much of it around the chair, she thought she would surely be
left with none at all, but she trusted Majella and gave in to this
new experience that was now her life.

After Majella had finished cutting, she reached for the
dryer and began to softly brush Mary Kate's hair, curling it
under and teasing it into a natural style.

'There,' she said, 'what do you think? Do you like it? Oh, I
do hope so.'

Mary Kate stared at the woman in the mirror. She didn't
recognise herself. Her once-dull hair was now as shiny as a new
penny, it framed her face and curled around her ears. She felt a
stinging behind her eyes and then she was crying.

Majella immediately knelt beside her and held her hands.
'Oh, Miss Ryan, don't cry, please don't cry. Do you hate it? Is it
not what you wanted?'

When she was able to speak, Mary Kate looked at the young
girl's anxious face. 'You have performed a miracle this day,
Majella, for I look almost...'

'Beautiful?' said Majella.

Mary Kate smiled at her and shook her head. 'I was about to
say normal.'

'Oh, Miss Ryan, there is nothing normal about you. In fact, I think you're magnificent.'

'Well, I've never been described as magnificent.'

'Shall we go the whole hog and put a bit of make-up on you?'

'I've never worn make-up, never in all my life.'

Majella grinned. 'Then maybe it's time you did.'

'All right, I'll give it a go. But I don't want to end up looking like yer women hanging on the wall.'

'Don't worry, Miss Ryan. No one will even notice you are wearing any. I will just enhance the beauty you already have.'

Her beauty? Her mother had been beautiful, but she had always known that her mother's beauty had never passed down to her.

Majella worked her magic again as she brushed mascara onto Mary Kate's lashes, smoothed blusher onto her cheeks and outlined her lips in the palest shade of apricot.

She walked down the steps of Clerys that day, feeling that she had left the old Mary Kate behind her and she felt... She felt magnificent.

That evening, she opened the new diary and started to write.

CHAPTER 8

The house on Merrion Square was hers; it was really hers. Mr Renson had got it at a good price because it needed so much doing to it.

'Now, I can recommend a good team of builders. The firm is owned by Sean Barry, he's done work for me and you will be in safe hands. There are some around here that I wouldn't recommend to my worst enemy, they'd take your money quick enough but the work would be shoddy at best. But Sean will see you right. Will I give him the go ahead?'

'Oh, yes please, Mr Renson, and thank you. I don't know what I would do without you.'

'I will help all I can, Miss Ryan, and it will be my absolute pleasure to be of assistance.'

'What about the furnishing of it? That is another area that I will need help with.'

'Without seeming forward, Miss Ryan, my wife Erin runs an interior design business with her sister, Gerry. They are very well thought of around these parts, in fact they've picked up the odd award. You could meet them and discuss what you have in mind, if that would suit.'

Mary Kate smiled. Everything was coming together, it really was going to happen. She really was going to be the owner of the best boarding house in Dublin.

'That would suit me just fine,' she said, 'and I'm obliged to you.'

And so began the work of bringing the house back to its former glory. Mary Kate visited every day and watched as it began to transform before her eyes. Each visit brought some new change that delighted her. At the beginning, she feared she had taken on too much, as windows were taken out and tiles ripped from the roof and all of it piled at the front of the house, ready to be carted away. Inside, floors were torn up and added to the growing pile outside the door.

Mr Renson had been right about Sean Barry, who was at the house almost every day, overseeing every little piece of work that was being carried out.

'Now there are some things that are worth saving,' he said. 'And I would strongly advise that you do. Some of the cornices are intact and the tiles in the hallway are the original ones. With some work and a bit of loving care, we can have them looking beautiful. This house has a history, Miss Ryan, and it would be a sin not to try to save what we can, if that is what you would like.'

Mary Kate smiled. She was in good hands. This wasn't just another building job to Sean Barry. He, like herself, was seeing the house as it used to be and she trusted him with her vision.

'Oh yes, Mr Barry. I would like to preserve all we can.'

'I thought you would,' he said, smiling at her.

'And Mr Barry?'

'Yes?'

'I want a plaque over the door and for it to say "cead mile failte".'

Sean Barry smiled at her. 'A hundred thousand welcomes? Now that would be grand.'

'And I want the door to be red.'

Sean grinned. 'Red?'

'Yes, red. Bright red.'

'Any particular reason?' he said, smiling.

'To remind me of my red-letter days, Mr Barry.'

'Then I'll make sure that you have the best red door in Dublin. And if anyone should ask me where Miss Mary Kate Ryan lives, I shall say, you can't miss it, it's the house with the red door.'

Oh, he was nice. Her grandfather would have called him a decent bloke and that's what he was.

Every day, at one o' clock, a car arrived from the Shelbourne hotel and delivered lunch for everyone, including a bowl of scraps for Mr Barry's dog, who seemed to take as much interest in the house as his owner.

Sean shook his head. 'There'll be no pleasing them now, Miss Ryan, for you have them spoiled. They'll be putting down tools and demanding their dinner from the Shelbourne at every job we take on.'

'Ah, they're good workers, Mr Barry, and deserve something nice at lunchtime.'

'You're very kind, Miss Ryan, but are you sure you should be feeding the dog too? You'll have him spoiled as well.'

'You don't mind, do you?'

'Now, why would I be minding? Sure he has as much right to a good dinner as the rest of us.'

Mary Kate knelt down and stroked the dog's head. He wasn't the handsomest dog she'd ever seen – his head was white and the rest of him was black, one of his ears lay flat against his head while the other one stood straight up, but his eyes made up for his looks, they were soft and brown and kind. Yes, he had kind eyes.

'What's his name?' she said.

Sean Barry laughed. 'Now how would I be knowing that?'

'But I thought—'

'That he's mine? You thought the dog was mine?'

Mary Kate nodded. 'I did, I mean, he's here every day.'

'That's because he's latched onto you, Miss Ryan. He knows a soft touch when he sees one.'

Mary Kate stood up and frowned. 'Is that how you see me, Sean Barry? As a soft touch?'

'I didn't mean to offend you, Miss Ryan, and I'm sorry if I did. I just meant that you are kind and the dog can sense it. Are you thinking of taking him on?'

The dog was staring up at her, as if he was waiting for an answer, how could she walk away from those eyes?

'But what would I do with him? I can't be taking him to the Shelbourne.'

'He can stay with me until the house is ready.'

'But won't your wife mind?'

'I don't have a wife, Miss Ryan.'

'Oh, I thought maybe you had. I don't know why I thought that, I just did.'

'I was married once, a long time ago, but my Lorna died very young and I have never felt the need or desire to replace her.'

Mary Kate could feel her face going red.

'Like I said. It was a long time ago.'

'I'm sorry for your loss.'

'It *was* a loss but I have learned to live with it. When you have no choice, there is nothing else to do, is there? Now, if you are determined to keep the dog, it'll need a name.'

'Polly,' she said. 'I've always liked that name.'

Sean didn't speak.

'You don't like it?'

'I like it fine but I'm not sure yer man would like to be called Polly.'

'It's a boy?'

'It is indeed.'

'Are you sure?'

'Trust me on this one, Miss Ryan,' said Sean, grinning. 'He's definitely a boy.'

Mary Kate could feel herself blushing. She cleared her throat. 'Then I'll need to think of a boy's name.'

'You will.'

'What do *you* think I should call him, Mr Barry?'

Sean put his head to one side and stared at the dog. 'Well, he puts me in mind of a pint of Guinness.'

Mary Kate laughed and grinned at the dog. 'Will that suit you, boy?' she said. 'Would you like to be called Guinness?'

The dog put a paw on her arm.

'You have him eating out of your hand already. I'd say you've found yourself a friend for life there,' said Sean.

A friend for life? She liked that, for it was something she'd never had.

'Guinness it is then,' she said, smiling at Sean. 'Guinness it is.'

When she got back to her room, she opened the new diary and wrote: 'I have a dog and his name is Guinness.'

A week later, she met Erin Renson and her sister Gerry outside the boarding house. They were both carrying cases.

'It's so good to meet you, Miss Ryan. My husband told me all about you and your plans. In fact, it's all he's talked about.'

'Good things, I hope,' said Mary Kate, smiling.

'Oh yes,' said Erin, 'all good. I felt I'd known you before I'd met you. This is my younger sister, Gerry.'

'Hello,' said Gerry, shaking her hand.

They were very beautiful and very alike, except for their colouring. Erin's hair was dark brown and came just below her ears while Gerry's was a mass of red curls, that tumbled about her shoulders, but it was their eyes that held Mary Kate's attention, for they were the colour of the grass on St Stephen's Green.

'We've brought some samples of fabric for you to look at,' said Erin. 'My husband gave us a sense of what you wanted. Soft and homely and welcoming. Was he right?'

Mary Kate nodded. 'That is exactly what I have in mind.'

'Then let's make a start, shall we?'

'Let's,' said Mary Kate, leading them up the steps and into the house.

They spent the morning walking through the rooms. Gerry took a tape out of her case and started measuring the walls and windows.

'Now,' said Erin, 'I would suggest a theme. We can select about six colours. Each room should have its own personality, its own individual feel. How would you feel about that?'

'I know nothing about these things but I do like the sound of it.'

Erin opened the other case. 'Take your time, Miss Ryan, feel the fabric, look at the paint samples and imagine what would best suit this beautiful house and, more importantly, what would best suit yourself.'

The case was packed with materials of all different colours. Blues and pinks, lilacs and soft greys. Cottons and velvets, satins and wool.

'They are all lovely, how will I ever be able to choose?'

'You don't need to make a decision right now,' said Gerry, smiling. 'And you can change your mind any time you like.'

Mary Kate laughed. 'Well, that's a relief anyway.'

'You can take all the time you like,' said Erin. 'Oh gosh, I'm talking as if we already have the job.'

'Oh, you do,' said Mary Kate, quickly. 'Of course you do.'

'Then I can assure you that by the time we've finished, you will have the best boarding house in Dublin and it's comfort and style will be talked about all over the county and beyond.'

Mary Kate smiled at them. They looked as excited as she did and, just like Sean Barry, she felt they cared about her boarding house and that it wasn't just another job to them.

'Now choose some colours and take them home with you, feel the fabric, hold it up to the light and we'll meet back here again tomorrow. Will that suit you, Miss Ryan?'

'It will and I'd like it if you called me Mary Kate.'

The three of them hugged at the bottom of the steps and she felt as if she'd made some new friends. She'd had no one she'd cared about before the money and no one who cared about her. She didn't feel alone any more, and she had a feeling that she never would again.

Mary Kate watched and waited as Sean, Erin and Gerry gradually brought the house back to life and, soon, the day she had waited so patiently for had finally arrived. The boarding house was ready and it was time to push open the red door and step into her new life.

'It's my red-letter day, Grandad,' she said. 'And I wish you were here beside me.'

CHAPTER 9

The young girl standing in front of Mary Kate was slight. She looked more like a young child than a girl of fourteen.

'I'd like you to meet Miss Ryan,' said Sister Luke, smiling at the girl.

She stood at the door, she looked terrified and was staring at her feet. Her dark hair fell across her eyes, so that Mary Kate could barely see her face.

'Jesus, Jessie, she's not going eat you,' said the nun. 'Now, will you come into the room and say hello to the woman.'

The girl moved slowly towards Mary Kate and gave a little bob.

'Miss Ryan is looking for a girl to help her in her boarding house. From what I've heard, the house is beautiful, it's the talk of Dublin. You would have your own room there, Jessie. Isn't that right, Miss Ryan?'

'Oh yes, of course,' said Mary Kate. 'You would have a lovely room.'

'This is a great chance for you, Jessie,' said Sister Luke. 'A great chance.'

'If you feel you would like to,' said Mary Kate, smiling at her.

The girl was still staring at her feet, she looked ready to run at any minute. Quietly, she mumbled something.

'Speak up now, Jessie, for myself and Miss Ryan here can't understand a word you are saying.'

'I'm sorry but I can't,' Jessie said louder. 'I can't come with you.'

'Can I ask why, Jessie?' said Mary Kate gently. 'It really is a lovely boarding house. I think you could be happy there.'

'I just can't, miss.'

'Oh, Jessie,' said Sister Luke. 'We've talked about this, haven't we? You don't want to be staying here with a load of old nuns for the rest of your life, do you? Of course you don't. May God forgive me but even I find it a trial myself at times. You need to get out into the world, you need to see a bit of life and Miss Ryan here is offering you a grand opportunity to do just that. You haven't suddenly found a vocation, have you, child?'

Jessie looked up for the first time. 'Jesus, no, Sister,' she said. 'I mean, I'm sure it would be great altogether to have a calling but I haven't had one, at least I don't think I have.'

'You'd know if you'd had one,' said the nun. 'And you'd have to follow it whether you wanted to or not. I had no desire to enter the religious life. I was all for having a great time with the lads but it wasn't to be, Himself upstairs called me and I had no choice but to do His will.'

'I definitely haven't been called, Sister,' said Jessie, with the mere hint of a smile on her face.

'So I'm guessing it's Abby, am I right?'

The girl nodded. 'I can't leave her, Sister.'

'I thought so. Would you step outside for a while, Jessie. I would like to have a word with Miss Ryan in private.'

The girl bobbed and quickly left the room. Mary Kate had never seen anyone look more relieved.

'Who's Abby?' she asked. 'Is she Jessie's sister? Because I wouldn't want to be responsible for taking her away from her sister. I really couldn't do that.'

'Abby is not Jessie's sister, Miss Ryan.'

'Then...?'

'Abby was but a toddler when she was found asleep on the steps of the abbey, hence her name. She hasn't spoken a word since the day she came to us, except to Jessie. Jessie is the only one she speaks to.'

'That is so sad, Sister.'

Sister Luke nodded. 'We've all tried, we've taken her to doctors but to no avail, she will only speak to Jessie.'

'How old is she?'

'About six now but we're not sure of her true age. Jessie was ten when Abby came to us. Adoption is out of the question, so unless something changes Abby will stay here with us, at the convent, and we are happy to have her for she is loved by us all. She is the sweetest child, Miss Ryan, but she is holding Jessie back. I was hoping that Jessie would come to you, for I would dearly love to see her settled outside these convent walls. This is no place for a young girl. But there, I've tried, what more can I do? Myself and the rest of the nuns have our knees only worn out, praying to Saint Jude for his intervention. I had my hopes up this time, we all did.'

'What do you know about Abby, Sister?'

'Nothing, nothing at all. It was winter when she was found, wearing only a thin dress, she didn't even have undergarments on her. If the monks hadn't found her when they did, I don't think she would have survived another night. I'd say she had a guardian angel looking out for her.'

'Does she go to school?'

'She is taught here by the nuns; the poor child would be eaten alive in a regular school, she wouldn't last a morning. So, no, we keep her here where she feels safe and as long as she has

Jessie close by she is as happy as the day is long, but it's not fair on Jessie.'

'So, you don't know if she has any parents?'

Sister Luke shook her head. 'We made enquiries at the time but no one came forward to claim her. We had to give her a surname. Every day a nun would come up to me with a name for her – they had my brain mashed. One of them said that Saint Athracht came to her in a dream, demanding that she be called after him. Well, he could demand all he wanted, but there was no way that I would be landing the child with a name like that, it sounded like some desperate illness.'

Mary Kate laughed.

'In the end we chose Boniface, after the blessed saint. The child is exceptionally beautiful, and we thought the name suited her.'

'And what of Jessie, Sister? What is her story?'

'Jessie's mother died when she was five and she was brought here by her father, who couldn't – or wouldn't – take care of her. He promised to come back when his circumstances changed but we've not seen hide nor hair of him since that day. We tried to track him down to sign a form, allowing Jessie to be put up for adoption, but the man had gone, so she has been with us ever since. At least she came with her own name, which is Logan.'

'And has she had an education, Sister?'

'Jessie is an exceptionally clever girl, Miss Ryan. God alone knows where she gets it from but she was already reading when she came to us. The child devours books and it's not just the reading that she excels in, she also has a great head for figures. With a college education, Jessie could go far and that is what we had always hoped for.'

Mary Kate took a deep breath. 'I would really like to help Jessie, Sister. I was given a chance myself; I would have loved to have given Jessie the same chance.'

'I believe that it is the Almighty Himself that guides people to our door. Would you like to meet Abby? If I'm not mistaken, she'll be outside with Jessie. The child follows her around like a little shadow.'

'But if I can't take Jessie?'

Sister Luke smiled. 'Sure what harm can it do to meet her? Our dear Lord works in mysterious ways, His miracles to perform, and who am I to stand in his path? I'll fetch her in, shall I?'

Without waiting for an answer, the nun rang a bell and Jessie came back into the room, still looking wary. Behind her was a little girl, barely visible behind Jessie's dress.

'Abby, this is Miss Ryan,' said Sister Luke. 'Would you not come out and meet her? Because she would like very much to meet you.'

Abby tugged at Jessie's dress and Jessie got down to her level.

'What, darling?' she said.

Jessie listened as Abby whispered into her ear. Jessie smoothed back the little girl's hair.

'You have no need to be scared, Abby. Yer woman is kind, won't you let her see your lovely little face and your new ribbon? I'm sure she would love to see your ribbon, wouldn't you, miss?'

Mary Kate smiled. 'Oh, I would, Abby, for I have a desperate weakness for ribbons.'

Slowly, Abby peeked out and gave a shy smile. Mary Kate took an intake of breath, for she had never seen such a beautiful child, not even in the films; she couldn't take her eyes off her. Mary Kate knew that no good ever came from judging a person by their looks but there was something about the child; she looked like one of God's own angels.

'Well, isn't that just the nicest ribbon I have ever laid my eyes on?' she said. 'And if I'm not mistaken it's velvet.'

Abby nodded her head.

'And did someone buy it for you?'

Abby smiled and looked up at Jessie.

'Jessie bought it for you?'

Abby smiled again.

Mary Kate walked across to Abby and knelt in front of her, causing the little girl to immediately disappear behind Jessie again.

'Abby?' Mary Kate said softly. 'I've a lovely house, not far from here. It's a big house and I am going to need some help, for I can't manage it alone. It would make me very happy if you and Jessie would come and live there with me and give me a hand.'

'Both of us?' said Jessie, with a smile that transformed her face. 'You'd take Abby as well?'

Mary Kate nodded. 'If she would like to come.' She was still kneeling in front of Abby and she slowly edged forward until she was almost touching her. 'I have a dog, Abby,' said Mary Kate. 'His name is Guinness. He's a lovely old thing, with big brown eyes and as gentle as a kitten. I think that you two would get along fine, for Guinness is in need of a friend and I need someone to look after him and give him his food. Do you think that you could be his friend, Abby?'

Abby stared at her for a moment, then tugged Jessie's dress and whispered something.

Jessie stood up and smiled. 'Abby says that she would like very much to take care of your dog.'

Sister Luke clapped her hands and everyone laughed.

'Ah sure, Saint Jude is a queer one all right,' she said.

'I'd say this has very little to do with Saint Jude, Sister Luke, and a whole lot to do with you,' said Mary Kate.

'Ah well, I might have nudged him along a bit.'

Mary Kate laughed. She had been hijacked good and proper.

'We have twenty more children running about the place, Miss Ryan, if you would like to cast your eyes over them.'

'I think I will just take the two for now.'

'Ah well, there is no sin in trying.'

'No sin at all,' said Mary Kate.

So, there it was. She had come to the convent with a mind to take on a girl to help her in the boarding house and she had come away with two. Mary Kate watched Abby skipping along the pavement ahead of her and she couldn't have been happier.

PART TWO

CHAPTER 10

Mary Kate gazed around the beautiful room. It was perfect, even more perfect than she had dreamed it could be. Sun streamed through the long windows, casting beams of April sunlight over the pale-cream walls. She looked around the room at her new friends – for they really were her friends. Mrs Leamy was sitting on the blue velvet couch next to Carla and Majella; Jessie was moving around, offering wine and nibbles; Mr Renson was leaning against the beautiful marble fireplace, puffing away on a cigar; Jenny and Duffy were standing at the window, looking out over the green; and Gerry and Erin were chatting to Sean Barry.

Erin beckoned her over.

'Well, I'd say this is a great success. You must be very proud this night.'

'Oh, I am,' said Mary Kate.

'You should be,' said Gerry. 'For it was you who chose every part of this room.'

Mary Kate smiled. 'Ah, sure no, it was yourselves that taught me how to use colour. Without you, I'd have had the place looking like a circus tent.'

'You do yourself an injustice, Miss Ryan,' said Erin. 'You have a natural flair for design – that can't be taught.'

'Well then, let's just say that the four of us created the perfect boarding house. The best boarding house in Dublin.'

'I'm surprised you didn't invite the delightful Mrs Gibb to the party,' said Erin.

'It's not too late,' said Gerry, grinning. 'You could send Jessie round to fetch her.'

'Do you know what?' said Mary Kate. 'I'm almost tempted, just to see her face turning green with envy.'

'She can't come then; she'd clash with the blue lamp. What a shame.'

'Do you like the room, Mr Barry?' said Mary Kate, turning to Sean.

'It's like a hotel, Miss Ryan. But, if I'm honest, I wouldn't have chosen these colours. I'd have gone darker.'

Mary Kate felt hurt, she wanted Sean Barry to like what she had done, it seemed important that he was pleased with what she had achieved.

'Why would I be wanting dark colours, Mr Barry?' she said sharply. 'I want light – lots of it – and soft colours and comfy couches and...' She paused. She could feel her eyes filling with tears, she was going to make a fool of herself in front of everyone. 'I've had my fill of living in the dark.' And with that, she hurried away from him.

'What did I say?' said Sean, looking completely bewildered.

Gerry shook her head. 'Honestly, Sean, can't you see that your opinion is very important to Mary Kate? More important than you realise, I'd say.'

'But all I said was—'

'We know what you said, Sean, and it has sent Mary Kate running off in tears.'

'I made her cry?'

'I'm afraid you have,' said Gerry.

'I must explain what I meant.'

'Then you'd best go after her,' said Erin.

Sean found Mary Kate sitting on the stairs, with Abby on one side of her and Guinness on the other. The dog had a paw on her lap and she was gently stroking his head. Sean felt awful that he had reduced her to tears.

'Can I have a word, Miss Ryan?'

'Abby,' said Mary Kate, 'would you be a love and take Guinness for a walk over the green?'

Abby stood up, tapped her side and Guinness followed her towards the front door.

Sean sat down. 'I've upset you, haven't I?'

'Not at all,' said Mary Kate. 'I just needed a bit of air. Didn't you find it rather warm in the room?'

Sean didn't speak right away and then he said, 'I have, haven't I? I've hurt your feelings?'

'Take no notice, Mr Barry, I expect I'm just tired. I barely slept a wink last night.'

'When I said I would have chosen darker colours, what I meant was, that with the people who will be staying here and Guinness, your beautiful furniture and pale carpets will be ruined within a month. I most certainly wasn't criticising your choice of décor, in fact I'm in awe of what you have done here. I was thinking of asking you to come around and sort out my place.'

'Really?'

'Yes, really. I'm an eejit, Miss Ryan, and I speak before I think. I wouldn't have hurt your feelings for the world. What you have achieved is nothing short of a miracle and you should be proud. I know I am.'

'I believe, Mr Barry, that if people are surrounded by nice things, they are more likely to have some pride in them. I shall train Guinness not to go on the furniture.'

'Good luck with that, Miss Ryan, for I couldn't keep him off my couch. But I'd say if anyone can teach him, you can.'

She smiled. 'I intend to,' she said.

'So, will you please forgive me for being such an eejit and come back to the party? For if you don't, I shall be sitting here beside you all evening.'

Mary Kate smiled. She should have known better than to have thought so badly of him. He was only trying to help, she understood that now. Sean Barry was a good man, she had known that the first time she'd met him and, much to her surprise, she would have been quite happy to have sat here on the stairs beside him for the rest of the evening, for she found him to be very easy company.

They walked back into the room together. Erin spotted them and winked, which caused Mary Kate to blush. Sean Barry might have thought he was an eejit but sure wasn't it herself who was the eejit this night? Sean Barry, indeed. Cop on to yourself, Mary Kate Ryan.

Mr Renson tapped his glass and the room fell silent. All eyes were on her and she wasn't used to the attention but she had something to say and she was going to say it. She took a deep breath and smiled at them.

'I want to thank you all for being here on this special evening, to celebrate the opening of my boarding house. I couldn't have done it without you. Each one of you, in your way, has helped to make this dream of mine come true. Mr Renson, you treated me with such dignity when first we met. You put me at my ease, when I felt so out of place, you made me believe that I had as much right to be sitting in your office as any other woman. No, not just any woman but a special one, yes, a special one – and I hadn't felt special to anyone in a very long time. Jenny, I will never forget your kindness and your welcome, even before you knew who I was. I'd say if it was the queen or a pauper that came through your doors, they would be treated with the same kindness that you showed me and that is a gift, Jenny. I still have your hankie with the letter J embroidered in the corner. I will never forget the day we spent in Clerys where yourself and Mrs Leamy helped me to choose a whole new set of clothes. Thank you, Carla, for sharing all the excitement with me and Majella for giving me a swish new hairstyle. What a wonderful day it was.'

Majella smiled. 'I'll put some highlights in next time.'

'And I might just let you.'

'I'll hold you to that, Miss Ryan.'

Mary Kate grinned and continued. 'Between you all, you turned that drab little woman into the vision of loveliness you see before you today.'

Everyone laughed.

'Duffy, the hug you gave me when I walked into the offices of Renson and Renson was the warmest I had had in a very long time. You gave something to a stranger, who so needed a hug that day. I will never forget it and I thank you from the bottom of my heart. Erin and Gerry, look around at what you have created. You were so patient with that country bumpkin who wouldn't have known style if it had smacked her in the face. You have worked wonders, you gave me everything and more to make this beautiful house into the home I wanted it to be. Thank you. And, Mr Barry, you have brought this house back to its original glory. You seemed to know exactly what I wanted. It was as if you could see what I could see the first time I laid my eyes on it. I hope I am not wrong in thinking that it became a labour of love.'

Sean Barry raised his glass. 'It did indeed, Miss Ryan, it did indeed.'

'Where's Jessie and Abby?'

'We're here, Miss Ryan, so is Guinness,' said Jessie from the doorway.

Mary Kate smiled. 'Then stand beside me.'

Jessie and Abby stood either side of her and Guinness settled himself at her feet.

Mary Kate paused. 'What I am trying to say is, that with you, my dear friends, and with Jessie, Abby and Guinness, I have found a family. And I'm going to stop there, before I start blubbing.'

'Or before we start blubbing,' said Erin. 'Now let us all raise our glasses and toast the best landlady in Dublin.'

Mary Kate smiled as everyone chorused. 'To the best landlady in Dublin.'

That's when she lost it.

CHAPTER 11

Moira

Moira Kent was sitting outside Miss Williams's door on one of the hard chairs that seemed to be favoured throughout the school. Miss Williams had been head teacher at Clifton College for twenty years and was about to retire. Moira herself had been teaching music there for almost thirty years and been deputy head for the last ten. She'd been passed over twice for the head-ship, even though her pupils achieved some of the best results in the county. She wasn't popular with the girls, she knew that, but she had never courted popularity and didn't care what they thought about her – not like some of them here, with their after-school clubs and dancing in the gym during the luncheon break. Well, she'd put a stop to all that once she was in charge, she was here to teach them, not mollycoddle them.

She'd tried to instil in them her love of the classics. Moira favoured the German composers, Beethoven, Bach and Wagner. She found Brahms to be a bit fey for her liking, a bit pretentious. Her favourite piece was Tchaikovsky's *Romeo and Juliet*. She would close her eyes and let the music carry her to a place where she forgot that she was ugly, forgot that there was not a living soul who even liked her, let alone loved her.

When she had first come to the school, she'd played it to the class, placing it reverently on the turntable, before standing with her back to the room looking out over the grounds. As the strains of the piece washed over her she'd felt again that feeling of hope, of a place beyond the narrow confines of the empty life she inhabited, a place of beauty she had never known; it touched her heart as nothing else ever had. She had almost forgotten the room full of girls behind her until she heard the muffled sound of giggling. She had been filled with such rage she could hardly contain it, she'd wanted to lash out at them and tell them what an ignorant load of buffoons they were. She had shared something of herself with them and they had thrown it back in her face. She'd ripped the record from the stylus, leaving a deep scratch across it, then she'd turned and faced them. She didn't speak, she'd just stared at them with utter contempt. The giggling stopped, except for the odd nervous muffled titter from the back.

The record had been ruined but she didn't care for she would never play it again. She pushed a stray curl behind her ear. The skitty girl at the hairdresser's hadn't cut it short enough and the curl was an affront to her senses. Moira Kent was plain, she knew what she looked like. How could she not when the mirror reminded her of it every day and her father was barely able to look at her?

Her sister Katherine, on the other hand, had been beautiful. Moira should have been jealous but she'd loved her from the moment she was born, for she was the sweetest, kindest little thing she had ever known. Everyone had loved Katherine and Moira didn't mind at all, for she was proud of her sister even though she had always been aware of the difference between

them. Katherine took after their mother, who had the same
dark-green eyes and beautiful red hair that she wore in a single
plait that reached halfway down her back. As a young child,
Moira loved nothing more than to stand behind her mother as
she sat at the dressing table. She'd gently loosen the plait and let
the hair tumble around her mother's shoulders in a cloud of red
that looked like the autumn leaves in the park then she'd brush
it until it shone. Her mother would smile at her and praise her
gentleness.

She could remember saying to her once, 'Why am I not
beautiful like Katherine, Mummy?'

Her mother had taken her on her lap and said, 'You have a
strong face, Moira, and it has its own beauty. It's what is inside
that counts and you are beautiful inside.'

'But no one can see the inside,' she'd said.

'Not now maybe, but one day they will. I promise you that,
my sweet girl.'

Well, that day had never come and no one had been interested enough to find the beauty behind the long pale face and
lank brown hair.

She'd had a privileged upbringing and had wanted for nothing. She'd attended a private school and been taught the piano.
She and Katherine would run around the long garden at the
back of their house, chasing after Dougal, their little black dog.
Then they would lay on the grass and look up at the sky and
make pictures out of the clouds. Katherine was deaf and at an
early age Moira had learned sign language. But the sisters didn't
need words to watch the clouds or to find joy in each other's
company, love needed no words. Back then, her father had a
good job in the bank and, although they had never been close,
he wasn't cruel to her.

All that changed when her mother and sister were taken by
an outbreak of scarlet fever. Moira's father was like a madman
in his grief and he turned to the drink. He would shut himself in

his room for days on end and she would stand outside the door, her back to the wall, not knowing what to do, waiting for a kind word that never came.

She had lost her beloved mother who could see the beauty inside her, and she had lost her little sister whom she had adored, yet there was no one to comfort her in her grief. No one to hold her in their arms and tell her that she was loved, no one who cared whether she was dead or alive.

One morning at the breakfast table her father announced that she would be going away to boarding school.

'Is it a nice school, Father?'

'What?'

'The boarding school, is it nice?'

Her father stared at her with such hatred in his eyes that she wanted to run from the room, to run as far away from him as she could get. Her eyes filled with tears as she stared at the piece of toast in front of her.

'Why were they taken and not you?' he'd spat.

'I'm sorry, Father,' she'd whispered.

'Not as sorry as I am,' he'd said.

That was the moment she made up her mind to never love another human being as long as she lived. She would never let anyone close enough to hurt her ever again.

But now, her life was about to change. Not only would she get the recognition she so justly deserved but she would move into the cottage in the school grounds that came with the position of headmistress of Clifton College.

Her backside was aching from sitting on the hard chair, what was the point of a bloody chair that gave no semblance of comfort? She stood up and rubbed her back, just as the door opened.

'Please come in, Miss Kent,' said Miss Williams, smiling.

Moira walked into the room and waited to be asked to sit down. The large desk which seemed to take up most of the space was covered in papers, some of which had slid to the floor. Cupboard doors gaped open and the windowsills were cluttered with dying plants that looked as if they had never been watered. How the woman managed to work in such a mess was beyond Moira. She couldn't wait to get some order in the place and she would – oh yes, she would – and the first things to go would be the bloody plants.

Miss Williams was shuffling papers, completely ignoring Moira. When she eventually looked up it was with such surprise, it was if she had just realised Moira was standing in front of her.

'Oh, do sit down, Miss Kent,' she said.

Moira lowered herself onto another hard chair and waited.

Miss Williams leaned forward and rested her arms on the desk and smiled.

Why doesn't she just bloody well get on with it?, thought Moira, staring at her.

'Now, Miss Kent, you'll be pleased to know that the governors were very impressed with your interview, very impressed indeed, you should be proud of the way you conducted yourself.' The headmistress was having trouble meeting Moira's eyes. She gave a small smile but her teeth seemed to be stuck to her lips. She took a deep breath and continued. 'But after much discussion they decided that it was time for a change.'

Moira stared at Miss Williams. Her heart was pounding, and she could feel a prickle of sweat under her armpits – this wasn't going the way it was supposed to go. The little cottage she had longed for, the place that she thought she could at last call her home, was disappearing before her eyes. It was all she could do to stop herself from leaning over the desk and putting her hands around Miss Williams's skinny neck.

She took a deep breath and tried to compose herself. 'What sort of change?' she almost spat.

'Someone younger, Miss Kent, someone who can identify

with the girls, take a more modern approach to their education. The new way of thinking is that we look at the whole child, not just the academic side of things.'

'What a load of utter rubbish,' said Moira. 'Our job is to teach them, not investigate their psyche. That's their parents' job, not ours.'

'I do understand your disappointment, Miss Kent, of course I do. But I hope that you will come to understand this and not take it personally.'

'Not take it personally? It *is* personal. How else am I supposed to take it? I've given thirty years to this school. That job was mine, it was mine.'

'I'm sorry you feel like that, Miss Kent.'

'Are you?' Moira stood up, almost knocking the chair over.

Miss Williams didn't like confrontation. 'Of course I am sorry and so are the governors. There is no doubt that you have been a great asset to the school, but times are changing and we must change with them. We do of course hope that you will continue as deputy head.'

The two women glared at each other, all pretence of any kind of a friendship gone. There had at one time been a modicum of respect between them but at that moment their dislike of each other was palpable and neither of them cared.

'I shall be giving three months' notice as dictated in my contract. I hope that will be satisfactory, Miss Williams.'

'There will be no need for that, Miss Kent,' said the head-mistress. 'I think it is in both our interests that you leave now, don't you?'

Moira Kent stalked out of the office, almost taking the door off its hinges, as Miss Williams took a bottle of whiskey out of the drawer and drank it straight from the bottle.

CHAPTER 12

Mary Kate was sitting in her favourite chair looking out over the green. The early-morning sun streamed through the long windows and a soft summer breeze lifted the hem of the beautiful curtains, letting them drop, only to lift them again and have them billow out into the room. She still couldn't believe how much her life had changed and she would be forever grateful to the mother she would never know. She hoped that her beloved grandparents could see her and knew she was happy and at peace and that every day was a red-letter day.

There were very few people on the green, just a couple of dog walkers and men in suits hurrying to work, clutching their briefcases. She could remember running across this very green towards whatever rotten job awaited her. In her wildest dreams she could never have imagined that there would come a day when she owned one of the beautiful houses that surrounded Merrion Square.

Just then there was a tap on the door and Jessie almost fell into the room, followed by Abby, who was followed by Guinness, who never left the little girl's side.

'You have a letter,' said Jessie, panting. 'Do you think it's about the rooms?'

Mary Kate stood up and took the letter from Jessie. 'Let's see, shall we?' she said, smiling.

'Wouldn't it be desperate exciting if it was, Miss Ryan?'

'It would indeed, Jessie,' she said, 'it would indeed. Shall we cross our fingers?'

Jessie nodded and whispered something in Abby's ear. The little girl grinned and crossed her fingers, holding them up so that Mary Kate could see.

'Here we go then,' she said, opening the envelope.

'Is it?' said Jessie, hardly able to contain her excitement. 'Is it about a room?'

Mary Kate looked up and smiled. 'We have our first guest, girls. A teacher. Now isn't that lovely?'

'What's her name?' said Jessie.

Mary Kate looked back at the letter. 'A Miss Moira Kent and, dear Lord, she's coming tomorrow.'

'That's grand, Miss Ryan, for everything is ready.'

'We shall give her the best room in the house – the one at the front, overlooking the green.'

Abby was tugging at Jessie's skirt.

'What, darling?' said Jessie, leaning down to her.

Abby whispered in her ear and Jessie straightened up and smiled.

'That's a wonderful idea,' she said.

'Can you share this wonderful idea?' said Mary Kate, grinning.

'Abby says shall we pick some flowers and put them in the new lady's room?'

Mary Kate could feel tears stinging the backs of her eyes. 'Oh, Abby, how clever of you to think of that. I'm sure Miss Kent will appreciate such a kind gesture.'

Abby smiled her sweet little smile and Mary Kate was once

again struck by the child's beauty. Oh, how she longed for the day when the little girl felt safe enough to speak to her. What a wonderful day that would be.

The next morning, Mary Kate was in the kitchen, going through the meals for the coming week. When she had mentioned to Erin that she would be needing a cook and someone to help in the kitchen, Erin had recommended a widowed lady by the name of Mrs Lamb and her daughter, Eliza. As soon as Mary Kate met Mrs Lamb she knew she had no need to look any further, for the two of them immediately liked what they saw in each other.

Mrs Lamb was small and round with the most beautiful blue eyes Mary Kate had ever seen. They crinkled up at the corners whenever she smiled and Mrs Lamb smiled a lot.

'Well, I hope Miss Kent isn't a fussy eater, Miss Ryan, for as I explained, I am a plain cook. But you can be sure that what I put on the table will be fresh, nourishing food that won't cost you the earth.'

'I have every faith in you, Mrs Lamb, for every meal you have made for us has been delicious.'

'I do my best, Miss Ryan, I do my best. Now, Eliza, we must away to the shops and I'm relying on you to take care of the list. Can you do that, love?'

Eliza smiled and nodded. 'I can look after the list, Mammy. I'll put it in me pocket.'

'Good girl,' said Mrs Lamb.

Mary Kate had known from first meeting her that Eliza, at twenty, was more like a child – an eager child whose main purpose in life seemed to be to please everyone she met. There was joy shining out of her eyes and an innocence that made you want to protect her for, God love her, she was a child in a woman's body.

'She's a hard worker, Miss Ryan, there's not a lazy bone in her body. She's just a bit slow, and if you have any misgivings about that, I will understand.'

'Oh, Mrs Lamb,' Mary Kate had answered, 'now why would I have any misgivings about Eliza? I can see that she is a sweet girl and what more could I ask for? I just hope that you will both be happy here.'

'Oh, we will, Miss Ryan, we certainly will.'

Miss Kent would be arriving at ten o'clock that morning. Mary Kate went upstairs to Miss Kent's room, just to check that every-thing was perfect. She had knots in her stomach. In the name of God, what did she have to worry about? Miss Kent wasn't the only woman who would be staying at the boarding house and she needed to cop on to herself or she'd be a blithering idiot by the time she got here. The room was perfect, with its pale-blue walls and crisp white bedding, nothing like the rooms she'd had to live in. Oh, she hoped Miss Kent would like it, she hoped Miss Kent would like *her*.

She gave one last look around the room, smiling as she spotted the sweet peas in a little glass jar beside the bed, then she went downstairs.

When the doorbell rang, she nearly jumped out of her skin.

'She's here, Miss Ryan, she's here,' shouted Jessie, running down the stairs. 'Shall I open the door to her?'

Mary Kate took a deep breath and smoothed down her dress. 'Thank you, Jessie. Yes, open the door for it's the only way she is going to get in.'

Jessie grinned. 'I suppose it is.'

Behind Jessie were Abby and Guinness. What if Miss Kent didn't like dogs? Well, if she didn't like Guinness there was no welcome for her here. Jesus, what was she thinking? The woman wasn't even over the doorstep and here she was, thinking of turning her away.

The doorbell rang again and Jessie still hadn't moved. Mary Kate gave her an encouraging smile and Jessie moved towards the door. She was just about to turn the handle when she looked back at Mary Kate. 'You should receive her in your sitting room, Miss Ryan. That would be only right and proper.'

Jessie was correct, the last thing her guest would want would be a pile of them gawping at her on the doorstep, so Mary Kate went into her room and closed the door. She could hear voices in the hallway – dear God she wished she'd asked Erin or Gerry to come over, it would have made the whole ordeal that much easier. The door opened and Jessie came into the room.

'Miss Kent to see you,' she said, standing aside to let her enter.

When Mary Kate looked at the woman standing in front of her, her heart sank. There was nothing soft about her, she was bone-thin, all angles and sharp edges. Her long nose dominated her face and, God love her, it was a face that was as plain as a pikestaff. Mary Kate wasn't one to judge a person by their looks, it was what was on the inside that counted, but she got the feeling that the inside of Miss Moira Kent would be as sharp as the outside. Nevertheless, she smiled at her.

'Do sit down, Miss Kent,' she said. 'I hope you had a decent journey here. We have all been very excited since we got your letter.'

'Excited?' said Moira, looking puzzled.

'You are our first guest, you see.'

Moira Kent didn't seem the least bit interested in this piece of information and clearly felt no need to comment on it. Mary Kate didn't know what to make of her, she wasn't a bit friendly and not the type that she had imagined living in her house.

'Have you come far, Miss Kent?'

'Not far. Now I'd like to see my room if I may, Miss Ryan.'

'Of course, of course. I'll get Jessie to show you and once you've settled in, come downstairs and I'll get you a grand cup and tea and some of Mrs Lamb's cake, straight from the oven.'

Miss Kent stared at Mary Kate. 'If I could just see my room,' she said.

'Just wait here a minute while I get Jessie.' Mary Kate went into the hallway, where she knew Jessie would be waiting, along with Abby and Guinness.

'Jessie, would you show Miss Kent her room? And, Abby, will you take Guinness into the garden?'

Abby nodded and walked away with Guinness at her heels.

Mary Kate went back into the sitting room. 'Jessie will help with your bags.'

'There's no need, I can manage.'

'Oh well, if you're sure.'

'I'm sure.' At the door Miss Kent turned around and looked back at Mary Kate. 'A cup of tea would be most welcome.'

'That's grand then,' said Mary Kate, smiling. 'I do hope you like your room.'

Miss Kent followed Jessie, upstairs.

'It's the best room in the house,' said Jessie, looking back at her. 'Miss Ryan said that as you were our first guest, you should have the best room. It's a grand room, Miss Kent, and it looks out over the green.'

'Are there any other rooms available?'

'Other rooms?' said Jessie, looking puzzled.

'At the back of the house.'

'But do you not want the room at the front?'

'I'd rather have a room at the back, one that looks out over the garden, if that is no trouble.'

'I'm sure it's no trouble at all but I'll have to let Miss Ryan know.'

'Of course.'

Jessie ran downstairs and into the sitting room.

Mary Kate looked up and smiled at her. 'Does she like the room?'

'I wouldn't know, she hasn't even looked at it.'

Mary Kate frowned. 'She hasn't looked at it? Why ever not?'

'She wants a room at the back of the house, Miss Ryan, one that overlooks the garden.'

'Well, Jessie, Miss Kent is a paying guest and, as such, she is entitled to whichever room she wants.'

'But don't you think that's awful odd?'

'Between you and me, Jessie, I think perhaps Miss Moira Kent is a bit on the odd side. But as my grandmother used to say, "Folk come in all shapes and sizes and that is all part of God's creation. It would be a dull old world if we were all the same."'

Jessie smiled. 'I'd say your grandmother was a wise soul.'

'She was. Now show Miss Kent a room at the back of the house and let's hope it's to her liking.'

When Jessie went back upstairs Miss Kent was nowhere to be seen. 'Miss Kent?' she called softly.

There was no reply. Jesus, this was ridiculous, how was she going to tell Miss Ryan that she had mislaid her first guest? Just then, she heard a noise coming from the floor above. She ran up the stairs. One of the doors was open and inside was Miss Kent, standing by the window. She turned around as Jessie came into the room.

'This will suit me very well.'

'But it's the smallest room in the house.'

'It will suit my needs. Jessie, is it?'

'Yes, miss.'

'If you can inform Miss Ryan of my decision, I would be most obliged.'

'I'll leave you to settle in then, shall I?'

'If you wouldn't mind.'

After Jessie had gone, Moira walked back to the window.

The eagerness of Miss Ryan had been unnerving, the kindness of the woman was not what she had been expecting. Moira Kent wasn't used to kindness, it touched something deep inside her, which she quickly pushed away. She wasn't here to make friends and she had no intention of encouraging it.

After Jessie had gone, Moira walked back to the window. She watched a little girl running around the garden with a black and white dog. Tears filled her eyes and ran down her cheeks. She wasn't used to crying but what she saw in the garden reminded her of another little girl, a little girl called Katherine.

CHAPTER 13

Colleen

Colleen Brenna was ready to go. Her bag was packed and hidden under the bed. She wasn't taking much, just a few clothes and the stash of items she'd managed to take from the house.

She'd lost count of how long she'd been locked in the room. She'd tried to keep track at the beginning but gradually the endless days ran into each other, and she had no idea what month it was, let alone what day. Her one distraction was her books; she loved to read, and she'd read and reread every one of them over the months, disappearing into a world of fiction that took her away from the reality that was her life. Her other love was writing. She wrote down her thoughts in her little notepad, which she kept under the mattress away from her parents' prying eyes. Putting down her thoughts was like sharing them with a friend. She wrote about Roibin, silly love poems that she would never show him. She was no great writer but that didn't matter, her words were hers alone and would never be read by anyone else. She gently placed her hands on her growing belly – it was this that had stopped her from going completely mad. She'd made a promise to this unborn child that she would protect her with every breath in her body and she would fight anyone who tried to separate them.

She pulled back the curtains and looked out at the dark silent street. She was only allowed to open the curtains when it was dark, for fear of anyone seeing her and knowing that she was not in England like her parents had told them. She wished she *was* in England; she'd be safe there, her baby would be safe there.

The only light was from the one street lamp outside Theresa bloody Mahon's house, may a swarm of wasps fly up her nose when she's asleep. It was her fault that Colleen was locked in this room.

Colleen pressed her face against the cool glass. She longed to breathe in some fresh air but her father had nailed the windows shut. She longed to be in Roibin's arms – Roibin, who smelled of the fields and meadows and life and the open road. She closed her eyes and pictured his face. The way his dark hair fell like a curtain over his forehead, the way he pushed it back, in that careless way he had about him, the way he teased her with his eyes and, may God forgive her, the way she felt when he touched her. She had let him do things that she never dreamed she would let any boy do. She was a good Catholic girl – at least, she had been.

It all began the day herself and Theresa Mahon had been picking berries in the woods. 'Mammy will be only delighted with this haul,' said Theresa, popping another one into her mouth. 'They're only delicious, Colleen, the sweetest I've ever tasted. Won't you try one?'

'I have no mind to try one, Theresa, until they are rinsed under the tap and the bird shite has gone from them. And if you keep stuffing them down your throat there won't be any left for your mother to be delighted with.'

Theresa bit into another one and Colleen watched as the purple juice ran down Theresa's good blouse.

'Yer awful fussy, Colleen Brenna. You talk as if you were highborn. A bit of bird shite never hurt anyone.'

It was then they heard wagons and the sound of horses' hooves on the stony path.

Theresa nearly chocked on the blackberry. 'Jesus, Colleen, it's the gypsies! Hide.'

All doors were firmly locked when they pitched up in some field on the edge of town. Popular opinion was that they were thieving Godless rogues that would take food out of the babies' mouths and ravage their innocent daughters without a care for the wrath of God on Judgement Day. Personally, Colleen had never heard of any girls in the town being ravaged by gypsies and as for taking the food out of the babies' mouths, the mammies would kill them stone dead if they went anywhere near them. But the gossips in the town spoke as if they knew something the rest didn't.

She peered through the bushes as the painted caravans passed by. It reminded her of when she had seen *The Wizard of Oz* in Horrigan's Picture House. The beginning of the film was black and white but when Dorothy landed in Oz, it was all technicolor, with bright-blue skies and green trees and a yellow-brick road. Suddenly her world seemed brighter and, somehow, she knew that her life was about to change, that from now on it would be in technicolor.

The first time she had spoken to Roibin was down the quay. It was early September and there was a chill in the air. The tide was in and the sea was choppy, splashing over the quayside and bouncing the little fishing boats around as if they were toys to be played with. Roibin was sitting on the wall, looking out over the water. There was a stillness about him, as if he knew who he was and had nothing to prove to anyone, unlike the boys in the town who were a bunch of eejits.

'There's one of them,' said Theresa, nodding towards the boy. 'He has a nerve sitting there as if he owned the place.'

Colleen couldn't take her eyes off him; it was as if she was mesmerised.

'Don't you think he has a nerve?'

'Jesus, Theresa, he's doing no harm. He has as much right to sit there as anyone else.'

'Well, I think he has a nerve.'

'So you keep saying. I'm going to go across and say hello.'

The way Theresa looked at her, you'd swear she'd just said that she had a mind to ravage Father Benny in front of the blessed sacrament.

'You're going to do what?'

'Say hello, what's so wrong with that? He's a stranger in the town and deserves a bit of human kindness.'

'You know very well what's wrong with that. He's a gypsy for God's sake, your reputation will be ruined and what would your mammy say?'

'I have no idea, but I might remind her that Jesus said: "We are to love others regardless, of their race or religion."'

'When did he say that?'

'In the parable of the good Samaritan.'

Theresa had gone red in the face. 'Well, get you, Colleen Brenna, quoting the Bible as if you were Father Benny.'

'I know,' said Colleen, grinning. 'Aren't I a great girl altogether?'

'You're a fool is what you are. Well, don't be asking me to hang around while you canoodle with yer man.'

'I wasn't going to.'

Colleen watched her stomping off across the quay and

didn't care. She wanted to speak to the boy on her own and hoped she wouldn't get struck down by lightning for being so brazen. She took a deep breath and walked across. She sat beside him and stared out over the water. She watched as the fishermen hauled their catch onto the quayside.

'They have a good haul,' she said.

The boy smiled at her, his eyes seeming to look into her very soul. Eyes that were as blue as a summer sky, fringed by dark lashes that would surely be the envy of every girl in the town. No boy had a right to look that beautiful.

'I'm hoping to buy some,' he said.

It was as if she'd swallowed her tongue but she managed to squeak. 'Well, they'll be nice and fresh.' Then she felt like an idiot.

He nodded. 'Indeed they will.'

They sat in silence, but it didn't feel awkward, she felt at peace beside this boy she hardly knew. If Theresa had been beside her she would have been yapping away about this one and that one. She would have taken no pleasure in the beauty of the River Blackwater, or the little white cottage on the far bank that stood alone on the tip of the ferry point.

He held out his hand. 'Roibin Carroll.'

'Colleen Brenna,' she said, smiling at him.

He kept hold of her hand. 'It's nice to meet you, Colleen.'

That was the moment she should have jumped off the wall and run for her life, but she didn't and she wouldn't have changed that for the world.

They met in secret places, in the woods and the dark corners of the town. Sometimes they would just sit on the banks of the river, not speaking but touching, always touching. She couldn't get enough of him, she ached when they were apart. It was as if she'd been newly born, as if she hadn't had a life before him. They made love amongst the ruins of the old abbey – she knew it was wrong, she knew she should have been racked with guilt, but what she felt was an overwhelming sense of happiness and joy.

By spring he was gone, as she knew he would. He left without saying goodbye and a piece of her heart went with him.

'That's the way of gypsies,' said Theresa. 'They ravage the girls and move on. I'd say there's a pile of dark-haired children in every county of Ireland wondering who their daddies are.'

'How come you're suddenly the expert on gypsies, Theresa Mahon?'

'It's a well-known fact.'

'It's an old wives' tale.'

'It is not, I heard it from my mammy and my mammy's mammy. Are you standing there and telling me that I come from a family of liars?'

'Of course I'm not, I was just saying.'

'Well, don't. Anyway, I think you're lucky to be shot of him. If anyone had seen the two of you canoodling, you'd be up before Father Benny and your name would be read out at Mass and your family shamed. You should be down on your knees thanking God and all the saints that he didn't take advantage of you.'

Colleen could feel her face getting hot and Theresa was looking at her as if she had two heads.

'You didn't, did you?' she said. 'Dear God, tell me you didn't.'

'What's it to you what I did, Theresa Mahon? It's time you stopped poking your nose into other people's affairs.'

'Well, you can be sure that I won't be poking my nose into your affairs again, Colleen Brenna. I have better things to do than associate myself with a fallen woman.'

'Oh, go fry yer nose,' she said.

. . .

She should have kept Theresa on her side but she hadn't and very soon Theresa had her revenge. She told Sister Concepta that Colleen Brenna had sinned against God and she'd felt it her duty to inform her. People had seen Sister Concepta running through the town like a banshee, with her black veil flying behind her. Father Benny's housekeeper had told her what went on next. Apparently, Father Benny had just sat down to his dinner when Sister Concepta burst into the presbytery and insisted he accompany her to the Brennas' house as one of his flock had fallen from Grace. Father Benny had never taken to Sister Concepta and he was none too pleased to be dragged from his dinner, it would be cold by the time he got back.

'You have to hear her confession, Father, for if she dies in the night, she will have a mortal sin on her soul and be denied a place at the Lord's table.'

Father Benny had put another forkful of the good beef into his mouth and stared at the nun. 'And what leads you to believe that she will die in the night? Is the girl ill?'

'Her very soul is ill, Father, her very soul is black with the pain she has inflicted on our Blessed Lord, she has to be absolved from the sin of debauchery. You have a duty to hear her confession.'

Father Benny didn't like to be told what to do and what not to do. Father Benny wanted to eat his dinner in peace and he wanted Sister Concepta out of his house.

Father Benny's housekeeper came into the room carrying the Father's bowl of apple cake and custard. 'You haven't eaten your dinner, Father,' she'd said. 'Is it not to your liking? The butcher assured me that it was the best cut of beef in the shop.'

'It is very much to my liking, Mrs Lacey, but I'm told that I must hear someone's confession right away.'

Mrs Lacey glared at Sister Concepta. 'What is so important that prevents Father enjoying his dinner?'

'A girl in the town has gone over to the dark side.'

'What in all that's holy are you talking about, woman? The dark side of what, for Heaven's sake?'

'She has turned her back on God and all His angels and has moved towards the Devil.'

'Well, the Devil will have to wait, Sister, for I will not have Father going without his dinner. You can wait in the hallway until he has finished.'

Father Benny smiled gratefully at Mrs Lacey. 'I will be as quick as I can, Sister,' he'd said.

'You will not, Father,' said Mrs Lacey. 'You will take your time. I'm not having you doubled up with indigestion and the Bishop arriving tomorrow.'

Sister Concepta had gone red in the face. 'But...?'

'But nothing. Go and wait in the hallway and let Father alone, he has a right to eat his dinner in peace.'

'This is urgent, Mrs Lacey. An innocent girl has fallen.'

'Fallen where?'

'From Grace.'

'For God's sake, woman, will you speak in a language that we can all understand.'

Father Benny continued eating his dinner, enjoying the drama that was unfolding before him. If he wasn't a priest ordained by God, he would have given Mrs Lacey a big hug.

Mrs Lacey glared at Sister Concepta. 'And why can't Father hear her confession here in the church? Why would he need to be running through the town, with his belly full of beef and apple cake? I assume she hasn't been rendered incapable of walking.'

'It's her soul that needs saving, Mrs Lacey, not her legs.'

'Then she can come here. And that, Sister, is my last word on the matter.'

. . .

Mammy and Daddy were none too happy to have Sister Concepta standing in their kitchen. Having a nun visit the house was usually an honour and the place would be cleaned from top to bottom. Her mammy would make sure that the neighbours were informed of the visit and the best china would be taken down from the dresser and a sponge would be placed on top of her grandmother's glass cake stand. As it was, her mammy's eyes were out on two stalks, staring at the nun and wondering why on earth she was standing, unannounced, in the middle of her kitchen that was in need of a clean and with not a cake in sight.

Sister Concepta took great delight in telling them that their daughter had brought shame on the house of Brenna by laying with a gypsy.

Daddy had been dozing by the fire and was none too happy to be woken by a nun talking a load of shite. 'Laying where?'

'Well, Mr Brenna, I am not privy to that piece of information but I have it on good authority that she's been laying somewhere with him.'

Colleen's mother had cried and her father had eaten the face off her and was all for giving her the beating of her life but Sister Concepta stood between them.

'It is not Colleen's fault, Mr Brenna,' she'd said.

'Then whose fault is it?' he'd shouted.

'It's a well-known fact that gypsies are in cahoots with the Devil. The boy put a spell on her.'

'The boy put a spell on her, my arse,' said her father.

From then on, her parents only spoke to her when they had to and when the sickness started they locked her in her room and told everyone that she had gone to England to stay with relatives.

Roibin had taught her a lot. She'd loved listening to his voice, it was like listening to poetry. He'd taught her the meanings of the patterns on the caravans and the ways of his people.

He'd told her that his mother's name was Rosa and his father's name was Tamas. But the most useful thing he had taught her was how to pick a lock. She hadn't asked how he knew about picking a lock but it was this that had enabled her to creep out of her room every night and steal anything she could sell. It was great sport listening to her parents arguing, blaming each other for the missing items.

'Where's my watch?' screamed her father. 'I left it on the dresser and now it's gone.'

'How would I know?' shouted her mother. 'I'm still looking for my silver thimble.'

And so it went on, and now she had enough to see her through for a while. She would leave the rest to God, if He was still talking to her.

Colleen stared out of the window at the dark night. The street was deserted, it would have been nice to see another human being, she wouldn't feel so alone in the world. It had been raining and the street lamp shone down on the puddles, turning them into iridescent little ponds, the spiny branches of the trees casting their reflection in the rippling water. It looked like a painting that had come to life.

She liked the darkness. She needed the darkness. Tonight, it would be her friend and it would cover her flight to freedom.

She could still hear her parents moving around downstairs. She could be patient – she had learned how to be patient. In a few hours, she would make her escape. In only a few more hours she would leave her childhood home and never look back.

She placed her hands on her tummy; she was not alone. 'We're going to be OK, little one,' she said gently. 'You and I are going to be OK.'

CHAPTER 14

Mary Kate sat at her desk and looked at the papers in front of her. Mr Renson had listed the properties that she now owned in London, and the money she had, in her newly opened bank account. The responsibility of so much wealth weighed heavily on her mind. The only thing she knew was that she wanted to make a difference, she wanted to share her good fortune with those in need – but how to go about it? Mr Renson had warned of the dangers of con artists who would take advantage of her naivety and her kind heart. He had advised – no, he had insisted – that she ran everything past him before making any decisions and she had readily agreed, for she was grateful for his guidance.

Just then there was a tap on the door. 'Come in,' she called.

'I hope I'm not disturbing you,' said Moira, stepping into the room.

Mary Kate was surprised to see her, for she was like a ghost going about the place who only spoke when she had to. She couldn't make her out at all. When she had thought about running a boarding house, she had imagined friendly people filling the place, delighting in the lovely bedrooms. She had imagined a kind of family, who would appreciate the comfort and beauty of the house, but Moira Kent avoided any kind of pleasantries; she wasn't the type of woman who went in for small talk. Mary Kate looked at her now, standing in front of her, so stiff and unyielding. Everything about her was grey, her clothes were old fashioned and worn, it was as if she wanted to disappear. Her hair was poker-straight and lank, framing such a plain face. She wondered if this woman had ever known love, ever known kindness or the touch of a gentle hand. She herself had known loneliness, she knew what it felt like to be without love or companionship, what it felt like to want to give up on life – her heart went out to this sad woman in front of her. She felt like putting her arms around her and telling her that things could get better but she would probably run for the hills.

'Please sit down, Miss Kent,' she said. 'Is something amiss?'

'No, Miss Ryan, everything is satisfactory.'

Mary Kate waited.

'It's about Abby,' she said.

'Is she bothering you? If she is, I will have a word with her.'

'Oh no, she is not bothering me, not at all. But I have noticed that the child doesn't attend school.'

'Abby couldn't cope with school, Miss Kent. She was abandoned at two years old; found sleeping on the steps of the abbey. The nuns took her in and cared for her as if she was one of their own. She hasn't spoken to anyone except Jessie from the day she was found.'

'Has she had any education at all? Can she read?'

'The nuns did their best but they are not teachers. I don't know if she can read. I will ask Jessie, she should know.'

'I would like to teach her, Miss Ryan.'

Mary Kate didn't know what to say. If it had been anyone else willing to help Abby she would have been only delighted but Moira Kent wasn't someone that a child could warm to.

'I'm not sure. As I said, she doesn't speak.'

'I don't need her to speak, Miss Ryan, only to listen. If it doesn't work out, we can abandon the idea, but the child needs an education and I can give her that.'

'I will speak to Jessie, because you are right, she does need an education.'

Moira stood up. 'I will wait to hear from you then and if you would like me to teach Abby, we can come to an arrangement regarding payment.'

'Of course, and thank you for your concern, Miss Kent. Abby is a sweet child.'

'I'm sure she is, but I'm afraid sweetness doesn't equate to knowledge and without knowledge, the child will be ignorant. I feel it is my duty to help.'

Once Miss Kent had left the room, Mary Kate breathed a sigh of relief. She felt as if she'd just been well and truly put in her place. The woman would give you a headache, she couldn't see gentle little Abby taking to her at all. Her duty, indeed? She didn't want Miss Kent teaching Abby out of some sense of duty, she wasn't a bloody project for her to practise on.

But she was being mean, when what she should be feeling was gratitude. She would have to go to confession on Saturday.

The more she thought about it, the more she realised that maybe Miss Moira Kent had a heart after all, because she didn't have to worry about Abby's education, did she? Maybe the word 'duty' wasn't such a bad thing, for wasn't it also *her* duty to do the best she could for both the girls? Sister Luke had said that Jessie was clever and what they wanted for her was to go to college. Well, that was something she could do and she felt ashamed that it had taken Miss Kent to remind her of it. Yes, Jessie would go to college.

She waited until the afternoon to speak to her.

Jessie stared at Mary Kate. 'Miss Kent wants to teach Abby?'

Mary Kate nodded.

'I can't see Abby taking to her at all, Miss Ryan, she scares the shite out of *me*. Sorry, miss.'

'That's all right, Jessie, she scares the shite out of me too.'

They both started giggling. 'I'll ask her,' said Jessie, 'but don't get your hopes up.'

'I won't. And Jessie...'

'Yes, miss?'

'Would you like to go to college?'

Jessie's eyes filled with tears. 'But who will help you in the house?'

'I'm sure we will manage.' Mary Kate took Jessie's hands in hers. 'So, would you like to go to college, Jessie?'

By now tears were running down Jessie's cheeks. 'I would love to go to college, Miss Ryan. Oh, I would love to go to college.'

CHAPTER 15

Orla and Polly

Mammy had been roaring crying all morning, setting the baby wailing in his basket. Daddy was poking at the fire as if his life depended on it, sending blasts of heat into the little room till they could hardly breathe. The baby's face was bright red and there were beads of sweat on his forehead.

'Will you stop with the poking, Paddy,' said Mammy. 'We're only melting here.' Mammy started crying again and dabbing her eyes on her apron. 'It'll be like a morgue here without the two of you.'

'Jesus, Mammy,' said Orla. 'We're going to Dublin, not the feckin' moon.'

'You'll have to mind your language at Clerys, girl, or you'll be thrown out into the street. You should be down on your knees thanking God for giving you this opportunity, not blaspheming and swearing.'

'I thought it was Uncle Jack that got us the job,' said Orla.

'But he was guided by God.'

'Don't worry, Mammy,' said Polly. 'I'll make sure she behaves herself.'

'Listen to you,' said Orla, glaring at her sister. 'Are you looking to be canonised or what?'

Orla and Polly were twins but they were as different as chalk and cheese, not only in looks but in every other way possible. Orla's hair was a deep auburn and Polly's was almost black. Orla was disgusted with her hair and envied Polly her beautiful dark locks. Polly had inherited her mother's looks and her gentle ways, whereas Orla had always been a bit on the giddy side. Orla got her colouring from their daddy, and all she could see was her red curly hair that was the bane of her life. And yet it was Orla who was the beautiful one. Her skin was like alabaster and the smattering of freckles across her nose gave her character. Her eyes were the colour of the sky, deep blue, fringed with golden lashes, that seemed to change with her mood.

Despite their differences, the girls loved each other, they loved their family and they loved the little cottage in Youghal that had been their home since they were born.

Mammy handed Polly a parcel. 'A bit of food for the journey, love,' she said.

'Thanks, Mammy.'

'The car's here,' said Orla.

The girls hugged their parents and kissed Billy's sweaty head.

'Don't wave us off, Mammy,' said Polly. 'Let's just say goodbye here.'

'And smile,' said Orla. 'We don't want to remember you with long faces. We'll be home again before you know it.'

They picked up their cases, gave a last look around the room and left the cottage, closing the door gently behind them.

Diddy Cronin was leaning against his car, puffing away on a fag. 'Good morning, ladies.'

'The station please, Diddy,' said Orla. 'We're off to Dublin.'

'I know where you're off to,' said Diddy, grinning. 'Sure, doesn't the whole town know where you're off to?'

Diddy Cronin was a small man, hence his name. No one knew what his real name was, for he had always been known as Diddy and he didn't seem to mind one bit.

'Are you scared to be going off to the big city, girls?' he said.

'Now why should we be scared? We're sixteen years old and not children any more,' said Orla.

'How about you, Polly?'

'I suppose I am a bit, Diddy. But sure I have Orla with me, I won't be alone. In fact, if I didn't have Orla beside me, I wouldn't be going at all.'

'I've a sister in Dublin,' said Diddy, 'and I've visited the place many times.'

'What's it like?' said Orla.

'Oh, it's a grand city. I'd say the two of you will be desperate homesick for a while but once you get over that you'll have a great time altogether.'

The girls fell silent and stared out the window. Diddy drove slowly across the old bridge and they looked back at the town. They could see the clock gate rising above the houses and the spire of St Mary's church, they looked down at the beautiful River Blackwater flowing gently beneath them and their hearts were full.

The truth was that the pair of them were terrified and the closer they got to the station the worse they felt. Polly was holding the parcel of food close to her heart, as if it was Billy she had in her arms. She had an awful lump in her throat but she knew that if she started crying, Orla would eat the face off her but her sister reached across and took hold of her hand as if she knew what Polly was feeling. They had always had this connection with each other, where they seemed to know what was in each other's heart. When they were children, Orla fell out of a tree and broke her ankle and Polly was limping for a week. If it had been Orla who was limping, Mammy would have just thought that she was looking for attention but she knew that Polly was in real pain. The whole thing worried her and she wanted to make sure it was not the Devil's doing, so she took herself up to the church to speak to Father Benny.

'You were right to come and see me, Mrs Dooley,' he'd said, 'for I can assure you that the Devil has no hand in this. Orla and Polly were in each other's arms for nine months and I'd say they got to know each other pretty well. This communication they have with each other is a blessing from God and who are we to question His ways? You believe in the Holy Ghost, don't you?'

'I do indeed, Father.'

'But you don't really understand it?'

Mammy had shaken her head. 'I don't.'

'It's a mystery all right, but we have faith. It's the same with your girls. We don't have to understand the ways of God, we just have to accept and trust in His goodness.'

She left the church with a lighter heart, knowing it was Almighty God and not the bloody Devil that had given her girls this gift.

Diddy stopped the car outside the station and lifted their cases out of the boot.

'May God go with you, girls, and make your mammy and daddy proud.'

'We will.'

'And don't go getting your heads turned in the big city.'

'We won't, Diddy.'

'And one more thing, girls. Don't get too excited about the boarding house you'll be staying in, for they are all shite in Dublin.'

Orla raised her eyes up to Heaven. 'Well, that will be something to look forward to, Diddy, thanks very much.'

As they were walking away, Diddy shouted after them, 'And don't miss Mass on Sundays.'

'We won't, Diddy,' called Polly.

They started walking across the platform.

'Have you ever seen Diddy at Mass?' said Orla, giggling.

Polly grinned. 'Never. He's always been a great one for giving advice, it's a pity he doesn't follow it himself.'

'Imagine Diddy Cronin having a sister in Dublin,' said Orla. 'I never even knew he had a sister.'

'I'd heard rumours,' said Polly.

Orla stopped walking and stared at her sister. 'What sort of rumours? And why haven't I heard any rumours?'

'I walked in on Mammy and Mrs Quinn once and they were talking about Diddy's sister bringing shame on the family. They stopped talking when they realised I was there.'

'And you didn't tell me? Why didn't you tell me? We tell each other everything.'

'Well, there was nothing much to tell.'

'There was enough, we could have found out a bit more.'

'I can't say I was that interested, Orla. Anyway, won't we be too busy with our own lives to be bothered about what Diddy's sister might have got up to?'

Orla smiled at her sister. 'You're right, Polly.'

'Grand so,' said Polly, smiling.

Doors were slamming shut and yer man was waving his flag. The girls ran across the platform and jumped into the nearest carriage.

'Jesus, Orla, we nearly missed the train.'

'Well, it would have been your fault if we had, going on about Diddy bloody Cronin's sister.' As the train started moving, Orla pulled down the window and shouted, 'Look out, Dublin, the Dooleys are on their way.'

Polly laughed. 'Oh, Orla, what would I do without you?'

'You'll never have to, Polly, for I'll always be with you.'

Polly closed her eyes and leaned back in her seat. They really were going to Dublin.

CHAPTER 16

Colleen was tired and hungry; she was desperate for a cup of good, sweet tea and a sandwich.

Dublin frightened her. At home she knew almost everyone in her little town. She'd sat beside them at school, they'd played together in the streets and run through the fields and woods where they had grown up. In this city she was a stranger, just another face amongst the hundreds of people that jostled her on the crowded pavements. At home, you couldn't walk down the street without someone saying hello and asking after the family but here, everyone was in a hurry, they had no time to stop and pass the time of day and, Jesus, she'd never seen so many cars, you took your life in your hands just crossing the road. She longed for the safety of home, where she was loved. Oh yes, she had been loved all right and she'd thrown it away for a gypsy boy called Roibin. She had nowhere to go and no one to care whether she lived or died but she couldn't go back, she couldn't ever go back.

For the last two nights she'd slept on a bench in the railway station. People passed her by, as if someone sleeping on a bench was an everyday occurrence. At home you'd be interrogated.

'Does your mammy know where you are?' Or 'Will I get Father Benny?' They'd live on it for weeks. 'Did you see the Brenna girl asleep on a bench for all the town to see? As brazen as you like, in front of Toomey's shop, with a statue of the Blessed Virgin in the window.' But this wasn't home, this was Dublin, where people minded their own business and left you to yours. During the day she'd walked the streets of the city, looking for somewhere to sell her stolen goods. She hadn't thought about how she was going to manage in a city where she knew no one and no one knew her. She had been turned away from every shop she'd entered, and she was getting desperate. She knew what she looked like – she'd caught a glimpse of herself in a shop window – she looked like a Hobo, no wonder people avoided her. There was no kindness here, it was a town without pity. No one was going to help her, she was going to have to help herself.

She smoothed her hair back from her face, pulled her coat tighter around her swollen belly and straightened her shoulders. That's when she noticed the man staring at her.

'Hello,' he said softly.

'I'm on my way home,' she said quickly. 'To my husband, he'll be waiting for me.'

The man smiled at her. 'You don't look as if you're on your way home.'

'Well, I am, I'm on my way home.'

'If you say so,' he said, grinning. 'But you look to me like a girl in need of a bit of help and a plate of eggs and bacon, am I right?'

The thought of a plate of eggs and bacon made her feel dizzy and she leaned against the wall.

'Come on,' he said. 'There's a café up the road that does a grand breakfast.'

'I don't have any money and I don't know you.'

'And you're right to be cautious. There's some in this town

who would take advantage of a young girl like yourself but I'm not one of them.'

She stared at the man. He didn't look Irish, his skin was a golden brown, a bit like Roibin's. She'd heard terrible tales of slavers that shipped young girls off to foreign parts, never to be seen again.

The man held out his hand. 'My name is Ashar Patel and you won't need any money as my family own the café.'

Colleen hesitated before she took his hand. The man had a kind face, there was something about him that she felt she could trust. 'Colleen Brenna,' she said.

He picked up her case and she followed him. Was she mad altogether, walking off with a man she didn't know from Adam? She could almost hear Theresa Mahon, may she die roaring, saying, 'Run for your life, Colleen.' Well, Theresa Mahon could go fry her nose. She needed to eat, if not for herself, then for her baby. Almighty God had given her two good legs, and if she had to run, she'd run, without any advice from Theresa bloody Mahon.

Her feet were killing her and she could barely keep up with Ashar. He noticed and slowed down.

'Not far now,' he said, smiling.

They left the main road and turned down a side street. It felt different here, friendlier somehow. There were people sitting on steps outside the shops, chatting and laughing. Men were standing in groups, smoking, and children were running amongst them, playing chase. They were speaking in a language she didn't understand, but it didn't matter, they smiled at her as she passed them and waved at the man beside her. It reminded her of home and her eyes filled with tears.

When Colleen didn't think she could walk any further, the man stopped outside a small shop. There was a closed sign on the door and when he opened it, her stomach groaned as the smell of fried food wafted out into the street.

'There's a child of Brahma here, who is in need of food,' he called.

A woman walked towards them, smiling. Colleen thought she was beautiful. Her hair was black and shiny, and she wore it in a long plait that reached down to her waist.

'Another lost soul, my son?' she said, putting her arms around him. 'You will have us all ruined.'

'Mother, may I introduce you to Colleen Brenna.'

The woman kissed her on both cheeks and sort of bowed. 'You are welcome in our home, Colleen.'

She'd been so strong, she hadn't had time to feel sorry for herself. What had kept her going through all those lonely months was the need to get out of that room and find a place of safety for her and her baby, but the kindness of these strangers touched her heart and all the sadness and fear that she had been holding in burst out of her like a broken dam. She sat down at one of the tables, put her head in her hands and sobbed.

Mrs Patel sat beside her, stroked her hair and murmured words in a language that Colleen didn't understand but which she still found soothed her. She leaned into Mrs Patel and for the first time in so long she felt at peace. She cried until there were no tears left and all the while she was held by this beautiful woman, who smelled of flowers and spices and love.

'Crying is good for the soul, little one,' Mrs Patel whispered.

Colleen dried her eyes on the sleeve of her coat. 'I'm sorry,' she said.

Mrs Patel shook her head. 'No need for sorry, you are amongst friends.'

Friends, thought Colleen, *what a lovely word.*

'Ashar,' said Mrs Patel, 'go into the kitchen and tell your father to bring us a meal fit for a king.'

Colleen looked around the room, she was just now noticing how beautiful it was. It was small and square, with wooden tables dotted about, each with chairs pulled up to its sides. Each table was covered in a cloth, placed diagonally, in a jewelled colour – vivid red, jade green, electric blue – and the edges of the cloths were fringed with spangles that caught the light and reflected it, sparkling, around the walls. In the centre of each table was a small candle on a saucer and a highly decorated ceramic elephant, with paper menus slotted into the place on its back where somebody riding it might have sat.

There were lights around the counter and every wall filled with pictures in the brightest of colours. Pictures that were strange to her and yet filled her with a kind of joy. The window looked out over the street, but inside the café was like being in a different place altogether than the cold, grey city beyond. Inside, it felt warm and welcoming and cosy. Although it was like no home Colleen had ever known, it felt like home.

Mrs Patel saw her looking at them. 'Come,' she said, taking her hand.

Colleen stood up and walked across to the wall.

'We are Hindus, Colleen, and these are some of our gods.' She smiled. 'We have many gods.' She pointed to one of them. 'This is Ganesh, he is the elephant God and lord of success, knowledge and wealth.' She stopped in front of a picture of a lady, sitting on a flower. 'And this one is Lakshmi.'

'She is beautiful,' said Colleen. 'But why does she have four arms?'

'A lot of our gods are shown with many arms. Lakshmi's arms depict the four important goals of life: morality, love, humanity and self-knowledge. Good things to aim for in our lives. We try but we are human and we don't always succeed.'

Colleen smiled. 'Neither do I,' she said.

'But there is always tomorrow for us to try again, yes?'

'Yes.'

Just then, Ashar came through the curtain, carrying a plate of food.

'And now you must eat,' said Mrs Patel, smiling.

Colleen sat down and Ashar placed the food in front of her. 'Don't worry, we won't sit and stare at you. We must open the café now.'

She had never tasted food like it and probably never would again. She ate as much as she could, then sat back in the chair and watched as the room started to fill with people. She noticed that when they said hello to Mrs Patel, they bowed, with their hands joined as if in prayer. There was something beautiful about these people, something calm and still and unhurried, she felt blessed to be amongst them. She didn't want to leave, she was warm and contented and at peace. She had seen another side of Dublin, a kind side, and it gave her hope. She stood up and put on her coat.

Mrs Patel came across to her. 'Do you have somewhere to sleep tonight, Colleen?'

It would have been so easy to say no and take advantage of such kindness but she had to do this on her own. She nodded, though she could tell that Mrs Patel didn't believe her.

'You will come and see us again?' she said.

'I will, I promise that I will.'

'And you will bring your baby?'

Colleen's eyes filled with tears. This lovely lady was not judging her, she spoke of her baby as if it was the most natural thing in the world. 'Of course I will.'

'My name is Sunni,' said Mrs Patel, kissing her cheek. 'May your God watch over you, Colleen, until we meet again.'

She left the comfort of the café with Mrs Patel's words in her head. Yes, tomorrow was another day and something told her that it was going to be a better one.

With a full tummy and hope in her heart, she headed back to the station.

CHAPTER 17

Orla gently nudged her sleeping sister. 'We're here, Polly,' she said.

Polly stirred and opened her eyes.

'Put on your coat, it's raining out there.'

Polly looked out of the window. 'I don't know whether I'm excited or terrified,' she said.

Orla smiled at her. 'As long as we're together, we'll be fine.' As the train pulled into the station, she lifted the bags down from the rack. 'Ready?' she said.

'As ready as I'll ever be,' said Polly.

They opened the carriage door and stepped onto the platform. The rain was coming down in sheets and people were hurrying for shelter.

'Jesus, we'll be drenched,' said Orla. 'This is a fine bloody welcome.'

'I don't think that we can blame Dublin for the weather, Orla.'

'OK, let's run for it, that looks like a café over there.'

Polly started to run after her, then she stopped.

Orla turned around. 'Will you come on, Polly, or we'll be arriving at the digs looking like two drowned rats.'

'Isn't that Colleen Brenna?' said Polly, pointing along the platform.

Orla peered through the driving rain at the figure on the bench. 'It can't be Colleen, she's in England, isn't she?'

'That's what I thought but it looks like Colleen.'

'We'd better check,' said Orla. They hurried across and looked down at the girl huddled over on the bench; she was coughing and she was soaked.

Polly touched her gently on the shoulder. 'Colleen?' she said softly.

Colleen's eyes flew open, she looked scared to death.

'It's OK,' said Orla, gently. 'It's only me and Polly.'

'I thought for a minute it was me daddy.'

'No, it's just us.'

Colleen stared at the girls. 'What in God's name are you two doing here?'

'We've a job in Clerys department store,' said Orla. 'But more to the point, what are *you* doing here? We thought you were in England.'

'It's a long story,' said Colleen.

'You better come with us,' said Polly. 'We're heading for the café. You can tell us everything over a grand cup of tea, you look as if you could do with one.'

Colleen stood up and rubbed her back; she was cold and stiff.

Polly picked up her bag and the three of them hurried across to the café. Its windows were so steamed up you couldn't see inside, and when they opened the door they saw why. There was steam coming off everyone, it looked as if they were all on fire.

'Sit down, Colleen, and we'll get the tea,' said Polly. They ordered tea and buns and waited at the counter. 'Oh, Orla, did you see her belly?'

'It would have been hard not to, the poor girl.'

'Do you think she's run away from home?'

Orla frowned. 'Well, something's not right, she looks exhausted and her hair's a fright.'

'What are we going to do with her?'

'We're going to look after her and if she has nowhere to go, we'll take her to the boarding house with us.'

'Do you think they'll let her in?' said Polly.

'Well, if they don't, we'll find a boarding house that will.'

They carried the tray to the table and sat down. Colleen was silent as she drank the tea and then, bit by bit, she told her story. Polly's eyes were full of tears as she listened and Orla couldn't take in what she was hearing.

'They locked you up?'

Colleen nodded.

'For how long?'

'I don't know.'

'Oh, Colleen,' said Polly. 'We passed your house so many times. If only we'd known. I'm so sorry.'

'They were going to take my baby away, I had to get out of there.'

Polly reached across the table and held her hand. 'Of course you did and you have been really brave, you should be very proud of yourself. *I'm* proud of you.'

'So am I,' said Orla. 'I'm guessing you have nowhere to stay, am I right?'

Colleen nodded.

'Then you'll come with us. You're not alone any more, you have me and Polly and together, we'll figure things out.'

. . .

There was great excitement in the house waiting for the girls to arrive, it would be lovely to have young people around the place. Miss Kent was no trouble, but she had brought very little joy with her. Mary Kate had never even seen the woman smile; she'd put you in a mood just looking at her.

Mary Kate remembered the day she'd spent in Clerys with Jenny and how wonderful she'd felt in the new clothes. She was no different inside, not really, but the clothes had given her a confidence that she had never had before. She wondered whether new clothes and a lovely hairdo would make a difference to Miss Kent. Not that she would ever suggest it, but she'd love to see her out of those dowdy clothes. She was on the plain side all right, but a softer hairstyle would surely improve her looks.

'Shall I put the girls on the top floor with Miss Kent, or the lower floor?' said Jessie.

Mary Kate smiled at her. 'I'm thinking they might be better on the lower floor, Jessie, don't you?'

Jessie smiled back. 'I was thinking the same, Miss Ryan.'

'There you are then, we're of the same mind.'

'We are, Miss Ryan. Will I give them the room at the front of the house?'

'I have a feeling they won't mind which room they have and the view will be lost on them,' said Mary Kate. 'Put them in the room next door, for it has single beds. I don't know much about sisters, but I imagine there will be times when they fall out with each other and may want a bit of space.'

'There were sisters at the convent,' said Jessie, 'who were always eating the faces off each other.'

'Well, there you are, the room with the single beds it is.'

Jessie was just about to leave when Mary Kate stopped her. 'Where's Abby?'

'She's up with Miss Kent.'

'And is Guinness with her?'

'He is, should I fetch him down?'

'No, leave him. I'd say, knowing Miss Kent, if she didn't want him there he would have been shown the door by now.'

Jessie laughed. 'I'd say you're right, miss. Actually, I think she likes the dog. I've seen her petting him when she didn't know I was watching her.'

'Well now, isn't that lovely?'

'It is, miss.'

After Jessie had left the room, Mary Kate sat back down in her favourite chair by the window. Something astonishing had happened between Abby and Miss Kent. Not only had the woman been teaching the child, but they had taken to going for long walks together and Abby seemed happy to be with her. Miss Kent would knock on the door and say, 'Myself and Abby are going for a walk, Miss Ryan, we'll be back by lunchtime.' She wasn't the sort to indulge in small talk, no mention of the weather, no good morning, she said what she needed to say and was gone. What would it take for the woman to unbend a bit?

Mary Kate would stand by the window and watch the two of them walking across the green, with Guinness running ahead of them. She tried to imagine them on their silent walks. It didn't seem to matter that Abby didn't speak, Miss Kent didn't say much either. It was as if they accepted each other and could be themselves.

Mary Kate didn't know Miss Kent's story, but she knew that this was a woman who had suffered. She knew that something had made her turn her back on the world. As for Abby, they would never know. They were two damaged souls who had found peace in each other's company and for that, Mary Kate was happy.

CHAPTER 18

Orla, Polly and Colleen stood on the green, staring across at the beautiful house.

'Are you sure this is it, Polly?'

'Yer woman said that it was the only one with a red door, so unless the address is wrong, it must be the one.'

'But Diddy said that all the boarding houses in Dublin were shite,' said Orla. 'This one looks like a hotel.'

'They won't let me in,' said Colleen. 'It looks too grand.'

'Well, if they don't, we'll find ourselves a shite one, where we will all be made welcome.'

'I think that you should go in alone,' insisted Colleen. 'I'll find another one.'

'You will not, Colleen,' said Polly. 'We'll all stick together and leave the rest to God.'

'I don't think God will be putting Himself out to help me.'

'When was the last time you went to confession?' said Polly.

'I don't know but it was a long time ago.'

'Then we'll find a church and you can confess your sin and be forgiven.'

Colleen didn't look convinced. 'What if my sin is too big to be forgiven?'

Polly smiled at her. 'Didn't God forgive yer man beside Him on the cross, and him a desperate sinner? And didn't he forgive Mary Magdalene, who was no better than she should have been? Jesus is a great feller for forgiveness. If he forgave those two, he's bound to forgive you. You were carried away by love, Colleen, and you couldn't help it.'

Orla stared at Polly. 'How come you're suddenly an expert on getting carried away, Polly Dooley? As far as I know, you've never been carried away in your whole life, unless you're not telling me something.'

Polly grinned. 'I read a lot.'

Colleen smiled as she listened to the banter between the two sisters and wished that she had had a sister she could have confided in.

'We'll take a chance then, shall we?' said Polly.

Orla took a deep breath and picked up her case. 'All right so,' she said, and the three of them walked towards the red door.

Jessie was looking out of the upstairs window when she saw the girls walking across the green towards the house. She tore down the stairs and burst into Mary Kate's sitting room.

'They're here, miss,' she said.

'The girls?' said Mary Kate, looking up.

'Yes, miss. I've just seen them walking across the square. They have cases, so it must be them.'

Just then the doorbell rang.

'Will I let them in?'

'Seems like the best way to get to know them, Jessie.'

Mary Kate smiled. Darling Jessie cared as much about her boarding house as she did. God must have guided her to the convent that day, for she'd grown to love both the girls. She wondered what her new guests would be like; she hoped that they would settle here.

There was a tap on the door and Jessie came in, she looked flustered.

'What's wrong?' said Mary Kate.

'I thought we were expecting two of them, Miss Ryan.'

'We are, Jessie.'

'Well, there's three of them in the hallway.'

'Three of them?'

'And one of them is...'

'Is what?'

Jessie's face was colouring up. 'Well, miss, one of them is...'

'Dear God, Jessie. Does the girl have two heads or what?'

'I think you'd better see for yourself. Shall I show them in?'

'I think you had better, so that I can see for myself what the poor girl's affliction is.' Mary Kate sat down and waited. There was obviously a problem with one of them but surely it couldn't be that bad and there was more than enough room for another guest?

The door opened and the three girls came into the sitting room.

Mary Kate could immediately see what the problem was, but she smiled at them and said, 'Sit yourselves down.'

The three girls sat down on the beautiful blue sofa.

'Now, which one of you is Orla and which is Polly?'

The young girl with the red hair pushed a lock of it behind her ear. 'I'm Orla.'

The girl is beautiful, thought Mary Kate. *I'll have to lock the door against the stampede of boys that would surely be making their way up the steps.*

'And I'm Polly.' Her sister had a softer beauty, one that could easily be overlooked beside Orla.

The other girl was looking down at her feet.

'And what is your name, dear?' said Mary Kate gently.

She looked up. 'Colleen, miss,' she mumbled.

'Well, girls, my name is Miss Ryan and I am the owner of this boarding house. I hope that you will enjoy your stay here.'

'I'm sure we will, miss,' said Polly. 'You have a beautiful house.'

'I think so too,' said Mary Kate.

'We'd heard that the boarding houses in Dublin were sh—'

Polly glared at her sister.

'Desperate places altogether,' said Orla, quickly.

Mary Kate smiled. 'You heard right, Orla, for I have stayed in most of them and, quite honestly, I wouldn't put a dog in them. Talking about dogs, we have a dog here called Guinness, I hope you are all right with dogs.'

'We have a dog at home,' said Orla.

'And I miss him already,' said Polly.

'Well, you can share Guinness.'

'Thank you, miss.'

'I believe that you are going to start work in Clerys?' she said, looking at Orla and Polly.

'We are, miss,' said Orla.

'I'd say you must be feeling a bit nervous?'

'We are,' said Polly.

'Speak for yourself,' said Orla. 'I'm not feeling a bit nervous.'

Mary Kate smiled; she could already sense the differences between the two of them, not only in looks but in personality. They reminded her very much of Erin and Gerry.

'Well, let me put your minds at rest.'

'You've been there?' said Polly.

'I have, Polly, and it is magnificent. You are very lucky to have landed a position in such a beautiful store.'

Polly's eyes were filling with tears. 'That's what Mammy said.'

'Now, girls, this must feel very strange being so far from

your family but I hope that in time, you will all get to feel at home here.'

Colleen's eyes filled with tears. 'All of us?' she said.

Mary Kate smiled at Colleen. 'All of you,' she said. 'You are all very welcome.'

'You're very kind,' said Colleen.

'Not at all,' said Mary Kate. 'Now, I will get Jessie to show you to your room and, Colleen, let you and I have a little chat.'

Once Orla and Polly had gone upstairs with Jessie, Colleen started to cry. Mary Kate handed her the white handkerchief with the letter J in the corner.

'I was given this by a girl called Jenny,' she said. 'It was a small kindness when I needed someone to be kind to me. Now I'm giving it to you.'

Colleen took the hankie and wiped her eyes, she reached out to give it back.

'It's yours now, Colleen, until the day that you can pass it on to someone else who needs a little comfort.'

'I'll understand if you don't want me here, Miss Ryan.'

'You are very welcome, love, but I do need to ask you a few questions.'

Colleen nodded.

'How old are you, Colleen?'

'I'm sixteen, miss.'

'And do your parents know where you are?'

Colleen shook her head.

The child looks worn out, thought Mary Kate. There was a sense of hopelessness about her, as if she'd given up on life. It reminded Mary Kate of the day she had almost jumped off the bridge and into the Liffey. It was the letter that had changed everything. The angels had come to her rescue that day and saved her life. If ever anyone looked as if they needed saving, it was this poor girl in front of her.

'Won't your parents be worrying about you?'

'They'll be angry.'

'You have to let them know where you are, they need to know that you are safe.'

Colleen, who had been looking down, almost jumped out of the chair. 'They mustn't know where I am,' she almost shouted. 'They'll lock me up again, they'll take my baby away.'

'They locked you up?'

Colleen started to cry again, covering her face with Jenny's hankie. 'I've been locked in my room for months. They said that I would never see my baby again, I would never get to hold her, I had to get away.'

Mary Kate couldn't believe what she was hearing. How could a parent do that to one of their own? She felt angry; a burning anger that started in the pit of her stomach and at any minute threatened to burst out of her. But this anger wasn't for herself, it was for this poor girl who had been denied a mother's love when she needed it most. She wanted to take her in her arms. She knelt in front of her and took Colleen's hands in hers.

'You are safe here, Colleen,' she said gently. 'And I give you my solemn promise that no one is going to take your baby away from you.'

'I don't know how to thank you, Miss Ryan, I really don't.'

'You have no need to. Now, Jessie will show you your room and I suggest that you sleep for as long as you need to. And, Colleen?'

'Yes, miss?'

'Buy yourself a diary.'

'A diary?'

'Yes, Colleen, a diary. For your red-letter days, for they will surely come.'

CHAPTER 19

James Renson was looking at Mary Kate, as if she had two heads.

'You want to buy a row of humble cottages?' he said.

'I do.'

'Wouldn't it be better to invest your money and let it work for you?'

'I don't need to make any more money, Mr Renson. I want to change people's lives, just like the money changed mine. I never knew my mother, but I would like to think it is what she would have wanted.'

'You are an amazing woman, Miss Ryan.'

'No, Mr Renson, just a lucky one.'

'But why those particular cottages?'

'Because that is where I was brought up. There is no water or electricity, the walls are running with damp, and the landlord doesn't care. Not only doesn't he care about the cottages themselves, he doesn't care about the people living in them. He has done nothing to improve their lives, he just keeps putting up the rents, and if they can't pay, they are thrown out onto the street. I intend to buy the whole row.'

James sat back in his chair and smiled at her. 'And what, may I ask, are you going to do with them?'

Mary Kate smiled back at him. 'I'm going to demolish them.' Then she started to laugh, until the tears ran down her face. 'I'm going to tear the whole lot down, till there's not one lousy brick left.'

James Renson started to laugh with her, even though he wasn't sure what he was laughing at. 'Of course you are,' he said. 'Of course you are.'

Mary Kate had returned to Tanners Row over the years. There had been times when her loneliness had overwhelmed her and she had been drawn back to her home and to the people who at least cared whether she lived or died. There was always a welcome to be had in Mrs Finn's cottage and her visits had given her the strength to live through another day. When she had come into her fortune, she still visited, but always dressed down and didn't tell her old neighbour about her bit of good fortune. They would sit together at the kitchen table and Mrs Finn would tell her about the goings-on in the town.

'Nothing's changed. We've been promised electricity and water for years but they are empty promises for it has never happened.'

'I'm so sorry, Mrs Finn.'

'Ah sure, it is what it is. A lovely God-fearing woman moved in a couple of years back and, God love her, her husband up and died on the front step, leaving her with five young ones, and that bastard of an Englishman threw her out into the lane.'

'Is he still alive?' she'd asked.

'Only the good die young, Mary Kate. That gobshite of a man would peel an orange in his pocket for fear he'd have to share it.'

Mrs Finn was desperate funny and Mary Kate always left Tanners Row smiling.

'So, Mr Renson, I need you to contact the owner and offer him whatever he asks for.'

'He'll be asking for more than they are worth, Miss Ryan, I can assure you of that.'

'I don't care what he asks, I am determined to buy those cottages at any cost.'

'I can see that, dear lady.'

'And I want it to be anonymous. I don't want anyone to know that I am the new landlady. Can you do that?'

'I most certainly can, but what I can't do is make the man sell them to you.'

'I have every faith in you, Mr Renson,' said Mary Kate.

'I think it's time that you called me James, for I feel that we have become friends. What do you think?'

'I think that would be lovely, for I too think of you as my friend. Please call me Mary Kate.'

James smiled at her. 'I would be delighted to. And what do you intend to do with the residents once you have demolished their homes?'

'I shall put them up in a hotel until the new houses are built.'

'New houses?'

'Yes. I am going to build decent houses for decent people to live in. Oh, and there is one more thing that I want you to do.'

He leaned forward and smiled. 'Surprise me.'

'There is land behind the cottages, I want to buy that too.'

'For more houses?'

Mary Kate picked up her bag. 'No, for gardens. A garden for each of the cottages. A place where they can grow flowers and vegetables. And somewhere for the children to play.'

James was smiling as the door closed behind her. A row of cottages, eh? What next? He thought back to the first time he had met Mary Kate Ryan, a shy woman who looked as if she had given up on life. That woman was gone. She looked different, she carried herself like someone who wasn't afraid of life. A woman who knew exactly where she was going. A woman who knew what she wanted. And James Renson was going to make damn sure that she got it.

Mary Kate was smiling as she walked across the square. To think that she, Mary Kate Ryan of Tanners Row, could count James Renson as one of her friends. And she had surprised him – oh, she had – and this was only the start, for there would be a lot more surprises to come.

She sat down on a bench and lifted her face to the sun. She felt such peace in her heart, as autumn leaves drifted about her shoulders. Reds and oranges, browns and golds dancing in the sky above her before drifting down onto the grass, turning the green into a patchwork of beautiful colours as if the hand of God had painted it in the still of the night, just for her.

She looked across the square at her beautiful boarding house. Its bright-red door, standing out like a welcoming beacon against the rest of the terrace. Oh, how she wished that her beloved grandparents could see her now and know that their daughter was the one who had made it all possible.

As she continued to stare at the house, she saw Jessie running down the steps, looking right and left, then running back indoors. Mary Kate knew there was something wrong. She hurried across the square to find the door wide open and Jessie and Mrs Lamb standing in the hallway. Mrs Lamb had her head in her hands and Jessie was comforting her.

'Oh, Miss Ryan, thank God you're back,' said Jessie.

'What's happened?'

'Eliza has gone missing.'

'She's never done this before,' said Mrs Lamb. 'Where can she be? Oh dear God, where is the child?'

'We'll find her, Mrs Lamb, we'll find her,' said Mary Kate. 'How long has she been gone?'

Mrs Lamb wiped away the tears that were running down her cheeks. 'I'm not sure, miss,' she said.

'Jessie, where's Abby?'

'With Miss Kent.'

'Run upstairs and tell Miss Kent what has happened, we need all the help we can get.'

Mrs Lamb was as white as a sheet and looked as if she was about to collapse. Mary Kate put her arm around her and guided her into the sitting room. The poor woman was shaking and wringing her hands as Mary Kate settled her in the chair beside the fire and tucked a warm blanket around her knees.

'She has never been anywhere without me, Miss Ryan. How is she going to find her way home?'

'She won't have gone far, we'll find her. Has the house been thoroughly searched?'

Mrs Lamb nodded. 'We've looked everywhere.'

Just then Moira came into the room and straight away knelt in front of Mrs Lamb. 'Now, Mrs Lamb, I want you to think of all the places that Eliza might go,' she said gently. 'Places you went together. Can you do that?'

Mrs Lamb carried on crying.

'Is there a favourite shop that she liked to look in? Could she have gone down to the river?'

Mrs Lamb looked up at her. 'I don't know,' she mumbled.

Moira touched her hand. 'Try and think, Mrs Lamb, it will help us to get her home quicker if we have some idea of the places you often go to.'

Mrs Lamb wiped her eyes. 'She likes going to the butcher's, she likes to look at the picture of a cow in the window.'

'That's good, Mrs Lamb. Now can you think of anywhere else she might have gone?'

'The man in the grocer's always gives her an apple, she

might have gone there. Oh, where could she be, Miss Kent? Where could my poor girl be?'

Moira stood up. 'We'll find her, Mrs Lamb, we'll find her. Right, the best thing to do is for us to split up.'

Miss Kent was taking control and Mary Kate was glad of it.

Colleen came into the room. 'Is she not back yet?'

'I'm afraid not,' said Mary Kate. She noticed Jessie standing at the door; she was as white as a sheet, there was something wrong. 'What is it, Jessie?'

'I can't find Abby.'

'I want you and Colleen to search the town. Miss Kent and I will take Guinness and hope to God that he can lead us to the girls. And, Colleen, I want you to call Sean Barry and tell him we need his help. His number is in my diary beside the phone.'

'Yes, Miss Kent.'

'Don't worry, Jessie, we'll find them. Now, let's all get going.'

CHAPTER 20

Claire

Claire Devlin stood by the window, looking out over the park. Everything had seemed so clear to her when she'd left Brooklyn: she would find her child and take her back to America.

Claire picked up her coat, said hello to the doorman and walked across the road to the park. There was a warm breeze that lifted the hair on the back of her neck and made her shiver, as if some unknown hand had touched her. She loved fall, it had always been her favourite season. She sat on a bench and lifted her face to the sun. The tall trees that surrounded the green were shedding their leaves, a kaleidoscope of colour that covered the grass and the sidewalks and drifted past her in a mad, swirling dance. It had been fall when she had left Ireland and maybe it was fall that had brought her home.

She had only been to Dublin once and that was when she had boarded the ship to America.

She thought back to the girl she had been, the girl who had

walked up that gangplank without a care in the world. She had been so young, so full of dreams, she was going to make something of herself. She was heading for a new life in America, where her beauty would be her passport to the fame and fortune that she deserved. How easily she had turned her back on the people who loved her, how easily she had turned her back on her precious baby. How stupid and shallow that girl had been.

From as far back as she could remember, she was told how pretty she was. 'One of God's own angels,' they said. 'Too beautiful for this world,' they said. She had grown up believing she was special, that she was destined for something beyond the humble cottage that had been her home and the small town where nothing ever happened.

Her prettiness made her popular. Everyone wanted to be her friend, but she only chose the girls that came from the rich part of town, girls whose daddies drove around in smart cars and whose mammies had their hair permed every week in Dublin. She had no time for the others, the hangers-on, the ones who were last to be picked for the team, in fact, she barely noticed their existence.

She grew to resent her parents and the simple lives they led. She was ashamed of the tiny cottage, with its statues of the saints on every bloody surface. St Anthony, who you prayed to when you lost something, not that he ever found it. Saint Patrick, with snakes crawling up his legs, that would put you off your dinner and a picture of the Crucifixion staring down at you over the fireplace with the blood trickling down his side. Did it not occur to them that this could damage a child for life? No, of course it didn't, for it had always been this way, it was all they knew, it was all they had ever known. Every good Catholic family in the town had a statue of 'The infant of Prague' somewhere in the house. She made her friends laugh when she told them that you had to chop it's head off and bury it in the garden the night before a wedding, it was supposed to ensure that the couple had a good marriage. The thing was that you had to stick his head back on again the next day, meaning the town was full of statues of the 'Infant of Prague' and they all had wonky heads. Oh yes, they had a good laugh about it and God forgive her, she had laughed with the best of them and she still felt ashamed when she thought about it.

On the day of her first holy communion she was only mortified, as she walked down the aisle with a bit of net curtain pinned to her hair with a couple of grips. She could barely look at her friends, whose dresses had been specially made for them in Dublin, and whose veils floated around their shoulders as they walked. They had almost reached the altar when her best friend Victoria turned around and smiled at her; she had smiled back but then saw her whisper in Pauline Butler's ear. The pair of them looked back at her and started to giggle. She knew at once that they were laughing at the bit of net curtain stuck to her head. Sister Joan ate the faces off them but that hadn't made her feel any better.

She was prettier than all of them but on that day, her beauty meant nothing to her. She was poor and she looked poor. She would never speak to them again.

Outside the church, the parents were all smiling and looking proud. 'You looked lovely, Claire,' said Mammy.

She had glared at her. 'How in God's name could I look lovely, with an old bit of net curtain stuck on my head?'

'Don't speak to your mother like that,' said her father. 'We can't afford posh veils and dresses, Claire, you know that. This is not a party where you parade around in fancy clothes. This is the day that you received the body and blood of Christ. Do you think that our dear Lord cares what you are wearing? What matters is what is in your heart, that's where real beauty lies. You have made me ashamed this day and you have broken your mother's heart. Do you care at all?'

She had stared down at her old black shoes and said nothing.

'Well, do you, Claire?'

'I suppose so,' she'd mumbled.

'Now apologise to your mother, for you have sorely hurt her this day.'

She hadn't wanted to say sorry; she was angry and anyway, why should she say sorry? It wasn't her fault that they were poor.

After that, she decided that she didn't need any friends, it was time to concentrate on herself. She went to the little picture house in the town whenever she could. She stared up at the screen, imagining herself in the beautiful gowns, imagining herself in the arms of Tony Curtis or Kirk Douglas. She was as beautiful as any of them, maybe even more beautiful. That's when she made up her mind, she would leave this dreary town and go to Hollywood. Every day after school she worked in the butcher's shop; she hated handling the slabs of raw meat, laid out on the counter looking like dead bodies. Her hands became rough and bloodied, but she would suffer it until she had saved enough for the boat fare to America.

And then she met Tom and everything changed. She forgot about Hollywood, she forgot about being a star, she forgot about everything, it was love at first sight. Tom was English and was touring Ireland with his parents and sister. They were staying at The Green Park Hotel on the edge of town. Tom sounded like Dirk Bogarde and David Niven and all the other dashing English actors on the screen in the little cinema, she could have listened to him all day. He and his family only stayed in the town for a few months. Claire's heart was breaking as they said goodbye.

Tom had kissed her cheek. 'I'll come back one day, Claire,' he'd said. She didn't believe him, she could tell by his eyes that he had already moved on.

. . .

Claire wasn't proud of the girl she had been. She wished she could go back and shake her by the shoulders until her teeth rattled. Did teeth rattle? It suddenly seemed terribly important that she knew. She would ask Ronald, he'd know – Ronald knew everything.

She had been so peaceful sitting on the bench but now she felt sweat forming on her upper lip and under her bra. She undid the buttons on her shirt and tugged at the straps. The cool air felt lovely on her skin, she pulled the shirt open a bit more.

A woman stared at her as she walked past. Why was she staring? Did she know her? She didn't think so. A minute or so later the same woman walked back and stood in front of her.

Claire looked up at her. 'Do I know you?' she asked.

The woman smiled and sat down beside her. 'I don't think so,' she said. 'But I couldn't help noticing that your blouse is undone. I hope I haven't offended you, but I'd want to know if my blouse was undone. There are some desperate odd fellers around here that might take advantage, if you know what I mean.'

Claire looked down. The woman was right, her blouse was gaping open for all world to see. She couldn't think how it had happened. She looked around her and frowned, what was she doing in a park? She couldn't remember getting there. Claire rubbed at her forehead with a balled fist. It was starting again, this horrible feeling of detachment, of feeling alone, even when she was surrounded by people she cared for. Ronald called them her funny turns, 'Nothing to worry about,' he'd say kindly, for he was a kind man.

His mother on the other hand said she was attention seeking. In fact, Ronald's mother didn't like her at all and sat through the wedding ceremony with a face like a melted wellington boot. She'd accused her of being a gold digger and she'd been right, what else was there to attract her to her son? He looked like a squashed frog and yet he was kind and gentle and she grew to love him in a way that she hadn't expected.

The woman touched her arm. 'Are you all right?'

Claire fumbled with the buttons but she was all fingers and thumbs, and she was doing them up all wrong. She kept stopping and then starting again.

'Let me help you with that, dear.'

The woman's fingers were so gentle as she carefully did up the buttons. 'There now, that's better, isn't it?'

Claire was mortified. Why had her shirt been undone in the first place? Her funny turns had been happening more often these days.

Ronald's mother said she was mad and there were times when she wondered if she was. She was never sure how long the funny turns lasted either. It was like waking from a deep sleep, knowing that something had happened but not knowing what it was. It was like she'd lost all sense of time.

Claire smiled at the woman. 'I get these funny turns,' she said.

'Are you going to be all right now?'

'Yes, and thank you for caring.'

The woman smiled at her. 'Sure it's a poor show, isn't it, if you can't help somebody along the way?'

Claire nodded.

'Now if you're sure you're going to be all right, I'll say goodbye and good luck.'

Claire watched the woman walking away. Would she have done the same thing for a stranger? She would like to think that she could do something kind, she didn't think that she was a very kind person – well, it wasn't too late, was it? She could change, she could be better, kinder.

Her mind was clearer now. She looked across the green at

the Shelbourne hotel... yes, that was where she was staying, she wasn't lost. Sometimes when she had one of her turns, that's how she felt: she felt lost.

She watched a little girl playing, running this way and that in the sunshine. It would be nice to be a child again – she would be a better child next time round, if she was given the chance. The girl seemed to be running towards her, she looked behind her but there was only herself in this part of the park.

The girl stopped in front of the bench. Claire smiled at her: 'Hello.'

The child stared at her but didn't speak. Claire found it a bit unnerving. 'Are you lost?'

The child shook her head.

'You're not lost?'

She shook her head again and pointed across the grass.

'You want to show me something?'

This time the little girl nodded and pointed again. Claire got up and followed her across the grass and into a wooded area that bordered the edge of the park.

It was old woodland, old trees with thick, gnarled trunks interspersed with younger ones that rose up high, and saplings, and beneath them all were bramble bushes and clumps of nettles. Stepping out of the open greenness of the park and into the dark shadows of the wood was like going from one world into another. A narrow path wound into the forest. Underfoot were fallen leaves and chestnut casings. The denseness of the trees allowed very little light to come through and there was a strong, dank smell of rotting vegetation. The child suddenly turned off to the left and Claire stumbled after her. The girl was agile and clearly knew where she was going, but it was harder for Claire, who found herself tripping over logs and bracken and slipping on damp leaves that squelched beneath her feet but she kept following her. At one point she startled a pigeon that flapped noisily up into the canopy, sending a flurry of red and gold leaves falling down. Now and then the girl turned round, making sure that she was still there. Sometimes she lost sight of her completely as the child ran ahead of her, leaping over fallen branches, dodging around rotten tree trunks, like some mystical creature.

It suddenly occurred to her that she could be in some sort of danger. Why was she following this strange child who hadn't even spoken to her? This could be a trap, she could be robbed and beaten and left for dead. Was she the biggest fool in Dublin or what?

She was about to turn back when a thin beam of light filtered through the trees, settling on the girl's shoulders, like a yellow shawl. Claire bent over, trying to catch her breath, while the girl stood perfectly still, beside what looked like a large round metal pipe. Claire straightened up and glared at her. 'Is this what you wanted to show me?' she shouted. The child just stared back.

'Is this why you had me running through a forest, in the pitch-black, to look at a bloody pipe?'

The girl nodded and crawled into the opening. Claire had no intention of going after her, so she waited. It was eerily quiet in the woods; only the occasional rustle of a bird or squirrel up in the branches, the scutter of some small creature dashing through the undergrowth. After a while the little girl shuffled out, she was very obviously in some distress. Claire softened: 'Can you tell me what is wrong, dear?' she asked.

The child shook her head.

'You can't tell me?'

She shook her head again.

'How can I help you if I don't know what's wrong?'

The girl pointed to herself.

'You?' said Claire.

The child smiled and nodded.

'Good girl, now we are getting somewhere. What more?'

Again, the child pointed to herself then put one finger up.

'One?' said Claire.

The child now pointed to the space beside her and put two fingers up.

'There were two of you?' said Claire.

The girl nodded.

'A child? Were you with another child?'

She shook her head.

'An adult?'

She nodded and then put her hand nearer the ground.

'She's small?'

Claire could see that she was desperately trying to get her to understand. She felt so sorry for her.

The girl shook her head, touched her tummy and then her forehead.

Claire couldn't make head nor tail of what she was trying to tell her. Then it came to her: 'She's small inside?'

The little girl looked so relieved that she wanted to hug her but of course she was a stranger and it wouldn't be right.

'Okay,' said Claire,'you were in the pipe with another person and now they are gone?'

The girl nodded.

'Girl or boy?'

The little girl pointed to herself.

'Okay. So, we need to find her. Now, I am aware that you can't tell me but I need to know her name.'

Claire held the palm of her hand towards her. 'Can you write it on here?'

Slowly and carefully, she wrote ELIZA.

'Eliza?' said Claire.'

She nodded, took Claire's hand and started to write again. Then pointed to herself.

'Abby?' said Claire. 'Your name is Abby?'

Abby nodded.

'Good girl, let's go find her.'

But where should they start?

Claire looked around. They were surrounded by forest; she wasn't sure which direction they'd come from and the branches overhead all but obscured the sky. The forest was a big place, and a frightening one if you were lost and alone. Claire remembered all the fairy tales she'd been told; all those little children being lost in deep, dark forests inhabited by witches and wolves and ogres. Poor Eliza! Where would she have gone?

'We need to stay together,' Claire told Abby. 'We don't want you getting lost too.'

Abby looked alarmed.

'Not that you're going to get lost,' Claire said at once. 'But stay close to me, all right? So you can see me.'

Abby nodded.

They started running, Claire calling Eliza's name as they ran but all was silent, the only noise coming from the breeze moving through the branches of the trees.

'Would she have tried to get home?'

Abby shrugged her shoulders.

'OK, let's keep looking, she can't have gone far.'

It was now late afternoon and what little light there had been was gone. She knew she had to find Eliza soon, or she would be out here all night and surely she must already feel frightened?

Claire kept shouting her name but there was no answering call, only the rustling of creatures in the undergrowth, going about their business.

As they went deeper into the wood, the tree roots became thicker and the brackens more dense. It was more difficult to walk. Every so often her feet sank into pools of dank, muddy water that smelled of cold tea and her ankles were scratched, her stockings torn to shreds. The path had petered out and they were now just stumbling along, not knowing where they were going. Claire held Abby's hand, for fear that, despite her earlier warning, she would lose her too. The trees were closer together here, making it almost impossible to see in front of them, and they had to keep walking around clumps of them, ducking beneath low-hanging branches, skirting puddles, and climbing over fallen saplings, thick, musty-smelling fungi climbing up their trunks. That's when she fell, the shock made her feel sick. What in God's name was she doing here? Was it another one of her funny turns? Maybe this was all in her imagination but no, all her senses were sharp. The smell of rotting vegetation, the cold, the wind rustling the leaves on the trees, the sound of creatures in the undergrowth and the pain in her leg. Abby sat down beside her on the muddy ground and put her arm around her shoulder.

She was cold and wet and so was Abby. Claire put her coat around Abby's shoulders. 'I think we're going to have to call it a day,' she said.

Abby shook her head.

'I'm sorry, Abby, but we need more help if we are going to find Eliza.'

Then she heard a kind of moan, it was probably nothing but she called out. 'Eliza? Is that you?'

They waited but there was no answering call. Claire stood up. 'We tried, Abby, we've done our best.'

There was a rustling sound. Claire took Abby's hand and held it tight. The rustling was coming closer, and a panting sound too. Something was approaching them. Claire tried desperately hard to put thoughts of witches and wolves from her mind. Abby whimpered.

'It's all right, Abby,' Claire said. 'I'm here; I'm going to look after you. We're going to be fine.'

Just at that moment a figure emerged out of the shadows; a young woman with a tear-stained face and torn clothing. Abby ran forward and threw her arms around the woman's waist.

'Eliza?' said Claire.

Abby nodded, smiling.

The young woman standing in front of her looked to be in her early twenties. She was covered in mud and looked terrified. Claire moved towards her. 'My name is Claire,' she said gently, 'myself and Abby have been looking for you, dear.'

Eliza stared at her. 'I got lost,' she said.

'I'm not surprised,' said Claire. 'It's very dark in here.'

'I thought you were the bad man. We had to run away from the bad man, didn't we ,Abby?'

'Do you know what I think, Eliza?'

Eliza shook her head.

'I think that bad man has gone home for his dinner.'

'I missed my dinner.'

Claire moved closer and took her hand. 'So did we,' she said, smiling.

'Mammy will be cross.'

'I'm sure she will just be happy to see you and I promise that you will be safe with me.'

Eliza looked at Abby, who nodded.

'Do you know your way home, Eliza?'

'I don't think so,' she said.

'How about you, Abby? Could you find your way home?'

Before the child could answer, there was the sound of barking and then a large dog came bounding towards them.

'It's Guinness,' said Eliza.

'Guinness?'

'Abby's dog.'

The dog was running around in circles, his tail wagging, ten to the dozen and Abby was laughing at him. It was lovely to hear her voice, even though there were no words. The child was beautiful, maybe her own child would be just as beautiful. The dog started barking again and almost at once, two women burst through the trees.

CHAPTER 21

Mary Kate watched as Abby ran towards Miss Kent, who lifted her into her arms. 'Oh, Abby,' she said, smoothing the child's hair away from her face, 'we've been so worried.'

Abby started tapping away with her fingers.

'What is she doing?' said Mary Kate.

'I hope you don't mind, Miss Ryan, but I have been teaching Abby to sign, so we could communicate.'

'Of course I don't mind, I think it's wonderful. What is she saying?'

'She says that she knew I would come.'

Mary Kate smiled; there was more than a friendship here, there was love. She went over to Eliza. She was shivering and crying.

'Is Mammy cross with me?'

Mary Kate took off her cardigan and wrapped it around Eliza. 'Why did you run away, Eliza? You know you are not allowed out of the house by yourself. We've all been worried sick.'

Eliza wiped her eyes on her sleeve. 'I wanted to show Abby the picture of the cow in the butcher's window.'

'Then why didn't you come straight home afterwards?'

'Because of the bad man.'

Mary Kate suddenly felt sick to her stomach. 'Did he touch you, darling?'

Eliza nodded.

Oh dear God, thought Mary Kate. 'Did he hurt you?'

'He tried to pull me away but Abby grabbed my arm and we started running.'

'Is that all he did?'

'Yes, but I was scared. He smelled bad and he had a furry face and I didn't like him.'

'You were right to run, Eliza, you did the right thing. Your mammy won't be cross with you, she'll just be happy that you are home. But promise me that you will never, ever go out on your own again.'

'I promise, miss.'

'Good girl,' said Mary Kate, giving her a hug. Shen then smiled at the stranger standing beside the girls.

Claire held out her hand. 'My name is Claire Devlin,' she said.

'She's been looking after us,' said Eliza.

'Then we are very grateful to you, Miss Devlin.'

'I'm glad that I was able to help,' said Claire.

'Your leg is bleeding,' said Mary Kate.

The woman looked down at her leg. 'I fell,' she said.

'Then please come back with us. We can clean that up and I think we are all in need of a good cup of tea.'

'If it's no trouble, I would like that very much.'

'Now why would it be any trouble? You looked after our girls, I think a cup of tea is the least we can do.'

Abby held Miss Kent's hand as they walked back through the park, with Guinness running ahead of them.

As they neared the boarding house, Mary Kate could see Jessie and Colleen sitting on the steps. They immediately jumped up and ran towards them. Jessie scooped Abby up into her arms and swung her around, making her giggle.

'Thank God you found them, Miss Ryan,' said Jessie. 'Mrs Lamb was about to ring the Garda.'

'It was Guinness who found them,' said Mary Kate.

Jessie put Abby down. 'You all look frozen. I've lit the fire, so you'll soon be grand and warm.'

'That was very thoughtful of you, Jessie, you're a great girl altogether.'

'Come on, Eliza,' said Jessie. 'Let's put your mammy's mind at rest before she has the whole of Dublin out looking for you.'

'Did you manage to get hold of Mr Barry, Colleen?'

'I did and he said he would get his workers on board. He's nice, isn't he, Miss Ryan?'

'He is, Colleen, he's very nice indeed.'

After they had warmed themselves by the fire, Mary Kate sent the girls off to have a good hot bath and a change of clothes.

'Miss Devlin, I've laid some clothes out for you on my bed. We're about the same size, I think they'll fit you.'

Claire smiled at her. 'That's very kind and I will of course return them as soon as I can.'

'No rush.'

Mary Kate took Claire upstairs. Claire picked up a cream blouse and pale-blue cardigan.

'These are lovely,' she said.

'I got kitted out at Clearys, they have a lovely selection of clothes there, I had the time of my life. Now please make use of the bathroom, Miss Devlin, and I will see you downstairs when you are ready.'

'You have a lovely home, Miss Ryan.'

'Thank you.'

Mary Kate ran downstairs to the kitchen, where Mrs Lamb was stirring something on the stove that smelled delicious.

'I thought some nice hot soup would be the order of the day, Miss Ryan,' she said, wiping her tears on her apron.

Mary Kate went across and took her in her arms. 'No harm came to her, my dear, and I think it's safe to say that Eliza's wandering days are over.'

'But anything could have happened. She might look like a woman, Miss Ryan, but she has the mind of a child. I have lived in fear that one day someone out there would take advantage of her innocence.'

'Well, I don't think your lovely girl will stray far from home after this little adventure. It was a hard lesson for her to learn, but maybe God, in His wisdom, was showing her that the world isn't always a safe place.'

'I hope you are right, Miss Ryan, because I don't think I could go through that again.'

'I don't think any of us could. But there, we have a happy ending and don't we all love a happy ending, Mrs Lamb?'

'We do, Miss Ryan, we do.'

Mary Kate went back upstairs to her sitting room. What a day this had been. She tried not to think what could have happened to those sweet girls. Mary Kate believed that an angel had been looking down on them this day and she thanked God for it.

She walked over to the window and looked out over the green; the nights were drawing in, winter was on its way. The street lamps cast long shadows across the square and over the leaves that had piled up at the base of the tall trees. Mary Kate knew all about living in the dark places, overlooked by everyone, as if she were invisible.

She closed the heavy velvet curtains and looked back into the room. It was so cosy, with the fire crackling away in the grate and the pretty lamps that dotted the room, bathing the pale-cream walls in a soft yellow glow. There were still days when the past lay heavy on her shoulders, the thought of what she had been about to do and the letter that had changed everything. The letter that had taken her out of the shadows and into the safety and warmth of this beautiful house, that had become the home she thought she would never find.

As she rattled the coals in the fire, sending a blast of heat into the room, there was a tap on the door.

Mary Kate smiled as Miss Devlin came into the room. 'Oh, I'm so pleased that the clothes fit you, I thought they would.'

'You have been very kind.'

'It's you who has been kind, Miss Devlin, for you didn't have to put yourself out for strangers. It's a good Samaritan that you have been to us this day, and I thank God for guiding you to the right place at the right time.'

Claire was frowning. 'I'm *Mrs* Devlin,' she said. 'Yes, I'm quite sure about that.'

What a strange way to put it, thought Mary Kate.

One by one the sitting room filled up, with Abby and Eliza, Colleen, Jessie and, finally, Miss Kent.

'Well, I have to say that you all look grand after your big adventure,' said Mary Kate.

'I don't think I like adventures, Miss Ryan,' said Eliza.

'And aren't we all glad to hear it,' said Miss Kent.

'Eliza?' said Mary Kate. 'Would you be a grand girl and tell your mammy that we are ready for the soup now.'

'I will, Miss Ryan.'

'And don't go taking any detours,' said Miss Kent.

Well, it's nice to see that the woman has a sense of humour, thought Mary Kate, *albeit a bit on the droll side*. In fact, she found herself warming to her. She had taken charge today and had gone about the business of finding the girls with a sensible head on her and not a bit of fuss whereas she herself had been all over the place and no use to anyone.

Mary Kate noticed the way Mrs Devlin was staring at Colleen.

'When is your baby due, dear?' she said.

Colleen looked uncomfortable, for none of them really mentioned the coming baby, it was just something they accepted without discussion.

'It must be soon,' said Miss Devlin, 'for you look quite large.'

'Yes, soon,' said Colleen.

'I was big when I was carrying my little girl.'

'You have a daughter?' said Mary Kate, smiling. 'Is she in America?'

'No, that is why I am here. You see, I had to leave her behind but I've come to collect her now.'

'You had to leave her in Ireland?'

'I didn't want to but I had no choice. I left her with the nuns.'

'In Dublin?'

Miss Devlin was frowning. 'I think so.'

'You think so?' said Mary Kate.

Miss Devlin nodded.

Mary Kate was getting more confused by the minute. The woman didn't know where she'd left her child? That isn't something you'd forget in a hurry.

'And how old would she be now?' said Moira, looking equally confused.

Mrs Devlin was twisting her skirt into a ball. 'Maybe four months,' she mumbled. 'Yes, I think so, about four months.'

Just then, there was a banging on the front door and Jessie ran to answer it. She came back with Sean Barry in tow.

'Oh, Sean,' said Mary Kate. 'I'd forgotten all about you. Have you been out looking all this time?'

He smiled at her. 'News travels fast around here. I heard

that you had found the girls, I am just calling in to check that everyone is OK.'

'Well, we are now. Will you stay for some soup?'

'I've never been known to turn down a bowl of soup, Mary Kate Ryan, and I'm not about to start now.'

'Grand. So, Jessie, will you help carry the soup upstairs?'

'Of course, Miss Ryan,' she said, smiling.

As they sat around the fire eating Mrs Lamb's tasty soup, Mary Kate couldn't get the conversation with Mrs Devlin out of her head – it just didn't make any sense.

Soon everyone drifted off and Claire got up to leave.

'You said that you were staying at the Shelbourne hotel?' said Mary Kate.

Claire didn't answer.

'You're staying at the Shelbourne?' repeated Mary Kate.

'Am I?'

'You said that is where you are staying.'

'Oh, yes, yes. I am staying there at the moment.'

'Sean? Would you mind giving Mrs Devlin a spin home? It's too dark for her to be walking alone.'

'No trouble, Mary Kate.'

Once they were gone, herself and Moira stared at each other in disbelief.

'Well, I've heard everything now,' said Mary Kate.

Moira shook her head. 'Unless it's the immaculate conception, I'd say the poor woman is demented.'

'I'd say you're right. How in God's name can she have a four-month-old child?'

'Well, obviously, she can't. The woman's fifty if she's a day.'

'I think she might need our help, Miss Kent.'

'I think you're right.'

'And, Miss Kent?'

'Yes, Miss Ryan?'

'I'd say it's high time that we were on first-name terms. What do you think?'

'I think that would be lovely.'

'Oh, I'm so glad, I'm so very glad. Now, how about something a bit stronger than soup?'

'You took the words right out of my mouth, Mary Kate Ryan.'

CHAPTER 22

Paddy the Postman

Paddy Cronin had been postman in the town for nearly twenty years. He knew everyone by name and they knew him. He was often the first to hear when new babies were on the way and the first to know when someone was nearing death. He comforted the mammies who had said goodbye to their beloved sons, leaving home to work on the building sites, and he shared in their joy when the sons' first letters arrived from England. Paddy liked to think that he brought some cheer as he delivered his letters, a laugh and a bit of a joke. He prided himself on being a good listener, for all some of them wanted was to reminisce about the old days. He had seen these people at their happiest and he had seen them at their saddest. They were his people and he cared about them.

Paddy the Postman loved his job, that was until this day. For this day he was carrying despair to the door of every family in Tanners Row, there was no doubt about it. In his bag he carried six letters – one for every cottage. It could only mean one thing: eviction notices. Yes, these cottages were a disgrace, but it was a roof over their heads and he was the one that was having to bring the news that they were going to be made homeless. What would happen to the O'Connells and their seven children? Mrs Coleman, struggling to care for a sick husband and a simple son? Mrs McCarthy and her dying mother? What was to become of them all?

This was his last delivery of the day; he only had the six letters in his bag and yet it had never felt so heavy, the strap was cutting into his shoulder with every step that took him closer to Tanners Row. He was so angry, and he was not an angry man. These were good people, kind people who helped each other out. Their only crime was that they were poor. Printed on the top of each envelope was the address of the sender: RENSON AND RENSON, SOLICITORS. He felt like ripping the letters up, but what good would that do? He would lose his job and, in the end, it wouldn't change a thing.

He stood at the top of Tanners Row, took a deep breath, and proceeded to post a letter into each of the cottages. After he had posted the last one, he sat on the wall opposite Mrs Finn's in case he was needed. Not that there was much he could do for the poor souls, but he might be able to bring a bit of comfort. He put his head in his hands and waited.

Almost at once Mrs Finn hurried across to him, she had the letter in her hand. 'Is something wrong, Paddy?' she asked.

Paddy looked up. 'Have you read the letter yet?'

Mrs Finn looked at the letter in her hand. 'Not yet, Paddy, why?'

'Because I have just posted the same letter to everyone in the row.'

'To everyone?'

'Yes, and I'd say it points to only one thing.'

'Dear God in Heaven,' she said. 'I always feared that this day would come but prayed that it never would.'

'I'm sorry for you, Mrs Finn. I'm sorry for all of you and I wish it hadn't been myself who had delivered the news.'

'It's not your fault, Paddy. It's the fault of that gobshite of a man across the ocean. May the good Lord see fit to screw his nose to the floor. Come in, lad, and we'll have a cup of tea. If I must face the worst, I'd rather face it with you across the table from me.'

They were just about to go into the cottage when Mrs O'Connell came running up the lane towards them, waving the letter and screaming. 'I can't open it, Mrs Finn, I can't.'

'Come in then, love, and we'll open it together.'

Mrs O'Connell was wailing. 'What are we to do? Where are we to go?'

Mrs Finn put her hand on her neighbour's shoulder. 'Well, as neither of us has read it yet, l think we should wait and see what it says, then we can talk about what we can do.'

'But we know what it says, we're going to be put out into the street.'

Mrs Finn thought the same but she wanted to give Mrs O'Connell a bit of hope before the poor woman collapsed on her doorstep.

'Will I put the kettle on?' said Paddy once they were in the kitchen.

Mrs Finn nodded. 'That will be grand.'

They waited until Paddy had put the tea on the table. The two letters sat between them, like a couple of unexploded bombs. Neither of them spoke as Mrs Finn tore open the envelope.

Mrs O'Connell was wringing her hands together. 'Are we going to be homeless? We are, aren't we? We're going to be homeless.'

Mrs Finn put the letter back on the table and wept.

'Dear God,' wailed Mrs O'Connell, 'we're all for the workhouse.'

Mrs Finn looked up and smiled through her tears. 'No, Mrs O'Connell, we are not going to be made homeless.'

'You're not?' said Paddy.

'We're not?' said Mrs O'Connell.

Mrs Finn picked up the letter and looked again at the words on the top of the page in big bold letters. **THIS IS NOT AN EVICTION ORDER**, it said.

'We are all to be given new houses, with gardens and lower rent. What you have brought us this day, Paddy Cronin, is a miracle.'

The three of them went outside to celebrate with the neighbours, who were out in the lane whooping and laughing and crying and hugging each other. Mrs Coleman was kneeling in the middle of the lane with her arms raised to the heavens, thanking God and all the saints. Mrs Finn walked over and helped her up and then they both cried in each other's arms.

Paddy Cronin stood watching them, then lifted his bag onto his shoulder and started walking home.

This day, that had started out so badly, had turned into one of the best days of his life. He would sit with his wife Molly and tell her all that had happened and how he thought that being a postman was the best job in the world.

CHAPTER 23

Diane

Diane Mason had been looking forward to getting out of the ugly green prison clothes, but as she stood in front of the governor, she felt that what she was wearing was all wrong. The colours were too bright, the skirt too short and the buttons on her blouse had barely done up from all the bloody porridge she'd put away. She wasn't the same woman who had strutted in there a year ago, thinking she was the bee's knees. Everything had changed; she had a purpose now and it didn't include wearing flashy clothes and high heels she could hardly walk in.

The governor smiled at her. 'Sit down, Miss Mason,' he said.

Diane sat down and returned the smile. Mr Tandy was OK, she'd known a lot worse. She had always found him to be a fair man. The first thing he had said to her was, 'If you play fair with me, I'll play fair with you,' and she had, because, over time, he had earned her respect and the respect of most of the women within these walls.

'So here we are saying goodbye yet again.'

Diane nodded. 'We are, sir, but it will be for the last time.'

Mr Tandy smiled. 'I wish you well, Diane, in whatever you are planning to do next.'

'I'm planning to have a decent cup of tea. Beggin' yer pardon, sir, but the tea in here tastes like cat's piss and that's doing a disservice to cats.'

'So I've been told,' he said, smiling. 'But we don't want to make it too cosy, do we?'

Diane stood up. 'Goodbye, sir, and thanks for everything.'

The governor came across the desk and shook her hand. 'Goodbye, Diane.'

She heard the clang of the heavy prison doors as they slammed shut behind her; she didn't look back, for she would never be going back again. She'd had an easy time in there, quite jolly, really. She had known a lot of the girls already and they looked out for each other, as they had always done.

She walked across the yard towards the big iron gates and her new life.

'See you soon,' said the guard, smiling. 'I'll make sure they keep your bed warm.'

'No need for that, Eddie, I won't be needing that bed again.'

'That's what you said last time, Dolly.'

'But this time is different.'

'You said that as well,' said Eddie, grinning.

Diane laughed. 'I expect I did but I mean it this time. You won't be seeing me again in this lifetime.'

Eddie Cooper put his arm gently on her shoulder. 'Then you'll be sorely missed, girl.'

'I'm sure that London is full of Dolly Masons. Anyway, isn't it time you retired and bought that boat you're always banging on about?'

He laughed. 'I'd have to win the pools first.'

'I'd give you a hug but I don't want you to lose your job, so let us just say goodbye and good luck.'

'Goodbye, Dolly, you won't be forgotten.'

'Goodbye, Eddie.'

He opened the gates and Diane walked towards freedom.

Frank was leaning against the shiny black limousine, smiling at her. She took off her shoes and ran to him, where she was enveloped in two big strong arms.

'Welcome home, Dolly,' he said.

He opened the car door and she stepped inside.

'Ready?' he said.

'I've never been more ready, Frank.'

'And are you sure that this is what you want to do?'

'I've had plenty of time to think about it in there, so yes, this is what I want to do. It's what I *have* to do.'

Diane gazed out the window as they drove down the Holloway Road. The familiar streets of London brought a lump to her throat; she'd miss it. When she'd first arrived all those years ago she'd found it to be a harsh, unfriendly place. She'd walked for miles looking for digs but even the most run-down houses had signs on the door that said, 'No blacks or Irish'. It was in the underbelly of this great city that she had finally found a welcome and it was there, amongst the gigolos and girls of the night, that she had found acceptance, friendship, loyalty and, yes, love. If London was the backbone of this great island of ours, then Soho was its heart and it was a heart that didn't judge, a place where you could be whatever you wanted to be, no matter what nationality you were, what deity you bowed down to, or what you were running from. It was here in the dark places and alleyways of Soho that your sins were wiped free, for everyone had their secrets and no one asked questions. You could be royalty or the dregs of life, but if you had money in your pocket then nobody cared. It was said that, at the right price, everything here could be bought, even redemption.

It was as the rest of the city slept that these streets became alive and for a while the world was a brighter place, a place of silks and satins, of feather boas and high heels. The air was filled with hope and possibilities, dreams and promises. Neon signs guided you down steep steps and through scarlet velvet curtains, where for a few pounds you could believe that the arms that held you thought you were a great feller altogether and for those few moments you felt like a king. Everyone was beautiful under the cover of darkness and, like vampires, they slipped away as dawn broke over the rooftops of Soho.

And so this had become her life and these people had become her family. She was on nodding terms with the spivs who lounged in doorways, with their smart Italian suits and slicked-back hair. She spent time with old Molly, who sat outside the strip clubs, taking the entrance money and knitting baby clothes for her beloved grandchildren.

It was Tony Marino who had taken pity on the homeless young girl that she had been, setting her up in a house in Greek Street and becoming her protector. At just sixteen years of age she had become not a prostitute, but the youngest madam in Soho. The girls became her family and she cared for them as if they were her children. Most of her clients were regulars and she made sure that her girls were safe. If there had ever been any trouble, she left it to Tony Marino to sort out.

Every so often the police would raid one of the houses and they'd all be hauled up in front of the judge. The sentences were always light but they had to be seen to be doing something about that shady little corner of London. Of course it changed nothing and life went on as before.

She lay back against the soft leather seats and closed her eyes. She was ready for whatever lay ahead of her. It was time to go home.

Frank pulled up outside his office and they went inside.

'Everything is packed and ready. Norma picked out the clothes for you. I wouldn't have had a clue.'

'Thank her for me, Frank.'

'I will.'

'Now, I need to get the smell of that place out of my nose.'

Once she had scrubbed herself almost raw in the shower, she put on the clothes and began to feel more like her old self. No, not her old self, her *new* self. The clothes were plain but of good quality, Norma had done her proud.

When she walked back into the room, Frank nearly choked on the wine he was knocking back. 'Dear God, Dolly, you could pass for gentry in that get-up, there's not a trace of Soho about you.'

'It's only clothes, Frank. I'm the same inside and Soho will always be a part of who I am, maybe even the best part.'

He handed her a glass of wine. It was cold to the touch, she lifted it slowly to her lips and it slipped down her throat like nectar. It tasted like her old life, a mixture of pleasure and a hint of danger. Wine would never taste this good again.

Frank raised his glass. 'Good luck to you, Dolly Mason, wherever your journey takes you.'

'Keep an eye on the girls, Frank, especially Dawn, I worry about her.'

'Of course I will, love.'

She had tears in her eyes as she put her arms around him. 'Goodbye, Frank, thanks for everything. I'll never forget you.'

'And I'll never forget you, Dolly Mason.'

As the taxi pulled away, Diane looked back at the brass plaque beside the door: FRANCIS MALLORY SOLICITORS. She smiled all the way to the docks. Francis Mallory, the dodgiest solicitor in London and one of the nicest men she had ever known.

· · ·

The next morning she was standing on deck, watching as the green hills of Ireland appeared through the mist. She was surrounded by people, all waiting to see the first signs of their homeland, some even crying quietly. Someone started to sing a rebel song and was soon joined by others. The Irish had long memories, passed down from generation to generation; if they weren't talking about the wrongs done to them, they were singing about them. Chesterton was right when he said, 'The great Gaels of Ireland are the men that God made mad. For all their wars are merry, and all their songs are sad.'

She breathed in the fresh air and the smell of the sea, the saltiness of it on her tongue and the clean spray of it on her skin. The stench of prison still clung to her. The air inside was always thick with stale cigarette smoke, overcooked cabbage and hopelessness. Even worse than the smell was the noise, day and night, screaming and doors banging, until your mind was mashed and you felt as if you were going mad.

As the ship pulled into Dun Laoghaire Harbour, she picked up her case and joined the queue of passengers moving slowly down the gangplank. The quayside was full of people welcoming their loved ones home.

But there was no one to welcome Dolly Mason.

She made her way through the crowd and hailed a taxi to take her to Dublin.

PART THREE

CHAPTER 24

The first time Orla walked into Clerys, it was love at first sight. That morning, she and Polly had left the boarding house so early that it was still pitch-black outside. They trudged over the hard, frozen ground till they couldn't feel their feet.

Polly shivered. 'Jesus, Orla, do you realise we'll be doing this every morning for the rest of our lives?'

'God, you can be very dramatic at times, Polly Dooley. I thought it was me that was the dramatic one.'

'But aren't you cold?'

'I'm bloody frozen but it can't be helped. What do you want me to do? Carry you?'

This had Polly giggling.

'We're nearly there,' said Orla, smiling at her.

'Aren't you nervous?'

'I am and that's only natural, but I'm excited too.'

Polly stamped her feet to try to get some life into them. 'I wish I was more like you.'

Orla took hold of her hand. 'You're perfect as you are, love, and there's nothing for you to worry about because we'll be together. We'll always be together.'

They crossed the road and stood looking up at the grand building that was Clerys department store.

'Deep breath,' said Orla, starting to walk towards the big double doors.

Polly pulled her back.

'What?'

'We shouldn't be going in this way, Orla, there must be another entrance round the back for the workers.'

Orla grinned. 'I have no doubt that there is.'

'Then why are we doing it?'

'I have a mind to see inside.'

'I don't think that this will make a great impression on our first day.'

'What are they going to do? String the pair of us up as a warning to any other brazen hussies that are bold enough to use the front door? Come on, we're going in.'

Polly made the sign of the cross and reluctantly followed her sister into the store.

Orla stood by the door gazing around her. It was like stepping into another world, a world of soft lighting and beautiful mirrors and the scent of flowers. It was more beautiful than she could ever have imagined. Long cabinets ran all the way down one wall, displaying the most beautiful jewellery; rings and necklaces, bangles and brooches, sparkled under the glass counters. Her two eyes were out on stalks, gazing at it all. It was like an Aladdin's cave, all it needed was the magic lamp.

She nearly jumped out of her skin when a raucous voice, in the form of a woman in a black suit, bore down on them. Polly stepped behind her.

'How did you get in here?' the woman demanded.

'Through the door,' said Orla, with an innocent look on her face.

'Who let you in?'

'No one let us in, the door was open, we let ourselves in.'

'Well, you shouldn't have, we're not open yet. Isn't Colin out there?'

'Who's Colin?'

'The doorman, that's who Colin is, and he should be on duty.'

'Well, as I am not familiar with Colin's comings and goings, I'm afraid I can't help you, miss.'

The woman was glaring at them now. 'If you want to buy something in Clerys, you'll just have to wait outside until we open.'

'Oh, we don't want to buy anything,' said Orla.

'Then what are you doing here?'

'We're going to be working here. This is our first day.'

The woman was almost puce-looking now. 'The workers' entrance is round the back.'

'Oh right,' said Orla. 'Sorry to have bothered you.'

Polly was now tugging at her sleeve.

As they opened the door, Orla turned back. 'Miss?' she said. 'What?'

'If we did want to buy something in here, would we use the front door then?'

Before the woman could think of an answer, Polly had dragged Orla outside. They were both giggling as they ran down some stone steps to the workers' entrance.

'Well, I hope she never becomes your boss, Orla.'

'Wasn't she an awful old baggage? You'd think she owned the place the way she was going on.'

'Did you spot her name?' said Polly. 'It was pinned to her jacket.'

Orla shook her head.

'Her name's Miss Pring. I think it suits her, don't you?'

'I can think of plenty names that would suit her better.'

Polly grinned. 'I bet you can.'

'Well, we might as well go in,' said Orla, opening the door.

'This is the first day of the rest of our lives, Polly, so we'd better put on a good show.'

Herself and Polly got a position working in the warehouse and they both loved it but Orla was determined that one day she would stand behind one of those glass counters in a smart black suit. Her job was to take in the boxes and parcels that arrived daily at Clerys. She knew the names of all the delivery boys and had great craic with them.

Polly worked in another department, unpacking the goods and checking them off against a list, making sure they had delivered the right stuff. Orla only saw her at break times and at the beginning she seemed to be enjoying it; on their way back to the boarding house they would chat away, talking about this one and that one and having a laugh. But these days she could barely get a smile out of her sister and they would walk home in silence that was louder than their laughter. Something was very wrong but Polly wouldn't tell her what it was. Even more worrying were the bruises that began to appear on her arms and around her neck, that she always had some lame reason for.

They had always shared everything, there had never been any secrets between them, and they had only needed each other to be happy; but for the first time ever, Polly was shutting her out and she felt helpless.

They were almost home when, suddenly, Polly sat down on a bench, put her head in her hands and cried as if her heart was breaking. Orla sat down beside her and held her in her arms.

'You have to tell me what's wrong, Polly, you have to. I'm going out of my mind with worry.'

'I can't, Orla, I can't. It will just make things worse.'

'Well, if you won't talk to me then I'm afraid that you will have to talk to Miss Ryan.'

'I can't.'

'You *have* to. Come on, we must sort this out one way or another and I trust Miss Ryan, don't you?'

Polly nodded.

'Come on then.'

They held hands as they walked through the autumn leaves towards home.

They went into the house and Orla tapped on Miss Ryan's door.

There was no answer.

'We won't worry her,' said Polly, looking relieved.

Just as they were about to go upstairs, Mary Kate opened the door. 'Sorry, girls, I must have dozed off.'

'Oh, we didn't mean to disturb you, Miss Ryan, we just wanted a word. We can come back later.'

'No, no, I'm glad you woke me. It's these dark evenings, my body thinks it's night-time.'

'It's fierce cold out there, Miss Ryan, the two of us are only frozen.'

'Come and get warm, girls, and then we will talk.' Mary Kate noticed that Polly was very quiet and it looked as if she'd been crying.

'There's something wrong with Polly, Miss Ryan, but she isn't able to tell me what it is and I'm terrible worried.'

'Do you think that you might be able to tell *me*, Polly?'

'I don't know, Miss Ryan.'

'I'll tell you what, Orla, pop down to the kitchen and get the three of us some tea. I can always think more clearly with a grand cup of tea in my hand.'

Once Orla had gone, Mary Kate waited for Polly to speak.

'Whatever you say to me, Polly, stays within these four walls. I don't know what is worrying you but I can see that you are very troubled and maybe it would help to talk about it.'

'I want to go home.'

'You're homesick?'

'It's not that.'

'What then?'

'I'd be safe at home. I just want to feel safe. I can't go back there, Miss Ryan, I can't.'

Mary Kate frowned, this was not what she was expecting to hear. 'You can't go back to Clerys?'

Polly started to cry. 'Please don't make me go back.'

'No one is going to make you do anything you don't want to do, but I do need to know who is hurting you, for I think that someone is. Am I right, Polly?'

Polly nodded.

'Can you tell me his name?'

'I won't have to go back?'

'Not if you don't want to.'

Polly took a deep breath. 'Maeve Lynch.'

Mary Kate was shocked. 'It's a woman that's hurting you?'

'Every day. I'm so scared of her, Miss Ryan. I try to keep out of her way but she finds me.'

'And has no one noticed?'

'She waits until I'm alone.'

Mary Kate felt like crying. This sweet girl had gone into work every day, knowing what she would be facing when she got there.

'She said if I told, she'd cut all my hair off.'

Just then, Orla came in with the tea. 'Who's going to cut your hair off?' she demanded.

Mary Kate looked at Polly, who shook her head. 'Do you want me to tell her?'

Polly nodded.

'Sit down, Orla,' said Mary Kate.

Orla sat down and held Polly's hand.

'Polly is being bullied at work by—'

'Tell me his name, Polly, for as God is my witness I'll kill him.'

'*Her* name, Orla, is Maeve Lynch,' said Mary Kate.

'A woman? It's a woman who's been hurting you? Why in God's name didn't you tell me?'

'I couldn't because I knew what you would do to her and you'd lose your job.'

'I don't give a damn about the bloody job.'

'But you love it there.'

'Look at me, love,' said Orla.

Polly looked at her sister, who gently took her face in her hands.

'There isn't a job in this land that I could love more than I love you.'

'Oh, Orla, I've been so frightened.'

Orla put her arms around her sister. 'We'll find another job, Polly. Sure, who wouldn't want two beautiful girls like ourselves working for them?'

'Hopefully, it won't come to that,' said Mary Kate.

'I feel like killing her,' said Orla.

Polly gave a sad little smile. 'That's why I couldn't tell you.'

'I can see that now, love, because, as God is my witness, I would have eaten the face off her.'

Mary Kate poured the tea. 'Leave it with me, girls, and in the meantime, I want you to stay here until this is sorted out.'

CHAPTER 25

It was a grey, misty morning as Mary Kate strode across the green. She was so angry, she didn't trust herself not to burst into Clerys and string Maeve bloody Lynch up by her ears. She wanted to make her pay for what she had done to Polly. She had hardly slept; it broke her heart to think of what that poor girl had been going through. She knew what it felt like to be scared, to feel so alone. Well, Polly wasn't alone and she thanked God for it. Polly had people who loved her and would protect her and she was going to make sure that spawn of the Devil knew it.

She breathed in the icy-cold air and tried to calm down. Anger wasn't the way forward; words were going to be her weapons this day and she was almost looking forward to it.

Mary Kate walked into Clerys and was relieved to find that it was Carla who was sitting behind the reception desk.

Carla smiled at her. 'Are you having your hair done today?'

'No, Carla. I need to see to see Mr Walsh on a very important matter, if he's available.'

'I'm sure he'll make himself available to you, Miss Ryan, if he's able to.'

Mary Kate sat down on the red velvet couch and looked

around the beautiful store. She remembered the first time she had sat here. She remembered how she had felt that day, in her old coat and unkempt hair. She had known she didn't belong and so did everyone who walked past her.

Today, people didn't give her a second glance, because today she looked like the sort of person who had every right to be sitting on a red velvet couch in Clerys department store. Today, Mary Kate was acceptable – yes, that was the word, acceptable – and that saddened her, for surely a person should be judged by who they were on the inside and not the expensive cloth they were wrapped in.

Carla interrupted her thoughts. 'Mr Walsh will see you now, Miss Ryan,' she said, smiling. 'If you'd like to follow me, I'll take you up to him.'

Mary Kate stood up. 'Your hair is looking as lovely as ever, Carla.'

'Thank you, I was just thinking the same about yours.'

'Well, aren't we the grand ones then?'

Carla laughed. 'Aren't we just!' she said.

When Mary Kate walked into Mr Walsh's office, he immediately came round the desk and shook her hand.

'Well, Miss Ryan, this is indeed a treat and I have to say you're looking very well.'

'As you are yourself.'

'But you look worried, am I right?'

'Yes, I am very worried.'

'And is it something that I can help you with?'

'That is why I am here, Mr Walsh, for I do need your help.'

'Then if it's in my power, I shall be honoured to do what I can.'

'I have two sweet girls who are guests at my boarding house. They came to Dublin to work here at Clerys. Their names are Orla and Polly Dooley, and they work in your warehouse.'

'Go on, Miss Ryan.'

'To begin with, they were both very happy, and Orla still is, but I'm afraid that Polly is too scared to come back.'

'Scared?'

'Yes, scared.'

'But what is she scared of?'

'I'm sorry to have to tell you, Mr Walsh, that for the last few months Polly has been bullied. Not only bullied but harmed. She has been coming home with bruises on her arms and on her neck. The poor girl has been terrified to come to work but too afraid to tell anyone for fear of what her sister would do to this person, and which would result in her losing her job.'

Mr Walsh stood up and started pacing around the room. 'I can't tell you how angry I am, and how shocked, to think that there is such evil in my store without me knowing about it. Tell me his name, Miss Ryan, and I can assure you that he will be sacked on the spot. In fact, I shall report him to the Garda, for what he has put that child through is a crime and it's a crime that he is going to pay for.'

'I think that you will be even more shocked, as I was myself, to learn that it is not a man, or a boy who has been hurting Polly, but a woman.'

Mr Walsh stopped pacing and stared at her. 'A woman? It's a woman who has been doing this?'

Mary Kate nodded. 'Her name is Maeve Lynch.'

Mr Walsh sat back down and stared into space. 'I have to take some of the blame for this.'

'But sure it's not your fault.'

'I'm afraid it is. My job is to see to the smooth running of this store but in doing so it seems that I have neglected the most important part of it, the wellbeing of my staff. But I can assure you, Miss Ryan, that from this day, that is all going to change.'

'Don't be too hard on yourself, Mr Walsh, for I too hadn't a clue what Polly was going through. If I had known, I could have stopped it sooner.'

'You are very kind, Miss Ryan, and I appreciate you bringing this to my attention.'

'Well, it was either speak to you or eat the face off her myself and I thought the sensible thing was to speak to you.'

'You did the right thing. I am just so sorry that this has happened. I hope you will not think too badly of Clerys.'

'Not at all. The Devil arrives in sheep's clothing and isn't always easy to spot.'

Mr Walsh picked up the phone on his desk. 'Hello, John, will you please send Maeve Lynch up to my office immediately, thank you.' He put the phone down and looked at Mary Kate. 'Do you want to be here when I confront her?'

Mary Kate smiled. 'Try and stop me, Mr Walsh.'

They didn't have to wait long before there was a tap on the door and a large woman walked into the room. She was smiling. *Well, she won't be smiling for long*, thought Mary Kate.

The woman went to sit down but Mr Walsh stopped her.

'Don't make yourself comfortable, Miss Lynch, for what I have to say won't be taking long.'

Maeve Lynch stared at Mr Walsh and then at Mary Kate, who glared at her.

'I don't understand,' she said.

'Are you standing there telling me that your conscience is clear?'

'I don't know what you are talking about, sir.'

'Well, let me make it clear, Miss Lynch. You are a bully and a coward, who has terrorised a young girl for no other reason than to satisfy your wickedness. Is that clear enough?'

The colour had drained from the woman's face. 'I'm, I'm sorry.'

'You are *sorry* because you have been caught.'

'I won't do it again, I promise I won't do it again.'

'I am sure that, given the opportunity, you most certainly *would* do it again but not in my store, madam, not in my store.

You are hereby dismissed. Collect your things and leave these premises and never step foot in Clerys again. Do I make myself understood?'

The woman started to cry great loud, shuddering sobs.

'Save those tears for Polly Dooley,' said Mr Walsh. 'And don't expect a reference. Now get out of my sight before I call the Garda.'

After she had gone, Mary Kate heaved a sigh of relief. 'Thank you, Mr Walsh, the girls will return to work tomorrow.'

'Let them have the week off, Miss Ryan, a bit of a holiday. Let them explore Dublin.'

Mary Kate stood up and shook his hand. 'You're a good man, Mr Walsh. I'm sure the girls will be delighted. Thank you.'

'It's the least I can do, Miss Ryan, and I hope that the next time we meet, it will be in happier circumstances.'

Mary Kate smiled. 'I'm sure it will.'

She couldn't wait to tell the girls about their unexpected holiday and to let Polly know that her tormentor was well and truly gone. And so it was with a lighter heart that she hurried across the square to the house with the red door.

CHAPTER 26

Colleen was standing in front of the mirror, smiling as she turned this way and that. Her tummy was so big now, she could barely see her feet. She placed her hands very gently on her bump as the baby moved. It was the strangest sensation, like a little butterfly fluttering away inside her, and she loved it.

'Are you a boy or a girl?' she said, smiling. 'Not that I mind, for I shall love you whatever you are, and I can't wait to meet you. I hope you'll like me.'

She knew that the baby must be due very soon, because she could barely get out of a chair with the size of her tummy. Miss Ryan hadn't taken a penny piece from her since she'd arrived. Colleen had tried to repay her by helping in the house and even then, Miss Ryan had insisted on paying her. Colleen thanked God every day for sending Orla and Polly to rescue her and to bring her to this boarding house where she had found kindness and shelter and not a word of judgement. The only thing Miss Ryan had insisted on was that she was not to sell the items she had stolen from home.

'You left your home because you were being held captive by your parents, who were intent on taking your child away from you,' she'd said. 'Running away was not a crime. The crime, Colleen, was that you stole from them and they could have the Garda out looking for you, if they haven't already done so.'

'But I had to, Miss Ryan.'

'I know you did and I'm thinking that had I been in your situation, I might have done the same myself.'

'Would you?'

'I would. But now you must – *you must* – put it right and return these items.'

'But if I send the stuff back, they'll know that I am in Dublin.'

'I've thought of that,' said Mary Kate. 'My solicitor often has to go to London on business. I shall ask him to post the parcel from there and I'll make sure that your parents have to sign for it. I'm not saying that they will deny receiving it but this way we can be sure.' She'd grinned. 'And that way, no one can accuse me of sheltering a desperate fugitive in my house. What do you think?'

'I think that is perfect, thank you, Miss Ryan. Thank you for everything.'

Colleen had decided to take herself into town to buy some clothes for the baby. She had been saving up for ages and if she didn't get some clothes soon, her little baby would end up as naked as the day it was born. Just as she was preparing to leave, Orla and Polly came running down the stairs.

'Hi, Colleen,' said Orla. 'Off somewhere nice?'

'I'm going into town to buy some things for the baby.'

'So are we, going into town, I mean. You can come with us if you like.'

'You sure you don't mind?' said Colleen.

Polly smiled at her. 'Sure why would we mind? The three of us will have great craic altogether.'

Although it was only November, Dublin was preparing for Christmas, and the shop windows were already beginning to sparkle with wreaths of tinsel and coloured baubles. Tiny strings of fairy lights glittered and shone onto the damp wintry streets, turning them into a kind of magical wonderland.

Polly smiled. 'Don't you just love Christmas?'

'I wasn't expecting to but now me and my baby are safe, I'm actually looking forward to it.'

'Oh, Colleen,' said Orla. 'I'm so sorry that happened to you. It must have been awful. I still can't believe your parents would do such a thing.'

'They said I'd shamed them, and I suppose I had. They're not bad people, just very set in their ways.'

'Not enough to lock you in your room. How did you get out?'

'I picked the lock,' said Colleen, grinning.

'You did what?' said Polly.

'I picked the lock.'

'Well, I'd say the nuns didn't teach you that at the Presentation Convent.'

'Roibin taught me how to do it.'

'Was that yer feller?' said Orla.

Colleen nodded. 'I met him when the gypsies came to the town.'

'I remember them coming,' said Polly.

Orla grinned. 'Well, aren't you full of surprises, Colleen Brenna? Cavorting with a gypsy lad and picking locks.'

'Was he nice?' said Polly.

Colleen smiled, remembering the kind, gentle boy she had fallen in love with. 'He was lovely, Polly.'

'I've heard desperate tales about them that would put the fear of God into you.'

'So have I,' said Colleen. 'But Roibin certainly wasn't the

type to go around ravaging young girls and taking the food out of babies' mouths.'

'Well, he ravaged *you*,' said Orla, grinning.

Colleen grinned back. 'I have a feeling that it might have been me that ravaged him.'

'Colleen Brenna,' said Orla, pretending to be shocked. 'Whatever next?'

'Nothing, I hope. I don't know what I would have done if you hadn't found me.'

Polly slipped her arm through Colleen's. 'Well, thank God we did.'

'You were a pitiful sight all right, we couldn't have left you there,' said Orla.

They spent the morning wandering around the shops. Polly and Orla bought Christmas presents for their parents and baby brother and Colleen found some lovely little outfits for the baby.

'Have you thought of any names yet?' said Polly.

'Well, if it's a boy, I thought I'd call him Robbie and if it's a girl, I thought maybe Rosa, after Roibin's mam.'

'They're lovely names,' said Orla.

'Oh, they are,' said Polly. 'Do you mind what you have?'

'No. As long as God in His goodness sends a healthy child, I don't mind if it's a girl or a boy.'

'It's in God's hands all right,' said Polly. 'But it wouldn't do any harm to go down to the church and light a candle, just to give Him a bit of a nudge.'

By midday they were all starving. 'Let's find somewhere to eat,' said Orla.

'I know exactly where we can eat,' said Colleen. 'It's a little Indian café. They fed me when I first arrived in Dublin and I'd love to see them again.'

'Lead on, my little lock-picking friend,' said Orla.

The three of them were giggling as they made their way to

the café. When they got there, Colleen was surprised to see a sign on the door that said CLOSED UNTIL FURTHER NOTICE.

'I don't understand this,' said Colleen.

'Maybe they've gone on holiday,' said Polly.

'I suppose they might have done.'

Just then she saw Ashar's mother, coming into the café, so she tapped on the door. Mrs Patel shook her head but then recognised her and hurried over.

'Colleen,' she said, smiling, 'how lovely to see you again.'

'I've never forgotten how kind you were to me that day.'

'You were such a sad little thing, but it looks as if life has been kind to you since then. I'm afraid I can't say the same for our little family, you have not come at the happiest of times.'

'I'm so sorry to hear that.'

'Come inside and we'll talk.'

'These are my friends, Orla and Polly.'

Mrs Patel smiled at them. 'You are very welcome in our home.'

They followed Mrs Patel through the café and into the back room. Mr Patel and Ashar were sitting at the table. They stood up as the girls came in.

'How lovely to see you again, Colleen,' said Ashar.

Colleen introduced Orla and Polly and they all sat down.

'I was surprised to see that you were closed,' said Colleen.

'We hadn't the heart to open,' said Mr Patel.

'Can I ask why?'

Ashar looked angry. 'Because the landlord is selling the place and we have four weeks to get out.'

'That's awful,' said Polly.

'Where will you go?' said Colleen.

Mr Patel shook his head. 'Four weeks, four bloody weeks and he couldn't even tell us in person. We got a letter. Six years we've been here and never missed a day's rent, and this is how we are treated.'

Mrs Patel touched his arm. 'Now, my love, we are just being shown another path.'

'And what will we find at the end of this path? Can you tell me that, Sunni?'

'We will find what we are supposed to find. We will be guided to the right place. Have faith, Mital.'

Suddenly, Colleen jumped up from the table. 'Dear God, I've wet meself, it's all over your floor. I'm so sorry, Mrs Patel, if you give me a cloth, I'll wipe it up.'

Mrs Patel smiled at her. 'When is your baby due, Colleen?'

'Is she having the baby?' said Polly. 'Is she having the baby now?'

Colleen suddenly screamed and doubled over.

'Ashar, get clean towels and sheets, quickly now.'

Colleen screamed again.

'Shouldn't we get her to the hospital?' said Orla, who had gone as white as a sheet.

Mrs Patel placed her hand on Colleen's tummy as another pain ripped through her. 'I don't think we will have time for that.'

'We need to let Miss Ryan know,' said Polly.

Mrs Patel held Colleen's hand. 'Is she a friend?'

'She's our landlady,' said Orla.

'And Colleen would want her to be here?'

'Oh yes, she would. I'll get her, the boarding house isn't far.'

Colleen screamed again.

'Run as fast as you can, Orla,' said Polly. 'Run as fast as you can.'

Orla could barely speak by the time she arrived at the boarding house and nearly fell into Mary Kate's arms.

'Dear God,' said Mary Kate. 'What is wrong, child?'

'Colleen needs you, Miss Ryan, she's having her baby.'

'Where is she?'

'In an Indian café in town.'

Mary Kate grabbed her coat and ran upstairs, calling out to Moira as she ran.

Moira appeared on the landing. 'Is something wrong?' she said, looking concerned.

'Not wrong exactly, Colleen is having her baby.'

'Downstairs?'

'No, in an Indian café by all accounts.'

'Well, I suppose that is as good a place as any to have a baby.'

'I suppose it is,' said Mary Kate. 'I just wanted to make sure that you would take care of Abby while I'm gone. Is she with you?'

'She's in the front bedroom, changing the flowers. Don't worry, I'll keep an eye on her.'

Mary Kate ran back downstairs, where Orla was waiting for her in the hallway.

'It's not too far,' said Orla.

'It was good of you to get me.'

'Colleen would want you there, Miss Ryan. I know she would.'

'Has no one called an ambulance?'

'Mrs Patel said there was no time.'

'Then we must hurry.'

Mary Kate could hardly breathe by the time they got there. The door was open, so they hurried through the café and Mary Kate followed Orla into the back room.

Colleen was lying on the floor. Her face was flushed and she was obviously in a great amount of pain. There was a woman kneeling beside her, speaking so gently, and placing a towel on her forehead. She looked up as Mary Kate came into the room.

'Miss Ryan?' she said.

Mary Kate nodded.

'I'm Mrs Patel, I'm so glad you are here. Colleen has been asking for you.'

Colleen screamed and Mary Kate knelt down beside her and held her hand.

'It's Miss Ryan, Colleen,' she said.

'Oh, Miss Ryan, I think I'm going to die. I'm in desperate pain.'

'You won't die, my love, for you are in safe hands. Very soon you will have your baby in your arms and all that pain will be forgotten.' Mary Kate looked around the little room. It was so peaceful, candles had been lit and it smelled gorgeous. She must remember to tell Moira that she had been right when she'd said that an Indian café was as good a place as any to have a baby.

Suddenly Colleen gripped her hand. 'I hurt so much,' she screamed.

'Just breathe, Colleen,' said Mrs Patel. 'This is natural and there is nothing to fear.'

'There's nothing natural about this.'

Mrs Patel lifted the sheet, she felt Colleen's tummy and looked between her legs. 'Now on your next contraction, I need you to push. Can you do that for me?'

'I don't know.'

'Your body is telling you what to do, just listen to it. Your baby is waiting to meet you.'

Colleen took a deep breath and started pushing. Her face was bright red and there were beads of sweat on her forehead. She pushed again, then laid back down on the cushion.

'I can't do it, I can't.'

'Yes, you can, you're doing beautifully. Now have a little rest until the next contraction. Miss Ryan, can you support Colleen's head?'

'Of course.'

'Oh, the pain is coming again.'

'Now, I want you to put your chin on your chest and push right down into your bottom.'

Colleen started pushing again.

'Good girl,' said Mrs Patel.

Polly, who had been massaging Colleen's feet, jumped up. 'Jesus Mary and holy Saint Joseph, I can see the baby's head.'

'Now pant, Colleen, very short little breaths, while I take a look.'

Colleen did as she was told.

'You are being so brave,' whispered Mary Kate.

'Now push,' said Mrs Patel.

Mary Kate supported Colleen's head as she started to push.

Mrs Patel was smiling. 'The baby's head is born. Now one big push and it will be here.'

And there it was, a tiny little thing with a mass of black hair, screaming its little lungs out.

'You have a little girl, Colleen,' said Mary Kate. 'You have a beautiful little girl.' At which point she was crying and so were the rest of them.

'Hand me the sari, Orla,' said Mrs Patel. 'It's there on the chair. The pink one, please.'

Orla handed her the most beautiful piece of cloth Mary Kate had ever seen and the woman tenderly wrapped it around the baby and handed her to Colleen.

Colleen gazed down at her little girl with such love. 'Hello, Rosa,' she said. 'We made it. We're safe and I shall never let you go.'

CHAPTER 27

Claire Devlin had been watching the house for weeks. She'd chosen a bench where she could see the front door, but no one inside could see her. It had become her routine, it gave her something to look forward to, it gave her a reason to get out of bed. She watched the comings and goings of her friends, for since that day, when she had been welcomed by them all and made such a fuss of, that's what they had become – her friends, the only friends she had. She couldn't remember their names, or even what they looked like, but none of that mattered. She remembered how they had made her feel and if she wanted to, she could walk across the green and knock on the door. So why didn't she? Why didn't she do just that? She frowned; had she been invited back? She couldn't remember and, until she could, it would be rude to assume that she would be welcomed back.

She'd watched the tall woman and a little girl going for their daily walk, always accompanied by a black-and-white dog racing around them. She'd seen an older woman and a young girl hurrying down the steps. She'd followed them one day, as they went into the butcher's and the grocer's – she'd enjoyed that day. They all looked so familiar to her but she didn't know where she could have known them from. Sometimes images would come into her head, little snatches of something, never the whole picture. Somewhere dark, somewhere cold and damp. She tried so hard to hang on to these images but just as they started to make sense, they were gone. The only thing that was real to her was the house and something else... something she had to do, something that would make everything better, something behind the red door.

Claire watched as a young girl raced across the square and into the boarding house. She didn't have to wait long before the door opened and the girl and a woman ran down the steps and headed towards town. Claire decided to follow them, keeping out of sight as much as she could.

Claire felt excited – it was like being in a movie. She hadn't enjoyed herself so much in ages. She suddenly had a memory of running away from something, maybe a place, a place where she didn't want to be. She hadn't been excited that day. She pushed it from her mind, but the memory had made her uneasy, it was as if a dark cloud had settled on her shoulders like a heavy blanket, making her doubt why she was here, running after these strangers. But she kept following them as they ran past the big stores and in and out of the crowds that filled the sidewalks. They didn't stop to look in the shop windows, even though they looked very pretty. They were in a hurry to get somewhere. They were definitely on a mission and she was determined to find out what it was.

Eventually, they turned off the main drag and down a side street. She watched as they went into a small shop. She didn't know what to do next, then she noticed an alley running down the side. The night was drawing in and though she felt safe under the cover of darkness, she looked around to make sure no one was watching her and, feeling confident they weren't, she walked down the alley.

The street had been bright, with lights shining out of all the little shops, but it was almost pitch-black down there and she stumbled over some boxes and nearly fell. She leaned against the wall and took a deep breath. She could hear screaming coming from inside. Had someone had an accident? Was that why the woman and the girl had been in such a hurry? The screaming stopped and for a moment all was silent. She groped her way along the wall until she was at the back of the house. She looked through the window into a little room – there were candles flickering, throwing soft beams of light into the yard, and then she heard it, the high-pitched cry of a new baby. She remembered that cry, it came to her at night, breaking her heart when she woke to find it had been a dream. Ronald would hold her until she was calm – he was a good man, a kind man, she missed him. The baby cried again, it filled her heart with such joy; this was real, this wasn't a dream. Now it was all making sense and she sighed with relief. Someone had guided her to this place, this was where she was supposed to be.

Rosa was beautiful. She had a mass of dark hair and the bluest of eyes, framed by silky lashes that rested on her pink cheeks like two curtains. Everyone had fallen in love with her. This new little life had brought something to the house, a feeling of hope and new beginnings and love. There was always someone gazing down at her, stroking her soft skin or holding her tiny hand.

Every little change in Rosa was noted and talked about at length.

'Do you see the way her eyes follow me around the room?' said Orla.

'I don't think she can do that yet,' said Polly, who had suddenly become an expert on all things relating to babies.

'And what would you know?' snapped Orla.

'I borrowed a book out of the library.'

'When?' said Orla.

'About a week ago.'

'And where was I?'

'I haven't a clue, Orla. I am able to go out on my own, you know.'

The sisters glared at each other and then burst out laughing.

'I suppose you are,' said Orla, smiling at her.

Mary Kate was fascinated by the baby, the way her hands worried at the cover and the way her tongue moved over her lips as if she was having a secret conversation. She was a time waster, that's what she was, and Mary Kate didn't mind one bit. Moira was just as besotted, they were like two mother hens; the child was going to be ruined but sure how could love ruin anyone?

Colleen was a natural mother, calm and capable and loving. The heavy load that she had been carrying on her shoulders for so long had disappeared with the birth of her child. Mary Kate thanked God every day for sending Orla and Polly to Colleen's side and bringing her here, to the house with the red door. She couldn't bear to think what would have happened to her if she hadn't been found.

Everyone had been so kind. Gerry and Erin had arrived with the biggest bouquet of flowers Mary Kate had ever seen, which had Mrs Lamb rushing to the shops for more vases. Flowers had also arrived from Mr Renson and Mr Walsh had sent a box full of the most exquisite baby clothes from Clerys. But the most surprising gift of all was from Sean Barry, who had turned up pushing a big shiny pram.

'I thought it would come in handy,' he mumbled. 'For wheeling her out, when the weather gets a bit warmer.'

Colleen was so overwhelmed by his gift that she immediately burst into tears. 'Everyone has been so kind,' she said. 'I hadn't expected such kindness.'

'I didn't know what else to get,' said Sean. 'But I thought I couldn't go far wrong with a pram. Doesn't every baby need a pram?'

'They do,' said Mary Kate, smiling at him. 'It was a very thoughtful gift, Sean, and one that I'm sure will get well used.'

'I was afraid that when I turned up there'd be a roomful of them and I'd look like a right eejit.'

'The other five are out the back,' said Mary Kate.

'The other five?' said Sean.

Mary Kate grinned. 'Just codding,' she said.

'I'll get you back for that,' he said, laughing.

'You can't cod a codder, Mr Barry.'

Sean winked at her. 'We'll see about that, Mary Kate Ryan.'

The way he said it with that twinkle in his eyes had her blushing to the roots of her hair. *Jesus, woman, cop on to yourself*, she thought.

Mrs Lamb had knitted a blanket and Eliza had embroidered the letter 'R' in one corner. Eliza had carried it into the room as if it was a piece of delicate china. She presented it to the baby and genuflected.

Mrs Lamb raised her eyes to the ceiling and smiled. 'That is not the baby Jesus in the cradle, Eliza, you don't have to genuflect.'

'I wanted to,' said Eliza.

'And it was a lovely gesture,' said Mary Kate.

'I thought so,' said Eliza, grinning.

The only one who wasn't besotted with the baby was Abby, who acted as though she wasn't there. Mary Kate noticed that it was worse when Moira was cuddling Rosa in her arms. The child was jealous and Mary Kate didn't know what to do about it.

. . .

One afternoon, Mr and Mrs Patel and their son Ashar came to tea. They were such lovely people, so sweet in their ways and so kind to each other, it was humbling.

Mrs Patel bowed and handed Mary Kate a tin. 'These are sweet cakes. We eat them a lot, too much,' she said, smiling. 'I hope you enjoy them.'

'I'm sure we will and thank you. Please sit down,' said Mary Kate, 'make yourself at home.'

'This is a beautiful room,' said Mrs Patel, looking around. 'You have very good taste, Miss Ryan.'

'Thank you, but I can't take all the glory, I had a lot of help.'

'But it was your design.'

'I suppose it was.'

'I'm sure it was, for there is an aura in this room that is all you.'

Mary Kate smiled. 'What a lovely thing to say.'

'I have done my best with our little place but the rooms are small and the top floor is not useable because of the damp.'

'Have you contacted the landlord about it?'

Mr Patel made what sounded like a snort. 'He said that it would cost too much and it wasn't worth it. I think what he meant was that we weren't worth it. Anyway, there is no point now. We have to be out in a week.'

Mary Kate smiled at him. 'I have learned that however bad something is, life has a habit of working out, and I'm speaking from experience. Now let us all have a cup of tea and one of those delicious cakes.'

CHAPTER 28

Mary Kate was sitting opposite James Renson in his lovely office.

'And once you have bought this Indian café, do you intend to demolish that too?'

Mary Kate laughed. 'I intend to renovate it and then give it away.'

'I would hardly call that good business, Mary Kate, and it's my duty as your solicitor to advise you against such a project.'

'And as my friend?'

He smiled. 'I have a feeling that whatever my opinion on the matter you will do it anyway, and I will of course help you all I can.'

'I thought you might,' she said, grinning. Mary Kate took a piece of paper out of her handbag and passed it across the desk. 'This is the name of the landlord who owns the building. Pay him what the building is worth, bearing in mind that the top floor is running with damp and it needs a new roof.'

'Now you are talking like a businesswoman.'

'I'm a late bloomer, James,' she said, laughing.

'And I wish you all the luck in the world. If anyone deserves it you do.'

At the door she turned around. 'And if you could keep my name out of this, I'd be grateful.'

'Of course.'

On her way out, she had a lovely chat with Jenny and then made her way to Clerys, where she was meeting Sean Barry for an update on Tanners Row.

It was a bright chilly day as she made her way across the park. She was early, so she sat down on a bench and looked across the green. The trees had shed their beautiful autumn leaves and the bare branches stood stark against a clear blue sky.

Oh, how her life had changed since the day she had learned that the mother she had never known had left her a fortune. At first, the thought of all that money had scared her. She'd never had money and she'd never missed it but suddenly she was rich and in less than a day she had moved out of Ginnetts Row and into the Shelbourne hotel. She should have been over the moon, she should have been down on her knees thanking God for such a blessing, but the truth was that it had made her sad. She would rather have met her mother and remained poor. Why hadn't she wanted to see her child, her own flesh and blood? Or visit her parents, who prayed for her until the day they died? Did she think that money could make up for missing all that?

This feeling of bitterness towards her mother had stuck in her throat for weeks and she'd hated herself for it. She was judging her when she had no idea what her life had been like or what had stopped her from coming home.

It was when she decided to do some good with the money that the bitterness eased. She was going to help people who were in need of a bit of luck, as she had once been, and she was going to do it in her mother's name and hope that she would have been proud of the baby she had abandoned.

Her breath billowed around her in the icy-cold air then

floated off over the park in a spiral of white smoke. She got up and hurried across the road to Clerys.

Sean was already there, and he stood up and smiled as she walked towards him.

'I'm sorry I'm late, Sean,' she said. 'I was daydreaming over in the park.'

Sean pulled out a chair for her. 'Nice daydreams, I hope,' he said.

'Just trying to make sense of all that has happened.'

'Well, I have some news regarding Tanners Row.'

'Good news?'

'I think it might be. Mrs Dunne at number five has passed away.'

'And that's the good news?'

'Of course not. I'm sorry, it came out all wrong. But it means that the cottage is empty. Now what you have to decide is whether you still want to build six small houses, or five bigger ones.'

'I think you already know the answer to that, Sean.'

'Five bigger ones?'

Mary Kate nodded. 'Definitely five bigger ones, it will give us so much more space. And apart from Mrs Dunne passing away, God rest her soul, yes, this is very good news.'

Sean stood up and moved to sit beside her, he unrolled a piece of paper and spread it out on the table. 'Here are the plans for the new houses and I hope they are what you had in mind.' He pointed to the drawing. 'You'll see that without number five, the rooms are much bigger.'

Mary Kate grinned. 'So, you already knew that I would want five houses?'

Sean tried to look shamefaced but didn't quite pull it off. 'I was hoping you would,' he said, grinning. 'So, lovely light sitting rooms, good-size kitchens, an upstairs bathroom and gardens back and front.'

Mary Kate's eyes filled with tears as she remembered the tiny cottage where she had been brought up. It was all she'd known and she had never wanted more. It hadn't bothered her that there had been no running water or electricity and, anyway, they had all been in the same boat – all poor but they had shared what little they had.

It suddenly occurred to her that these new houses might change the people of Tanners Row. And could these lovely new houses spark envy in the rest of the town?

'What are you thinking?' said Sean.

She frowned. 'Am I doing the right thing, Sean? Or am I just trying to be Lady Bountiful?'

Sean covered her hand with his. 'You couldn't be Lady Bountiful if you tried, girl. You are changing people's lives here, what they do with those lives is up to them. You have given from the heart, without looking for thanks or gratitude, and that is a rare thing indeed.'

Sean's hand had stayed covering hers and Mary Kate had let it rest there. It felt safe and solid and the warmth of it made its way deep into the secret corners of her heart. She wanted time to stand still, she wanted to take this moment and put it in a box and carry it home.

She knew that she was alone with these feelings but suddenly it didn't matter, it was enough that he was here beside her, she didn't expect anything more. Mary Kate had never been in love and through the years she had convinced herself that she didn't care, she hadn't time for it, she didn't need it. But now she understood and she thanked God for bringing her such a gift. Mary Kate Ryan from Tanners Row loved Sean Barry and she would take her secret to the grave.

Sean smiled. 'A penny for them,' he said.

'Oh, I was just wondering, how is the building work at the café going?'

'It's going well and I'd say that it won't take long. The Patels are staying with friends for the time being. They're lovely people, aren't they?'

'That's why I wanted to help them, Sean.'

'You are changing lives, Mary Kate. What you have done has brought them peace and a secure future and I wish that I could tell them that it's yourself that has made it happen.'

'Dear God, no, I don't want them to ever feel beholden to me, Sean.'

'You're a kind woman, Mary Kate Ryan, and I shall say no more on the matter.'

Mary Kate grinned. 'I'd be obliged, Mr Barry.'

Sean stood up. 'I'm afraid I have to leave you, Mary Kate, as I have some houses to pull down. Do you want to be there?'

'My grandfather told me that no good came of living in the past, but it will still be sad to see the cottage torn down, for I was so happy living there.'

'Of course, how thoughtless of me. I'm so sorry.'

'No need to be sorry.'

'Are you going home?' he said.

'I thought I'd have a look round the store.'

'I'll say goodbye then and hope to meet up again soon.'

'That would be grand, I shall look forward to it.'

As Mary Kate made her way downstairs a woman passed her. 'Claire?' she said. 'Claire Devlin? I didn't know you were still in Dublin.'

Claire looked at her as if she didn't have a clue who she was.

Mary Kate thought that was awful odd but she smiled at her. 'Colleen had her baby,' she said. 'A little girl. You would be most welcome to come and visit her when you have the time. I'm sure she would be delighted to see you, and so would Abby and Eliza. Do come, Claire.'

'Oh, I will, I most certainly will and thank you, Miss... umm.'

Mary Kate could see that Claire was struggling to remember her name. 'Ryan,' she said. 'Mary Kate Ryan.'

'Of course,' said Claire.

'We'll see you soon then?'

'You will.'

The encounter with Claire had unsettled Mary Kate so much, she no longer felt like shopping. It was obvious that Claire hadn't known who she was – how in God's name could that be? She'd go home and talk to Moira about it. She remembered that it was Moira who had said the woman was demented, and Mary Kate was beginning to think she might be right.

CHAPTER 29

Jessie

'See you tomorrow,' shouted Aishling, as Jessie started walking across the square towards home.

It had started to snow, soft little flakes of it, swirling around in front of her and settling on her shoulders. She pulled the sleeves of her coat over her cold hands and hugged the books to her chest. It had been so warm in the lecture room that stepping outside felt like stumbling into a block of ice.

Jessie had never been so happy in her life; she felt like spinning around, with her arms wide and her mouth open, letting the cold icy snow sit on her tongue. Sometimes, when she was sitting in the classroom, she would catch Aishling's eye and that happiness would bubble up inside, making her want to laugh out loud with the pure joy of it. She felt like a young girl, which sounded daft because she *was* young, but she had never really felt it.

The convent had been lovely and she'd been safe and cared

for, but there were times when the silence felt almost alive, like it was pushing her down. The soft footsteps of the nuns, as they glided past her, the swish of the black habits that made them all look the same, as if they were one person, with no thoughts or feelings of their own. The only music she knew was the hymns and the chanting of the nuns, echoing through the long corridors. She knew nothing about the latest songs or the latest fashions and she'd accepted, that for her, this was the way it had to be, this was her life, she had known nothing else.

Jessie often thought about the father who had left her at the convent but never returned to claim her. She wanted to think well of him, she wanted to think that life had not turned out the way he hoped it would and that he decided she would have a better life with the nuns than he could ever have given her. It had been Sister Hilda who had taken her in that day and met her father, and when Jessie lived at the convent, she was always asking her what he looked like.

'Was my daddy tall, Sister?'

'You have your own growing to do, Jessie,' she said. 'No matter how tall your father was.'

In the end, Sister Hilda drew a picture of him. The nuns had it framed, and it had hung above her bed throughout her childhood. To begin with, that had been enough, she had a picture of her daddy and she was proud that she had a daddy, while most of the kids in there had no one. But as she grew older, she began to hate it. They say that the eyes are the windows of the soul but the eyes in the drawing were dead, she couldn't see his soul, she didn't know what was in his heart. It was just a bloody drawing, it wasn't even a good one, it wasn't her daddy. She took it off the wall and shoved it under her bed. She hadn't taken it with her when she'd left the convent.

She had no idea what her mother had looked like. There was nobody to say, 'You have your mother's eyes, Jessie. You have her smile, you have her laugh.' She had hazy memories of being held, memories of feeling safe and loved, but she had very few memories of her father – perhaps he hadn't loved her at all, perhaps he couldn't wait to get rid of her. By the time she was fourteen she'd stopped caring; she was alone, and she always would be.

And then there was Abby, sweet Abby, who followed her around like a little lost puppy. God forgive her but there were times when she had resented her, while at the same time loving her so much that it broke her heart. She didn't just have *her* voice, she was also the keeper of Abby's. The nuns spoke to Abby but they were actually speaking to Jessie. They would kneel down, so that they were at the little girl's level, they would ask her questions, then wait for Jessie to answer them. There were times when she had felt invisible.

But now she had friends of her own and she was slowly learning how to be a teenager and she loved it. Most days after school they would head for the café and drink coffee and listen to the jukebox that played the popular songs of the day. Her best friend was Aishling. She'd never had a best friend before and she liked everything about her.

They'd met on her first day of college. Aishling was hurrying up the steps in front of Jessie when she'd tripped, sending her books – and Jessie's – flying in all directions.

Aishling had started laughing. 'Jesus,' she'd said. 'I'm terrible sorry, me mammy says I have two left feet. I even fell over walking down the aisle at my first holy communion. The bloody veil fell off me head and me candle landed up at the Bishop's feet. The mammy was only mortified. By the way, my name's Aishling Hurley.'

Jessie had smiled, the girl was like a breath of fresh air. 'Jessie,' she'd said. 'Jessie Logan.'

They'd gathered up the books and Aishling had linked her arm through hers. 'We'll be best friends,' she said, grinning. 'And there's nothing you can do about it.'

'I don't want to do anything about it,' she'd said.

Aishling was beautiful, with eyes the colour of the sea and a head of wild black hair that she hated but was the envy of every girl in the college. She drew people to her like a moth to a flame and soon she and Jessie had their own little group. Everyone wanted to be Aishling's friend, but it was the outsiders and not the popular girls that she chose.

'I can't be doing with those baggages, prancing about the place like bloody film stars. Their heads are full of horse manure, there isn't a decent brain cell amongst them.'

There was Greta, who blushed like the rising sun whenever anyone spoke to her. Maggie, who was always apologising even though she had nothing to apologise for, and Breda, who had the most infectious laugh Jessie had ever known.

'I went to me uncle's funeral last week,' Breda once said. 'And I laughed all the way through the Mass.'

'Why in God's name did you do that?' asked Aishling.

'There was a new priest taking the service and his wig kept slipping down over his eyes. My mammy says it was all due to my nervous disposition, but it wasn't, it was the bloody wig.'

'Well, I don't mind if you laugh all through my funeral,' said Aishling. 'In fact, I insist on it.'

'Oh, I'd be too sad to laugh at yours, Aishling,' said Breda.

'Weren't you sad at your uncle's funeral?'

'No, he was a gobshite,' she said, giggling.

Jessie loved being part of the little group, she couldn't wait to get to college every morning, she couldn't wait to be with her friends.

They were all studying English Literature. Greta wanted to be a writer, Aishling wanted to be a journalist and Breda just wanted to get out of the house and away from her seven brothers and sisters, who she said did her head in. Jessie just liked words, especially the Irish poets. 'The Lake Isle of Innisfree' by William Butler Yeats touched her heart like no music ever could.

Jessie stood still as soft flakes of snow whirled about her in the cold breeze, and she thought of his beautiful words.

> *I will arise and go now, for always night and day*
> *I hear lake water lapping on the shore;*
> *While standing on the roadway, or on the pave-*
>   *ments grey,*
> *I hear it in the deep heart's core.*

She knew that she would never come up with words like that, words that lifted you up out of the darkest of places. But she loved to read them and remember them.

She looked across at the boarding house that was lit up like a Christmas tree and she felt blessed. They were a great bunch, there wasn't a bad egg amongst them. Miss Kent had been a bit stiff when she'd first arrived and Jessie wasn't sure she was going to take to her, even Miss Ryan had her doubts about the woman, but she'd gradually softened and was now respected and liked by them all. It had been a kind of letting go when Miss Kent had taken Abby under her wing, maybe even a bit of jealousy on Jessie's part, but it was a gentle letting go and she had known that it was time. Colleen had found shelter for herself and her baby. Eliza had been accepted by everyone for the sweet girl that she was and it gave Mrs Lamb some peace. As for Orla and Polly, well, they were great craic. It was as if the house held a kind of magic that affected everyone who stepped beyond the red door.

She knew it was just a boarding house and not their real home, and that one day they would all move on, but she hoped that whoever replaced them would find the same comfort and joy as she had.

The wind had got up and the snow was whipping about her

in a mad dance, swirling this way and that under the lamplight, as if it couldn't decide which way it wanted to go. It was getting in her eyes and stinging her face. She was shivering inside her thin coat and hurried across the square to the boarding house, where she knew there would be a grand warm fire in the grate. She was about to walk up the steps when out of the corner of her eyes she saw something move.

She looked across the green – there it was again, a shadow moving amongst the trees. She walked back across the square, there was someone there. As she got closer, she called out.

'Hello.'

There was no answer and then she heard a rustling as a figure darted out from behind a tree and started running. She couldn't tell if it was a man or a woman and she had no intention of hanging around to find out. She hurried back across the square.

Now who in their right mind would be skulking behind a tree on a freezing cold night like this? Well, at least she had something to tell the girls tomorrow at college. She ran up the steps and into the warmth of the boarding house.

CHAPTER 30

Mary Kate hurried through the gate towards the mourners gathered around Mrs Dunne's grave.

Mrs Finn beckoned her over. 'I was hoping that you'd be here, Mary Kate, I have so much to tell you. You won't believe what has happened.'

Mrs Dunne's daughter glared at them.

'Will you look at her, dressed up to the nines as if she's royalty,' said Mrs Finn. 'She ran around Tanners Row with a bare backside the same as the rest of us. You can put a silk dress on a goat, Mary Kate, but it will always be a goat.'

The daughter turned around and shushed them.

'Oh, go fry yer nose,' whispered Mrs Finn. 'Her mother could talk the hind legs off a donkey, who is she to shush us?'

Mary Kate was trying to stifle a giggle. 'She's burying her mother, Mrs Finn.'

'That doesn't give her the right to be shushing people, as if she owns the graveyard.'

'I think that maybe it does.'

'Ah sure, you've always seen the best in people, girl.'

They stayed until the coffin was lowered into the ground.

Mrs Dunne's daughter was holding court with a little gaggle of woman around her, dabbing at her eyes and looking into the hole as if she intended to jump in after her mother.

'Will you look at her,' said Mrs Finn. 'Acting as if she gave a hoot about the poor woman, who she hasn't visited in twenty years. She must have had to turn sideways to get her fat arse up the gangplank.'

'You have a great way with words, Mrs Finn.'

'Don't all the Irish, Mary Kate?'

'I'd say you're right.' Mary Kate knew that she was going to have to put on a good show when Mrs Finn told her about Tanners Row. 'Umm, I expect Mrs Dunne's daughter will be staying at her mother's cottage, until she goes back to England.'

'Now, I don't want this to come as too much of a shock to you, Mary Kate, but Tanners Row has been pulled down. Razed to the ground and not a wall left standing.'

'So where are you living?'

'We're all staying at the Castle Marta hotel. It's great craic. We have lovely clean sheets and soft pillows, and they even give us our dinners. It's like being on holiday, Mary Kate, and it's not costing us a penny piece.'

'Well, you certainly seem very happy about it, Mrs Finn.'

'And why wouldn't I be? They are building brand-new houses for us all, we will even have gardens. It's as if one of God's own angels came down to earth and performed a miracle. We have no idea who the landlord is, but my wish is that whoever it is arrives at the gates of Heaven half an hour before the Devil knows he's dead.'

They walked towards the gate and said their goodbyes.

'It's been lovely to see you, Mrs Finn, and I'm so happy for your bit of good fortune.'

'Come and visit when we're settled.'

'Oh, I will, I certainly will.'

'May God bless you, Mary Kate.'

'And may God bless you too, Mrs Finn.' She started to walk away when she heard her name being called. She turned around to see Mrs Finn staring at her. 'I mean it, Mary Kate, may God bless you.'

She couldn't have guessed, could she? She smiled. 'God gives His blessings to those who deserve them, Mrs Finn, and who are we to question His ways?'

'Who indeed, Mary Kate Ryan? Who indeed?'

She hadn't had the heart to watch her old home being knocked down but today she had an urge to go there, today she felt strong enough. She stood at the end of what would have been the row of cottages. It was still a shock to see the huge empty space where they had once been. The land behind had been fenced off, ready to be turned into gardens. She was happy for them all and the lovely houses they would be returning to but there was sadness too, for all that had now gone.

Babies had been born inside those tiny rooms and old ones had died. Each brick held a memory, each piece of broken glass had witnessed happiness and despair and the hopes and dreams of all who had lived within those walls.

'Mary Kate Ryan?' shouted a woman running towards her. It was Kathleen Riley, who she'd gone to school with and hadn't seen for years. 'It *is* Mary Kate, isn't it?'

She smiled. 'You're looking grand, Kathleen.'

'You don't have to be kind. I'm as fat as a house and I know it. Five kids have ruined the figure, but there, I wouldn't be without them. Now you really *are* looking grand, the years have been kind to you, Mary Kate. Didn't you used to live in the cottages?'

'I did. In fact, I'm standing in what was once our front room.'

'It's a sad day all right,' she said. 'And I've heard that that gobshite of a landlord is going to build a grand mansion here.'

'Who told you that?'

'Oh, you know, the whole town is talking about it. The butcher's wife says she has it on good authority that His Holiness the Bishop is going to live in it. Which I suppose will be an honour but what about the poor devils who have been turned out into the street? The cottages were a disgrace, but they were their homes.'

'Maybe it will all turn out for the best; life has a habit of doing that sometimes.'

'I hope so, anyway it was great to see you.'

'It was great to see you too, Kathleen.' She watched her walk away and smiled. She'd always liked her, she'd been great craic at school. Five children, eh? God had indeed been good to her and she wished her well.

She gave one last look around the empty space that had once been her home, where she had been so happy, and made her way back to the boarding house.

As she crossed the square, she saw a woman sitting on a bench; as she got closer, she could see that it was Claire Devlin.

'Hello, Claire?' she said.

The woman nearly jumped out of her skin.

Mary Kate sat down beside her. 'I'm sorry to have given you such a fright. Would you like to come in for a cup of tea? You must be cold sitting here. You could see Colleen's baby.'

Claire Devlin smiled. 'That would be lovely,' she said, standing up. 'I'm very fond of babies.'

CHAPTER 31

Claire had just gone. Guinness was stretched out in front of the blazing fire and Abby was sitting beside him.

'That woman is awful odd,' said Colleen. 'Don't you think so, Miss Ryan?'

'She's more than odd,' said Moira. 'She's unhinged is what she is.'

'I do think that there is something wrong there,' said Mary Kate.

Colleen stroked the baby's head. 'Did you see the way she grabbed at Rosa? I don't think she even said hello to the rest of us. She gives me the creeps, Miss Ryan, she does that. I had to almost prise the child out of her arms. And did you notice that when she picked her up, Guinness growled at her?'

At the mention of his name, Guinness raised his head.

'Animals can sense when there is evil in the room,' said Moira.

'Isn't that going a bit far?' said Mary Kate. 'I feel sorry for her in a way, she seems like such a lost soul. But I don't think I will be inviting her in again.'

'Good,' said Colleen, 'because I don't trust her.'

Abby started to sign.

'Abby says she doesn't trust her either,' said Moira.

'You're a wise little girl, Abby,' said Mary Kate.

Abby started to sign again.

'She says she's not little,' said Moira, grinning.

Mary Kate smiled at her. 'I'm sorry, Abby, of course you are not little. Am I forgiven?'

Abby grinned at her and nodded.

'Where did you bump into her?' said Moira.

'She was sitting on a bench in the square. She nearly jumped out of her skin when I approached her.'

'Don't you find it very strange, Mary Kate, that the woman would sit out there in the cold? What would make someone do that?'

Loneliness, thought Mary Kate, *loneliness and despair*. Having no one to talk to, to welcome you home or to have a bit of a laugh with; no one who shared your history or took the trouble to find out. To be surrounded by people and yet walk as if invisible through a crowd, to carry an ache in your heart that becomes so heavy that jumping off a bridge is better than the thought of facing another day. If she had never known loneliness, then perhaps she would never have recognised it in Claire.

'I think I will go and visit her at the Shelbourne,' said Mary Kate.

'Then I'm coming with you,' said Moira.

Mary Kate laughed. 'What do you think she's going to do, murder me?'

'I wouldn't put it past her. Abby?' said Moira. 'Let's go down to the kitchen and ask Mrs Lamb if you can bake some cakes for our tea. It will give us something to look forward to when we come home.'

Abby smiled and followed Moira downstairs.

. . .

They were frozen by the time they arrived at the hotel and were glad to get inside. Mary Kate recognised the young girl behind the desk.

'Hello, Miss Ryan,' said the girl. 'Are you wanting a room?'

Mary Kate smiled and shook her head. 'We were hoping to see a Mrs Claire Devlin, I believe that she is staying here.'

'I'm afraid you've had a wasted journey, Miss Ryan. Mrs Devlin checked out not more than half an hour ago.'

'Did she say where she was going?'

'No, she just paid her bill and left. I thought it was unusual, as most people give us a bit of notice.'

'I know this is a strange question,' said Mary Kate, 'but what was her manner?'

'What do you mean?'

'How did she look to you?'

'It's funny you should say that.'

'Why?'

'She seemed flustered, as if she couldn't wait to get out of the place. She was drumming her fingers on the desk while I made out her bill and then she almost threw the money at me. She gave me too much, I called after her but she ignored me.'

Mary Kate smiled at her. 'Thank you, dear.'

'It was lovely to see you again, Miss Ryan.'

'And it was lovely to see you.'

'Well, let's hope that's the last we hear of her,' said Moira as they walked down the steps. 'She's not your responsibility any more, Mary Kate, so you can forget the woman.'

As they hurried home, Mary Kate had a feeling that it wasn't the last they were going to see of Claire Devlin.

CHAPTER 32

James Renson was on the phone when Jenny knocked on the door. Once he'd finished the call he stood up and let her in.

'There's a woman here who wants to see you, Mr Renson. She doesn't have an appointment, I'm afraid.'

'Well, that phone call was a client cancelling a meeting, so I could see her now. What's her name, Jenny?'

'Her name is Miss Ryan.'

'Mary Kate?'

'No, not Mary Kate.'

James walked towards the woman standing at the desk. She was tall and well dressed and there was an air of confidence about her.

'Do come in,' he said, shaking her hand. He couldn't help noticing that her handshake was surprisingly firm for a woman.

James ushered her into his office, offered her a seat and waited for her to speak.

'My name is Agnes Ryan,' said the woman.

James had heard that name before, but surely it couldn't be the same woman, that would be an impossibility. The Agnes Ryan he knew of was dead.

'My daughter is Mary Kate Ryan,' she said.

James Renson couldn't understand what was coming out of the woman's mouth. He stared at her. What on earth was going on here? Was this some sort of scam? Was she pretending to be Mary Kate's mother, so that she could get her hands on the money?

'Mary Kate Ryan's mother is dead,' he said in a stony voice.

'I'm sorry to disappoint you, but as you can see she is very much alive.'

There was a coolness in his voice as he said, 'And what do you want?'

'Don't worry,' she said, 'I'm not after her money, if that's what you think.'

'How do you know she has money?' he snapped.

'Because I gave it to her.'

'If you really *are* her mother, why would you give her all that money when you are still alive?'

'I think that is my business, don't you?'

'Why are you here then? And why now?'

She was quiet for a while, as if she was thinking. 'When you get to my age, Mr Renson, you feel the need to put things right. A bit late, I know, but you don't live this long without having some regrets.'

'Like abandoning your child?'

'I didn't abandon her. I left her in the care of my mother and father, who I knew would give her the life that I never could or even wanted to.'

'And her father?'

'I have walked amongst the lowest of the low, Mr Renson, and felt cleaner than the day I walked away from him.'

'If I am to believe that you are indeed Mary Kate's mother – and I'm still not sure – then let me ask you this: How could you walk away from your own flesh and blood?'

'She repulsed me.'

James stared at the woman in front of him. He had never heard anything like it in his life; it went against everything a mother should be. He wanted to walk out of the room to distance himself from her. 'Repulsed you? Your baby repulsed you?'

'I've shocked you, haven't I?'

James pictured Mary Kate's sweet face, her kindness, her generosity and here was this woman telling him that she had repulsed her. He felt physically sick. 'Yes, you have.'

'She repulsed me because she was part of him.'

'But that wasn't Mary Kate's fault.'

'I know that. I suppose I have always known it. But don't expect me to be sitting here in sackcloth and ashes, because that is not who I am.'

'This man,' said James.

'What about him?'

'Did he...?'

'It doesn't matter what he did, Mr Renson. I've lived a lifetime since then and I have no intention of playing the victim now.'

He couldn't make the woman out. She seemed such a cold fish and yet he felt a strange sort of respect for her. She wasn't looking for forgiveness, she wasn't making excuses for what she had done, she spoke her truth and he believed her; he believed that the woman in front of him was indeed Mary Kate's mother.

'Your solicitor led me to believe that you had died and that is what I had to tell your daughter. I think that was a terribly cruel thing to do to her.'

'Maybe it was but it seemed the best thing to do.'

'So, what do you want from me?'

'I want to pay for your time, sir.'

'I still don't understand.'

'I want you to tell me about my daughter and I will pay you for it.'

She gave a half smile and for a split second it was as if he was looking into the face of Mary Kate.

'So, do we have a deal?' she said.

'You have put me in a very difficult position, Miss Ryan. Mary Kate is not just a client of mine, she is a friend, a very dear friend, and I will not be party to her being hurt.'

'What she doesn't know won't hurt her.'

'But *I'll* know. How am I supposed to live with that?'

'That is not my concern. I shall say goodbye and leave you to battle with your conscience. Personally, I find it easier not to have one. I'm staying at the Grand. If you change your mind, you can reach me there. Goodbye, Mr Renson.'

'Goodbye, Miss Ryan.'

CHAPTER 33

Mary Kate and Sean Barry drove out of the city and into the countryside. They sped past white frozen fields that sparkled like a blanket of diamonds under a thin wintry sun.

'Oh, this is beautiful, Sean.'

'It's beautiful all right.'

She smiled to herself as she watched fields and cottages fly past the window. It was warm in the car but she wouldn't have minded if it had been freezing cold – just being beside him was warmth enough. She felt so comfortable with this lovely man and so safe. If Him upstairs had decided that they would just be friends, she would accept it and not complain. She had never known love, not romantic love, anyway. She had loved her grandparents, but that was a different kind of love. 'The saddest thing is to love and not be loved in return.' She'd read that somewhere and had thought it was probably true, but now she knew different – loving was enough.

Sean turned and looked at her. 'Happy?' he said.

Happy couldn't describe what she was feeling. 'Yes,' was all she said.

'I'm glad.'

'Will you be getting a tree yourself, Sean?'

'I haven't bothered with a tree since Lorna died. She loved everything about Christmas, she was like a child on Christmas morning, squealing with excitement at every gift she opened. On Christmas Eve she would make me go to bed before her and in the morning, she would make me cover my eyes as she led me into the room to show me the tree. Every branch would be hung with baubles and covered in twinkling lights. I haven't had the heart to get one since then.'

Oh, to be loved like that. 'She sounds lovely, Sean.'

'She was, and I was lucky to have had her for as long as I did. My beautiful girl died two days before Christmas and our child died with her. So, you will understand that I haven't much of an appetite for fairy lights and tinsel.'

Mary Kate's eyes filled with tears. 'I'm so sorry, Sean.'

'It was a dark time, and I'm not proud of the man I became. I'd eat the face off anyone who tried to help me. I just wanted to be alone and I didn't want anyone's help. In the end I'd pushed them all away and I didn't care. Without Lorna, everything seemed pointless. I lost myself in the bottom of a whiskey bottle, it was the only friend I needed and the only thing that prevented me from jumping off a cliff.'

Mary Kate knew that feeling because she too had given up. This was the most that Sean had ever told her about his life and she felt privileged that he had trusted her with something so painful.

'Hold onto your hat,' said Sean, turning into a gateway and bumping across a field. He parked the car and helped her out. There were lots of people wandering around, with rosy-cheeked children running between them.

'How on earth do we pick one?' said Mary Kate, gazing at the rows and rows of beautiful trees.

'Ah, there's a knack to it,' said Sean. 'Lorna always said that I could pick the perfect tree from a mile away.'

'Then I'll leave it up to you.' They walked together through the trees. 'How about this one?' said Mary Kate, stopping. 'It's lovely and bushy.'

'It might be bushy at the top but look at the bottom of it. See? It's all brown, it looks as if it's about to meet its maker. We'll find a better one, sure, we have all the time in the world.'

All the time in the world? How perfectly wonderful.

Grey clouds drifted across an almost-white sky, and as they walked through the avenue of trees it started to snow, icy little flakes that stung her cheeks and clung to her eyelashes. The air was filled with the sweet smell of pine and lemons. It smelled of Christmases past and the innocence of childhood. It took her back to the little cottage and her beloved grandparents; it smelled of home.

It felt as if they'd been walking for hours. She stood still for a moment, taking in the winter wonderland that surrounded her. Snow had covered the branches, making them look even more beautiful than before. She had never felt closer to God.

Sean was calling her name and she hurried towards him. He was standing beside a tall tree, looking delighted with himself. The snow was falling about his shoulders, settling on his head, turning his dark hair almost white. He looked so proud, you'd have thought he'd grown the tree himself.

He grinned at her. 'Well?'

'It's the most perfect tree in the whole forest,' she said.

'I'm glad you like it, Miss Ryan.'

'I do, Mr Barry.'

'We'll get yer man to cut it down for us and then I think I need to get you home, you look frozen.'

'I am.'

'Come here.'

She walked towards him and was enveloped in his arms.

'Better?' he said, wrapping his coat around her.

They stood perfectly still, in a silence louder than the words that sat on her tongue. As the soft flakes of snow drifted around them it felt as if they were the only two people in the world. She knew that this moment would return to her every snow-filled day for the rest of her life.

CHAPTER 34

Agnes

Perhaps if she'd been softer, a bit more vulnerable, maybe then that solicitor would have taken to her. Her cold manner had put him off, he didn't like her and he didn't trust her – and who could blame him? He wasn't a bad guy, he was just looking out for her daughter, his fondness for her was obvious. He was trying to protect her from some hard-nosed woman who had flounced into his office announcing that she was Mary Kate's mother. Perhaps if she'd told him her secret – that leaving her baby was the worst mistake she had ever made and she had lived with the guilt every day of her life – maybe then he might not have seen her as a threat, he might even have agreed to tell her a bit about her daughter. Had life been kind to her? Had the money come as a blessing, or a burden? But she'd shocked him with her lies.

She wondered what he intended to do now he knew that Mary Kate's mother was very much alive. Would he keep it from her? Or would that conscience of his get the better of him?

She shouldn't have come back; it was just a fancy she'd had. Mary Kate had been fine without her all these years, why would she have need of her now? And yet she had a desire to see her, not the baby she had turned her back on, but the woman she had become. They might not even like each other, she couldn't expect some sort of instant bond between them. Just because the same blood ran through their veins didn't mean they were going to fall into each other's arms like in the films. Would she see herself in her daughter's face? Or would she see him? Even that didn't matter much any more.

Perhaps she would stay a few days, maybe visit Tanners Row. She might even walk up to the graveyard and pay her respects to her parents. She had been a young girl when she'd left, so she had no fear of being recognised now.

Without realising it, Agnes found herself close to her old home. She turned the corner into the lane and stopped. She stared at the piles of rubble where the six cottages had been. Her home had gone. She felt something twist in her heart as if a part of her, the best part of her, had been ripped away, as if it had never existed. She felt a stinging behind her eyes; it was a strange feeling, she couldn't remember the last time she'd cried.

She walked along the row and stopped at the place where her home had once stood. Oh, to walk through the door and into the little room, to see the picture of the Sacred Heart above the fireplace and the smiles on her parents' faces when they saw her. But there was no door, no little room, and no loving arms to hold her. There was nothing left of the life she had so easily walked away from.

She picked up a small piece of brick and held it in her hand, turning it over and over. It was cold, as cold as her heart. She threw it back down and headed for the graveyard, leaving her home for the last time.

. . .

She avoided the town and took the backstreets. Nothing much had changed here, she'd known every family that had lived in these little houses, she'd played in these streets with her friends. Where were they now? What had their lives been like? What would her life have been like if she'd stayed? She stopped outside St Mary's church, where she had spent so much of her childhood. She remembered Sunday Mass, the Stations of the Cross at Easter and the nativity scene at Christmas.

On an impulse, she climbed the steps and pushed open the heavy wooden doors, and there she was, the child she had once been, sashaying down the aisle in her Holy Communion dress like a small bride, thinking she was a grand girl altogether. The smell of incense filled the empty church and caught in her throat as it always had. She looked up at the choir stalls, high up in rafters, where she and her best friend Eileen Burke would sing their hearts out every Sunday morning. The pair of them used to feel so important way up there above the congregation, staring down at the lads they fancied and giggling behind their hymnbooks. They hadn't a clue what they were singing about because it was all in Latin, but it didn't matter, it was what they knew, it was familiar. It was as much her home as Tanners Row.

There was no doubt in her mind that she would have had a simpler life here in this town where she'd been born, maybe even a happier one, but at sixteen she hadn't wanted simple, she'd wanted adventure, she'd wanted excitement. And then her mind had been made up for her when she found herself pregnant. In her heart it wasn't a baby she was bringing into the world but a lock and key that would chain her to this backwater of a town forever. Maybe if she'd loved the boy it could have been different, but she hadn't and she'd wanted no reminder of what that vile excuse for a man had done to her.

She walked down to the side altar, where she knelt in front

of the statue of Our Lady and lit a candle. She'd lost her faith a long time ago but she had always had a soft spot for Mary. She stayed for a while, enjoying the peace and the silence and then reluctantly stood up.

'See ya around, Mary,' she said. Her words echoed around the empty space and bounced off the old stone walls as she pushed open the door and walked back down the steps.

She stood by the gate and looked across at the hundreds of graves, scattered across the cemetery. She hadn't a clue where her parents were buried, what on earth had she been thinking? That the name Ryan would be emblazoned in lights?

She wandered amongst the headstones, some so old that they had caved in, while others lay on their side. Most of them were covered in moss and lichen that obscured the names of those buried beneath the soil, long forgotten with the passing of the years. At the far end, by the old stone wall, there was a woman kneeling on the ground. She stared at her. It couldn't be, could it? Now that would have been too much of a coincidence, and yet there was something about her. Maybe she was being fanciful.

She knelt beside a grave some distance away but where she could still see the woman. She traced the name on the head-stone with her finger. MICHAEL JAMES COLLINS. AGED FIVE. BELOVED SON, TAKEN TOO SOON, NOW IN THE ARMS OF THE ANGELS. FOREVER IN OUR HEARTS.

Agnes remembered Michael, a lovely little boy who had fallen off the quay and drowned. The town had been in mourning for months, his poor parents bowed down with grief at the loss of their only son.

There was an icy wind blowing across the field, numbing her fingers and toes, but she kept watching. It seemed an eter-nity before the woman stood up, made the sign of the cross and started walking back up the path towards the gate. Agnes bowed her head as she passed by, then went down to the grave. Her heart was thudding in her ears as she read the names of her parents on the grey stone.

The woman was just going through the gate – it had to be her daughter, didn't it? Who else would be visiting the grave?

She took a deep breath and started to follow her.

CHAPTER 35

Mary Kate couldn't wait to get home and into the warm. It had been so cold up at the graveyard, but being there always gave her comfort. She spoke to her grandfather as if he was still beside her. She told him all about the boarding house with the red door and all the people who lived there with her.

'They are like family, Grandad, and I am so happy. It was your daughter that made it happen, you must be very proud of her. Please give her my love if you bump into her up there and let her know how grateful I am. The money not only changed my life but it is changing other lives too. I expect you already know this, but I still buy a new diary every year, just like you told me to. Give Grandma a big kiss from me.'

As she neared the house, she saw Eliza running towards her, before the girl almost fell into her arms.

'It wasn't my fault, Miss Ryan, it wasn't my fault,' she screamed.

'I'm sure it wasn't, Eliza. Now calm down and tell me what an earth has happened.'

'Colleen told me not to let go of the pram and I didn't. I'm a good girl, Miss Ryan, don't I always do as I'm told?'

'You do, Eliza.'

'I didn't let go of the pram, but yer woman took the baby. Colleen never said anything about keeping hold of the baby.'

'Someone has taken Rosa?'

'But not the pram, Miss Ryan. I kept hold of the pram, just like Colleen told me to.'

Mary Kate took Eliza's hand and started running. There were two Garda cars outside the house, one of the guards tried to stop her going in.

'I live here,' said Mary Kate, pushing past him and running up the steps.

Moira was in the hallway with Abby at her side. 'Dear God, Mary Kate, how has this happened? The child is gone, Colleen is demented.'

'Where is she?'

'In there,' she said, nodding towards the sitting room. 'A guard is trying to talk to her. They tried to talk to Eliza as well but she ran off.'

'Moira,' said Mary Kate, 'can you phone Sean and ask him to come over?'

'I already have, he's out looking for the baby.'

Mary Kate opened the door. Colleen was sitting beside the fireplace with her back pressed against the wall. She had her knees tucked under her chin, as if she was trying to make herself as small as possible. She was hugging a blanket and the little woollen hat Moira had knitted for Rosa. The sound coming from her was something Mary Kate would never forget. It was guttural, coming from a place deep inside that was neither human nor animal.

A guard was kneeling beside her. He was a big man, making Colleen look even smaller. 'I can't get anything out of her,' he said gently.

Mary Kate sat down and took Colleen into her arms. 'We'll find her, my darling, and we'll bring her home, we will bring Rosa home. Now let's get you upstairs where you can rest.'

Colleen allowed herself to be helped up. She was still holding the blanket and the little woollen hat, as Moira led her out of the room.

'I'd like to speak to Eliza,' said the guard.

'You will have to be very gentle with her,' said Mary Kate.

'Yes, I know and I will.'

Mrs Lamb was sitting on the stairs, she had her arms around her daughter, who was still crying. 'The guard needs to speak to Eliza, Mrs Lamb.'

'I don't want to,' said Eliza, looking terrified.

Mrs Lamb held Eliza's face in her hands. 'Listen to me, Eliza.'

'I will, Mammy, but I don't want to go in there.'

'I know you don't, my love, but sometimes we have to do things we don't want to do. We have to do them for someone else. You want to help Colleen find her baby, don't you?'

Eliza nodded.

'Then be a brave girl and tell the Garda what you saw.'

'Will you be with me, Mammy?'

'I will of course. And, Eliza?'

'Yes, Mammy?'

'You have done nothing wrong.'

'I didn't let go of the pram, did I?'

'No, you didn't, my love. You didn't let go of the pram.'

Mrs Lamb held her daughter's hand, as they went into the sitting room and sat together on the couch.

The guard moved a chair and sat down in front of them. 'Thank you for speaking to me, Eliza,' he said gently.

'Mammy said I have to be brave.'

'And you are,' he said, smiling at her. 'Now, I just need you to tell me exactly what happened. Can you do that?'

Mrs Lamb held Eliza's hand. 'You can do it, love.'

'It would really help, if you could try,' said the guard.

Eliza took a deep breath and started to speak. 'Me and Colleen were going to take Rosa for a walk. I helped her down the steps with the pram.'

'And the baby was in the pram?' said the guard.

Eliza nodded.

'What happened next?'

Eliza frowned.

'Can you remember?'

'Yes, I can. Colleen said that it was very cold and she needed to go indoors and get another blanket and a woolly hat for the baby.'

'So, you were left alone?'

'Yes. She told me not to let go of the pram.'

'You're doing really well, Eliza. Now I want you to think very carefully about what happened after that.'

'The bad thing?'

'Yes, the bad thing.'

'The lady came over.'

'Was it someone you knew? Or was it a stranger?'

'It was the kind lady.'

The guard looked across at Mary Kate.

'Eliza, was it the lady who helped you and Abby that day in the woods?' asked Mary Kate gently.

'Yes.'

'Then what happened?' said the guard.

'She took Rosa out of the pram and walked off with her.'

'Did she say anything to you? Did she say why she was taking the baby?'

'She said that the baby was hers, and I said, "No, it's not your baby, it's Colleen's baby."'

'Now, this is a very important question, so I want you to really think about it. Are you sure that the lady who took Rosa from the pram was the same lady who helped you in the woods?'

'Yes, she had the same face.'

'You've been a grand girl, Eliza,' said the guard. 'Now, I may need to speak to you again, will that be all right?'

Eliza smiled at him. 'Yes, mister. And, mister?'

'Yes?'

'I like you.'

'And I like you too, Eliza.'

Just then Sean came into the room, he looked frozen and headed straight to the fire. 'Jesus, it's Baltic out there. I'll just get warm and head out again.'

'It's very good of you, Sean.'

'We have every man available looking for her,' said the guard. 'What we need is some sort of a lead, she could be anywhere.'

'Oh, and, Mary Kate,' said Sean, 'there's a man outside who says he needs to see you. The guard won't let him in.'

'I'll come out.'

'Is it OK if I get myself a hot drink?'

'Of course.'

The tall man standing on the steps smiled at her. 'Miss Ryan?' he said.

'Yes?'

'I can see that this is a bad time and I don't want to intrude but I'm hoping that you can help me.'

'You had better come in,' said Mary Kate.

He followed her into the room. 'It's freezing out there.'

'It is,' said Mary Kate.

The man was tall, nicely dressed and she noticed that he had an American accent.

'Now, how can I help?'

'My name is Ronald Devlin; I believe you know my wife, Claire. I am hoping you can help me find her.'

CHAPTER 36

BROOKLYN

Ronald

Ronald had been sitting at his desk eating his lunch, when one of the girls came and stood next to him. He looked up and smiled at her.

'Nice sandwich, Ronald?' she said.

He looked at the half-eaten cheese sandwich in his hand. Was it a nice sandwich? 'I suppose it is,' he said.

She sat down opposite him. 'I've been watching you all morning.'

'You have?'

'Yes, I have, and you look as if you lost a shilling and found a penny. I don't want to pry but is something wrong? You don't have to tell me if you don't want to but sometimes it helps.'

He looked at the young girl in front of him. She seemed truly concerned and he surprised himself by saying, 'Yes, I'm afraid that something is very wrong, Rita.'

'Well, throw that bloody sandwich in the bin and come and have a plate of shepherd's pie.'

'Oh, I don't know. My mother made it for me.'

Rita looked around the office. 'Well, as far as I can see, your mother's not here, so if you don't tell, neither will I.'

Ronald stood up, threw the sandwich in the nearest bin and followed Rita upstairs to the canteen.

At first, the noise made him step back – the chatting and the laughter, the sound of knives and forks clattering against china plates hit him smack in the face as if he'd been punched.

'Jesus, Ronald, they're not going to kill you. Go and find a table and I'll bring the food over.'

He found a table by the window and waited for Rita to come back. He looked around the room at these people he had worked beside for years and wondered why he had felt the need to distance himself from them. They were just people, with the same hopes and dreams, the same worries and problems, why had he thought they were any different to him?

Rita came back with the food and placed it in front of him; it smelled delicious.

'Tuck in,' said Rita, smiling.

He didn't need to be told twice, he picked up his fork and did indeed tuck in.

Rita grinned at him. 'You've got gravy on your chin, Ronald.'

He grinned and wiped it away with the back of his hand. He could almost hear his mother's voice, *You mean they don't supply napkins?*

'Now,' said Rita. 'Tell me what is wrong.'

'Oh, you don't want to hear my problems.'

'That is what friends are for, a problem shared and all that.'

Ronald smiled at her. 'Friends?' he said.

Rita smiled back. 'Yes, Ronald, friends.'

'It's about my wife.'

'Claire?'

He nodded.

'What has happened?'

'She left me.'

'Oh, I'm so sorry, Ronald, I really am. How long ago?'

'A couple of weeks. It was a Wednesday. I particularly remember it because that's the day we have sausages.'

'And do you know why?'

'Why we have sausages?'

'No, Ronald, why she left you?'

'Not really. We live with my mother because Claire is ill and couldn't be left alone. My mother said that she just packed a case and left.'

'And she didn't leave a note?'

Ronald shook his head. 'No note, no explanation. My mother said that she just left without a word.'

'So, tell me, what are you doing sitting here?'

'What do you mean?'

'Why aren't you out there looking for her?'

'Well, that's the thing you see, Rita, I don't know where to look.'

'Did she get on with your mother?'

'My mother didn't like her and I think that poor Claire was frightened of her.'

'Has it occurred to you that your mother might be holding something back?'

'Oh, I don't think she would be so cruel, she knows that I'm out of my mind with worry.'

'Have you tried talking to her about it?'

'Well no, no, I haven't. She's very difficult, you see, and set in her ways. She never approved of Claire.'

'I think you need to talk to her, Ronald, like right now, today. And then spend your time looking for your wife.'

'But what about my job?'

'Sod the job, Ronald. Finding your wife is more important than anything else.'

'You must think me a very pathetic little man, Rita.'

'Of course I don't. And just for the record, you will be missed.'

'Now what have I ever brought to the table that you could possibly miss?'

Rita smiled at him. 'Yourself. Your kindness, your honesty, your Ronaldness.'

He laughed. 'My Ronaldness? Is that even a word?'

'It is now. I wish you could see yourself as others see you. You don't have to come to the pub to be one of the gang, you've always been one of the gang.'

'Have I really?' he said, surprised.

'Yes, really,' said Rita, smiling. 'Now for heaven's sake, go and find your wife.'

Ronald stood up. 'Say goodbye to the others for me.'

'I will, of course.'

'Tell Nora that I hope her mother returns to good health. Tell Peter to give his marriage another go – Molly is a good girl – and tell the rest of the gang that it has been a privilege to know them all these years.'

'What shall I tell the boss?'

Ronald gave a sad little smile. 'I doubt he will even notice I have gone. Take care of yourself, Rita, and thank you.'

'For what?'

'For giving me the gumption to throw away the bloody sandwich. Shall I tell you a secret, Rita?'

She nodded.

'I hate cheese.'

He could hear her laughter as he ran down the stairs.

. . .

Ronald hurried home, feeling lighter than he'd felt since the day Claire had left.

As he opened the front door his mother called out, 'Is that you, Ronald?'

As he walked into the lounge, he was immediately hit by the smell. His mother was sitting in her usual chair by the fireplace. There was a cigarette hanging out of her mouth and the inevitable glass of bourbon on the table beside her.

'Why are you home, Ronald? Are you sick?'

'I don't think so, Mother.'

'Oh, Ronald, you can be so tiresome.'

'So you keep telling me, Mother.'

His mother stared at him and took a long drag on the cigarette. She stubbed it out in the ashtray and stood up, letting the blanket and the ash fall onto the floor. She walked across to the window and stared out at the garden. Then she turned around and faced her son.

'I did it for you, Ronald, and don't expect me to be sorry, because I'm not.'

Ronald stared at her with something verging on loathing. So, Rita had been right, his mother knew where Claire had gone.

'Where is she?' he almost spat. 'Where is Claire?'

His mother smiled but it was more of a sneer, her thin lips curling back to reveal yellow teeth. The stench of her breath seemed to suck the air out of the room.

'You married a madwoman, Ronald, you should be down on your knees thanking me.'

'Did she take her tablets with her?'

'How should I know? I wasn't standing over her while she packed.'

Ronald turned away from her and started to leave the room.

'Where are you going?' said his mother.

'I'm going to find my wife.'

'Well, good luck with that, you couldn't even find your way to school. I had to tag along, like a good mummy, holding your little hand. You were ten at the time, it was embarrassing. How do you think you're going to find her in Dublin?'

As soon as she said it, she had lost him. He closed the door on his mother. He would find his wife and he would never come back.

CHAPTER 37

Ronald sat in the departure lounge. It felt good to be doing something. He'd always known that he had been a disappointment to his mother and that in her eyes he was a failure. He didn't let people trample all over him, but he stepped aside and let them pass. All he had ever wanted was a peaceful life, he had no great passions or ambitions.

And then he'd met Claire, sweet Claire, who'd brought joy and happiness into his lonely life. They were two damaged souls who'd found love and acceptance in each other's arms and hearts. It was a simple, uncomplicated love, that began to heal the damage of the chaos that had been his childhood.

Their first few years together had been the happiest of his life. They liked the same things, they would read poetry aloud to each other, they could walk for hours without speaking and yet feel comfortable in their silence. They both loved the cinema and would sit in the darkness holding hands, laughing at the funny bits and crying at the sad ones. They were like two halves of a whole, that had somehow, amid the hundreds of people who crowded the sidewalks of Brooklyn, found each other.

From childhood he had loved books, and he would lose himself between the pages when life became unbearable. He would hide away and disappear into a world of fantasy that was better than the world he lived in. That's how they'd met, at a book club in the basement of St Peter's church. No matter what the weather outside, it was always freezing in there, but he loved it.

One week they were asked to bring along their favourite book and read a small excerpt from it. A woman stood up, she was holding a book close to her heart, as if it were a beloved child.

'*The Little Prince*,' she'd said in an Irish lilt so soft she could barely be heard.

'Speak up, dear,' said the guy leading the group.

She'd cleared her throat. '*The Little Prince*,' she'd said again. 'By Antoine de Saint-Exupéry.'

'And you have a favourite quote for us?' said the guy.

'I have many favourite quotes,' she'd said softly.

'Just the one will do, dear,' he'd said, which caused a few people to titter. 'And don't forget to speak up. We all want to hear you.'

Ronald had felt like hitting the man. He reminded him of his mother – that smug, patronising voice that he hated so much. He watched, as the woman took a deep breath and began to read.

'"Where are the people? Resumed the little prince at last. It's a little lonely in the desert. It is lonely when you're among people too,' said the snake.'"

There was silence in the room as she'd sat back down, then a woman at the back had said, 'That was lovely, Claire, thank you for sharing it with us.'

'You're welcome,' she'd said, smiling shyly.

'Now, Ronald,' said the obnoxious man, 'what gem have you got for us?'

'I've actually brought along the same book,' he'd said, smiling across at Claire.

'Not the same quote, I hope,' the man had said, laughing.

Ronald had felt like throwing the book at him. 'Actually, it *is* the same quote, so I think I'll decline this time.'

At the end of the session, Ronald had waited for her.

She'd smiled at him. 'We like the same book,' she'd said.

He returned her smile. 'We do.'

And that was how it had started, as simply and as uncomplicated as that. Neither of them trying to impress, neither of them pretending to be somebody they weren't. They just knew and that was enough.

He couldn't remember exactly when the crying started, or why. He'd tried to help but without knowing what was making her so sad, all he could offer was comfort. Day by day he felt her slipping away from him as her unhappiness permeated every corner of their home. Ronald knew she couldn't be left alone when he was at work and he decided to sell the little house where they had been so happy and move in with his mother. It hadn't taken long for him to realise that it was the worst decision he could have made.

His flight was being called. He picked up his bag, slung it over his shoulder and walked towards the boarding gate.

As the plane thundered down the runway, he felt the tension gradually leaving his body. He would find Claire, even if it meant scouring every hotel and guest room in Dublin. He would find her and he would never let her go again.

CHAPTER 38

Ronald was sitting on the couch with his head in his hands. 'And you really think it's Claire who took the baby?'

Mary Kate nodded. 'Yes.'

Ronald shook his head. 'I am so terribly sorry. I had no idea that it would come to this.'

'What made you come *here*, Mr Devlin?'

'I've been in Dublin for four days, trying to locate her. I've lost count of how many hotels and guest houses I've visited. I've just come from the Shelbourne and they mentioned your name as someone who might be able to help me.'

'I wish I could, because if we can find your wife, I am certain that we will find the baby.'

'She wouldn't hurt her, I know that much.'

'We only have your word for that, Mr Devlin,' said Mary Kate.

'I know, I know, but Claire has always loved babies. We both wanted a family but sadly it wasn't to be. After numerous tests it turned out to be that Claire couldn't conceive.'

'But what about the child she came here to find?'

'Claire has never given birth to a child.'

Mary Kate shook her head. 'Poor woman.'

'Thank you for saying that, Miss Ryan. Claire became fixated on the idea that she'd had a child, it seemed to give her peace and I hadn't the heart to take that away from her. Maybe if I had, this wouldn't be happening. I am not excusing what she has done, Miss Ryan, but my wife is ill, she is not in her right mind and I am worried sick about her.'

Abby, who was sitting on the floor with Guinness, got up and whispered in Moira's ear.

'What is she saying, Moira?' said Mary Kate.

'She says that she's always out there.'

'Do you mean Mrs Devlin, Abby?'

Abby nodded.

'You've seen her out there before?'

Abby nodded again.

'On our walks?' said Moira.

Abby started whispering again.

Moira frowned. 'Are you sure, Abby? Are you sure that is what you saw?'

'What?' said Mary Kate.

'Abby says that the woman followed you and Orla on the day Rosa was born. She says that she went into the front bedroom to change the flowers and saw her from the window.'

Mary Kate knelt in front of Abby. 'Are you sure it was the day that Colleen had her baby?'

'I remember that day, Mary Kate,' said Moira. 'You asked me to look after Abby and I said that she was changing the flowers in the front bedroom.'

'Moira?' said Mary Kate, looking puzzled. 'Is Abby speaking to you?'

Moira stroked Abby's hair and smiled. 'She is.'

'That's wonderful.'

Just then Sean came into the sitting room.

Mary Kate looked up. 'We might have a lead, Sean,' she said.

'Go on.'

'On the day Colleen gave birth to Rosa, Abby saw Claire outside the house. She then saw her follow myself and Orla. I don't know that she followed us all the way to the café but she might have done.'

'It's worth a look,' said Sean.

'We should tell the guards,' said Moira.

Ronald almost leapt out of the chair. 'Please don't do that.'

'But shouldn't they know, Mr Devlin?' said Mary Kate.

'If she is indeed at this café and the police descend on the place, she will run. She must already be scared and confused; she needs gentleness.'

'Gentleness, my eye,' said Moira. 'She's stolen a baby, Mr Devlin, or had you forgotten that bit?'

'I understand that you are angry, you have every right to be, but the best way to be sure of that baby's safety is not to frighten Claire.'

'What do you think, Sean?' said Mary Kate.

'I think he's right but we'll have to get past the guards first.'

'We'll go out the back way,' said Mary Kate. 'Will you come with us, Sean?'

He nodded. 'I'll drive the van round the back and pick you up.'

'Moira, will you phone the college and get Jessie home?'

'I'll do it right away.'

'And will you phone Clerys and ask them to send the girls home too? Tell them it's a family emergency.'

As Mary Kate and Ronald hurried down the garden, she thought about what she had just said. 'Tell them it's a family emergency.' They *were* a family, that is what they had become, and she cared about every single one of them. It was how she'd dreamed her boarding house would be, not just somewhere to lay their heads but a home. And now something dark, something evil, had invaded their lives and she wanted everyone to be under one roof. She needed to know that they were all safe. Dear God, let the baby be safe.

Sean was waiting for them outside the garden. Guinness was sitting in the front seat next to him.

'He followed me out of the house and before I'd realised, he'd jumped into the van.'

Mary Kate and Ronald climbed into the back and Sean sped towards town. Having managed to park quite close, they hurried towards the café. The little street was crowded with Christmas shoppers, and they had to keep stepping into the road to get past them. Guinness was running ahead but kept turning around to make sure they were following.

Mary Kate knew that work would soon be starting on the house, so she wasn't surprised to see lots of building material outside. But she was surprised when Guinness pushed against the door and it opened.

'The builders must have forgotten to close it,' said Mary Kate.

They stepped into the hallway and listened. There wasn't a sound, it was completely silent.

Mary Kate sighed. 'I had hoped,' she said.

Sean gave a sad little smile. 'I think we all had.'

'I don't know what to do next,' said Ronald.

Guinness, who had been sitting at the bottom of the stairs, started to whine, then went across to Mary Kate and put his paw on her arm.

'Have you heard something, boy?' said Sean.

'I think he has,' said Mary Kate.

Guinness ran up the stairs and they followed him. He sniffed around on the landing then ran into one of the rooms. He was still whining.

'Where is she?' said Sean.

They watched Guinness circle the room. Everyone held their breath as he began clawing at a cupboard.

Sean gently pushed the door and there was Rosa. She was wrapped in a coat, her eyes closed.

Sean lifted her from the cupboard and held her in his arms.

Tears ran down Mary Kate's cheeks. 'Is she breathing, Sean? Please tell me she's breathing.'

Rosa stirred and looked up at him.

'She's grand,' he said, stroking the baby's face. 'She's grand, Mary Kate.'

Ronald picked up the coat that had fallen onto the floor. He held it against him. 'This is Claire's,' he said softly. 'This is Claire's coat.'

Sean looked angry. 'But where the hell is she? Your wife left this baby in a cupboard. God only knows what would have happened if we hadn't found her.'

Ronald shook his head. 'I'm sorry.'

Sean took a deep breath and tried to calm down. 'I know you are, Ronald, I know you are.'

Rosa began to make little mewing sounds.

'She's soaking wet,' said Sean. 'And she doesn't smell too sweet.'

Mary Kate took her from Sean and held her close.

'Do you think we should be taking her to the hospital?' said Sean.

Mary Kate looked down at Rosa, who had her fist in her mouth. 'Well, right now, all she needs is feeding and a clean nappy. I think we should take her home to Colleen.'

'Are you coming with us, Ronald?' said Sean.

He shook his head. 'I have to find my wife.'

Mary Kate stared at him. 'And what are you going to do if you find her?'

'I'm going to get her the help she needs.'

'The guards will want to speak to her,' said Sean.

'No,' said Mary Kate.

'But she kidnapped a child, are you suggesting that she just walks away from this?'

'The woman is ill, Sean, she needs help. What good will locking her up do?'

'I think it might do Colleen a bit of good.'

'All Colleen wants is her baby back in her arms. Revenge will be the last thing on her mind.'

Sean shook his head. 'You never cease to amaze me, Mary Kate. I'm not saying I agree with this, but I can see that your mind is made up and it would take a braver man than me to try and change it.'

Mary Kate smiled at him. 'Wise decision, Mr Barry.'

She smiled at Ronald. 'I doubt that we will meet again.'

He took her hand. 'I'll never forget your kindness.'

'Where do you think she is?'

'I don't think that she will have gone far. I'll try all the shops in this street to start with and hope that she will be in one of them, or that someone has seen her.'

Mary Kate handed him a piece of paper. 'It might just help. Goodbye, Mr Devlin, and may your God go with you.'

'Goodbye, Mary Kate Ryan.'

CHAPTER 39

Claire sat shivering in a shop doorway. She couldn't remember where she'd left her coat. She rubbed her forehead with the heel of her hand, trying to think, trying to think. Had she done something wrong? She felt as if she had. Ronald would know; Ronald understood her, even when she didn't understand herself. The noise, the lights, the smells coming out of the shops just added to her already confused mind. She closed her eyes, put her hands over her ears and started rocking backwards and forwards, backwards and forwards.

'Can I help you, missus?'

Claire looked up at the man staring down at her. 'I don't know.'

'It's terrible cold today, isn't it?'

Claire nodded.

'Too cold to be without a coat, I'm thinking.'

'I must have lost it,' she said.

'Sure it's not a great day to be losing your coat.' he said. 'Look, why don't you come inside? There's a grand fire in the back room and I'm sure my wife will make you a hot cup of tea. What do you say?'

'Do you think that I should?'

'I think it would be better than sitting out here shivering. My name is Andrew and my wife's name is Alana. We are the owners of this little shop and I'm sure my wife would be only delighted to have some company.'

'In that case, I will come in.' Claire followed the man through the shop and into a room at the back. It was lovely and warm.

'This is... I'm sorry, what is your name?'

'Claire.'

'This is Claire and she is in need of some warmth and a grand cup of tea.'

Alana smiled at her. 'You poor thing, you look frozen to the bone. Do you not have a coat?'

Claire frowned. 'I had it this morning.'

'Have you left it in a shop?' said Alana.

Claire stared into the fire, the flames soothed her and warmed her cold body. 'I forget things,' she said softly.

Alana gently touched her shoulder. 'Sure don't we all, love?'

Claire was having trouble keeping her eyes open, the warmth in the room wrapped around her like the lost coat. The coat was still worrying her; it seemed important, but she felt too tired to try to figure it out.

'I think that what you could do with is a nice sleep,' said Alana.

Yes, that is what she needed, a nice sleep. Maybe she would wake up in a place that was familiar to her and perhaps she would remember where the coat was.

'There now,' said Alana, helping her onto the couch and covering her with a blanket. 'You stay there as long as you like.'

Claire fell asleep as soon as her head touched the cushion.

. . .

Alana had been watching Claire for over an hour. It was hard to put an age on the woman, there were hardly any lines on her face and yet she looked to be about fifty. She wondered what her story was, for there surely was a story here. And what were they supposed to do with her when she woke up? Andrew had a habit of scooping up waifs and strays, for he was the kindest man she knew. Mostly, they just needed a bite to eat and a warm drink and maybe a bit of company, then they'd go happily on their way, but this was different, they were going to have to make a decision and they were going to have to make it soon.

She stood up and stretched, then walked across to the window. It was early evening but it was almost pitch-black outside. Small flakes of snow had begun to settle on the windowsill and on the street. This was not a night to be wandering around alone, it was a night to be inside in the warm. This was one waif and stray who was going to need more than a bite to eat and a warm drink. God, in His wisdom, had guided her to their door and, for good or bad, they were now responsible for her.

Just then Andrew came into the room, followed by a tall man.

'This is Claire's husband, Alana.'

Ronald had gone into all the shops that surrounded the café and had finally got lucky. He went across to the couch and knelt beside his wife. 'Thank you for taking care of her.'

Andrew smiled at him. 'You are very welcome,' he said.

'Has she been all right?'

'She's very confused,' said Alana. 'We didn't know what else to do.'

Ronald stared down at Claire and gently kissed her warm cheek. 'You have taken a stranger into your home, when many would have turned her away. You have kept her safe and I will be forever in your debt.'

'I'd say the hand of God had a bit of a say in it,' said Alana, smiling.

Claire began to stir as Ronald brushed her hair away from her forehead. 'Hello, sleepyhead,' he said softly.

Claire rubbed at her eyes and then opened them. 'Ronald?' she said.

'Yes, it's me, my love.'

'I've been very tired.'

'I know, my sweet girl, but everything is going to be all right now, because I am going to take care of you.'

'I think I might have done something wrong.'

'Now what makes you think that?'

Claire frowned. 'I don't know.'

'Well then, we won't worry about it now.'

'Right,' said Alana, smiling. 'How about a cup of tea?'

'That would be just the ticket,' said Ronald.

Andrew put his arm around his wife. 'We'll leave you alone then.'

Once they'd left the room, Ronald took Claire into his arms. 'I've missed you,' he said.

Claire stared at him. 'You found my coat.'

'I did,' said Ronald, smiling.

'I lost it.'

'But now we have found it and we have found each other. Aren't we clever old things?'

'Oh, we are, Ronald.'

Alana put her head around the door. 'Do you both take milk?' she said. 'I've heard that you Americans have your tea with lemon, although I can't for the life of me think why.'

Suddenly Claire jumped off the couch. 'Milk,' she said. 'I was going to get milk for...' She shook her head, trying to remember. 'For the baby. Oh, Ronald, I have to get back to the baby, we have to go now. I was only leaving her for a short while, to get the milk and some nappies and then... Oh, Ronald, I, I forgot. I forgot about her. How could I have forgotten her?'

Ronald eased Claire back onto the couch and took her hands. 'The baby is fine,' he said gently.

Tears ran down Claire's cheeks. 'She wasn't mine, was she? She wasn't my baby?'

'No, my love, she wasn't yours.'

Alana and Andrew were staring at them.

'She left a baby somewhere?' said Alana, looking shocked.

Ronald shook his head. 'Not really,' he said. 'Now, I think we've imposed on you good people long enough and it's time we headed home.'

'To America?' said Andrew.

'Yes,' said Ronald. 'To America.'

'May God watch over you,' said Alana.

Once outside, Ronald hailed a cab. As they drove through the centre of Dublin, Ronald put his arm around his wife.

'Where are we going?' she said.

'I'm not sure.'

'I don't want to go back to your mother, Ronald.'

'Neither do I.'

'Couldn't we stay here?'

Ronald shook his head. 'It's not safe to stay here. We have to get away.' He remembered the piece of paper Mary Kate had given him. He took it out of his pocket and smiled. 'We are going to see a solicitor, Claire.'

'Why?'

'To collect some keys.'

'And what are we going to do then?'

'We are taking the night sailing to England and then we are going to stay in London.'

'In a hotel?'

'No, in a house owned by Mary Kate Ryan.'

CHAPTER 40

'So, you say the baby was all alone?' said the guard. 'There was no one else there?'

'No one,' said Mary Kate. 'Just the baby.'

'I'm not doubting your word, Miss Ryan, but it all sounds a bit odd to me.'

'Indeed,' said Mary Kate. 'But doesn't the Lord work in mysterious ways? And it's not up to us to question it.'

'Well yes, of course. But what am I supposed to tell my superiors?'

'You tell them the truth, that Rosa is safely home in her mother's arms. Colleen has gone through enough without the law coming round, asking questions she can't answer. Our blessed Lord guided us to that place and if there's a choice between Himself and the law, I'm inclined to rely on Himself.'

'Well, if you are sure.'

Mary Kate smiled at him. 'I am.'

'I can't promise that this will be the last of it, it all depends on them upstairs. It's not often we get a real live kidnapping around here, they'll be mighty put out.'

'I'm sure that a grand feller like yourself can assure them

that the baby is safe and well, and, after all, isn't that the only thing that matters?'

'But what about the woman who took the child?'

'We'll never know, will we? But I'd say she'll be long gone by now and no harm has been done.'

The guard certainly didn't look convinced. 'I suppose not,' he said. 'But that doesn't take away from the fact that a very serious crime was committed here.'

'Oh, I agree with that all right and it's going to take us a long time to get over it, so we would appreciate your understanding at this difficult time and give us the peace and privacy we will need in the coming months.'

'Well, I'll leave you to it for now, Miss Ryan, and hope that when we meet again it will be under happier circumstances. Goodbye, Sean.'

'Goodbye, Michael.'

There was a moment of silence in the room after the guard had gone. And then they all started speaking at once.

'Jesus, Mary Kate,' said Moira, 'you should be on the stage, you'd make a great actress.'

'Do you think he believed you?' said Colleen.

'I went to school with yer man,' said Sean. 'There's no harm in him, but intelligence was never his strong point.'

Mary Kate sat down beside Colleen. Rosa was asleep in her arms, looking none the worse for what had happened to her. 'Do you mind, Colleen? Do you mind that you won't see justice done this day?'

Colleen looked down at her baby. 'I won't lie, Miss Ryan, I wanted to kill her, I did. She took my child and broke my heart. But she is ill, isn't she?'

'Ill?' said Moira. 'The woman is mad.'

Mary Kate smiled. 'But aren't we all a bit mad?'

'Maybe we are, but we don't go around kidnapping other people's children.'

'What about her baby?' said Colleen. 'The one she was looking for?'

'Claire Devlin has never given birth to a child.'

Colleen's eyes filled with tears. 'Then I suppose she is more to be pitied than judged.'

'You are a strong girl, Colleen, and a kind one. You'll be going straight up to Heaven in a velvet lift, girl.'

'I doubt that,' said Colleen, making a face. 'Do you think we will ever hear from her again?'

'I shouldn't think so.'

'I very much hope not,' said Moira.

'I feel kind of sorry for her though, don't you?' said Colleen.

'And did you feel sorry for her when your child was gone, and your arms were empty?'

'No, Miss Kent, I wanted to take the head off her.'

'Well, there you are, so let that be the end to all this goodwill. I'd be happier if the woman was locked up.'

There was a tap on the door and Mrs Lamb and Eliza came into the room. Eliza was hanging back and staring at the floor.

Colleen handed the baby to Mary Kate and walked across to her. 'Look at me, Eliza,' she said gently.

'I did a bad thing, didn't I?'

'What happened to Rosa wasn't your fault.'

Eliza looked up. 'Wasn't it?'

'No, sweetie, it wasn't. You have nothing to feel bad about, you did nothing wrong. In fact, if it wasn't for you, we wouldn't have known who had taken the baby. You were the hero of the day.'

Eliza smiled. 'I've never been a hero before.'

Colleen put her arms around her. 'Now I don't want you worrying about it any more. OK?'

'OK.'

'Thank you, Colleen,' said Mrs Lamb softly.

'You're welcome.'

'Now,' said Mrs Lamb, 'there is a fine pan of soup down-stairs on the hob and a grand apple sponge fresh out of the oven. If I'm not mistaken, I'd say you lot could do with some food in your bellies.'

'You think right, Mrs Lamb,' said Sean.

'Moira, would you mind telling the girls that the Garda has gone and they are to join us down here for some food. They must be starving.'

'Now before they all come in, let us have a moment's silence and thank Almighty God for keeping Rosa safe and for bringing her home to us,' said Mary Kate

'Amen,' said Colleen.

CHAPTER 41

It was a week before Christmas and there was great excitement in the house. Mrs Lamb had been cooking all week; the smells coming up from the kitchen were making everyone's mouths water.

Sean's perfect tree stood in front of the window, filling the room with the sweet smell of pine and reminding Mary Kate of that magical day in the forest. She could still feel it, the cold, the silence, the soft snow falling around them and the roughness of Sean's shirt against her cheek as he held her in his arms. She would remember that day as long as she lived.

The girls had had great craic, hanging baubles from the branches and draping the silver tinsel over the green leaves. Moira had lifted Abby up, so that she could place the silver star on the top. The tree's lights shone out over the dark square outside, like a beacon guiding the traveller home.

It felt like a million years ago that she had spent Christmas in that cold and lonely room in Ginnetts Row. How her life had changed and how blessed she felt as she looked around the room at these wonderful people who, by the grace of God, had found their way to her door.

. . .

The general opinion in the house was that Rosa was the most perfect baby that had ever been born. Every small change was commented on.

'Her eyes are definitely going to stay blue, Colleen,' said Jessie.

Colleen smiled as she looked down at Rosa. 'Roibin's eyes were the most beautiful blue, she is going to look like her daddy.'

'Well, her daddy must be desperate handsome.'

'Oh, he is.'

'Isn't it an awful pity that he can't see her?'

'Theresa Mahon, may she die roaring, said that there's a pile of dark-haired children in every county of Ireland wondering who their daddies are.'

'She's an expert on the subject, is she?'

'She's a baggage, Jessie. It was her that told the nuns that I was a fallen woman.'

Mary Kate, who had been listening to the conversation between the girls, laughed. 'I've always thought that's an awful strange thing to say. Does it mean that every poor woman who happens to fall over will be judged? Would they be looking at her lying on the ground and saying, "I know what you've been up to?"'

Colleen laughed so much, tears rolled down her cheeks. 'Oh, that's funny, Miss Ryan. I wish I had said that to Theresa bloody Mahon, it might have shut her up.'

'She sounds like a right snitch,' said Jessie.

Colleen nodded. 'She's that all right. It was because of her that my parents locked me up.'

'My grandfather always used to say that when you do something bad, it will always come back and bite you on your bottom,' said Mary Kate.

'Well, let's hope that our dear Lord in His wisdom takes a great chunk out of hers. Now I'll leave you to it, I've homework to do,' said Jessie.

'Are you still enjoying college, Jessie?'

'Oh, Miss Ryan, I love it. Everyone is so friendly and I'm learning something new every day and it's all thanks to you.'

'Your happiness is thanks enough, Jessie.'

Colleen hadn't left Rosa alone for even a second since that awful day when they feared that she was lost to them forever. Even if she just needed to go to the toilet, she would make sure that someone was minding the baby. Mary Kate had even put a lock on Colleen's bedroom door to give her some peace of mind.

'How can I take her out, Miss Ryan? What if someone else tries to steal her away?'

'I do understand your fears, my love, but sure none of us would do anything if we thought like that. There are good and bad people everywhere, but I'd say that there are more good ones than bad ones out there.'

'Maybe, but I'm just not ready.'

'Well, when you *are* ready, I will be right beside you. And if anyone lays a finger on the child, I'll take the arm off them.'

'So would Ashar,' said Colleen.

Mary Kate smiled. 'Am I right in thinking that yourself and Ashar are getting close?'

Colleen could feel herself blushing. 'He's awful nice, Miss Ryan. I trust him, he makes me feel safe.'

'I'm no expert in the ways of the heart, Colleen, but I'd say that's a good start.'

'And he loves Rosa.'

'And isn't that the most important thing?'

Colleen nodded. 'It is. Miss Ryan?'

'Yes?'

'There is something that has been worrying me for a while.'

'Do you want to talk about it?'

Colleen nodded. 'I haven't given you a penny piece since I came here, and I don't know when I will be able to. You've given me so much, Miss Ryan, and I have given you nothing in return.'

Rosa, who had been happily gurgling away, started whingeing. Mary Kate walked across and lifted her out of the pram. She smelled of milk and wee and there was no perfume in the world that could have smelled lovelier. She waited as Colleen put Rosa to her breast. The baby immediately latched on and closed her eyes. Her heart was so full of love as she watched Rosa gently squeeze Colleen's soft flesh with her pudgy little hand. Mary Kate would have loved a baby of her own but it was not part of God's plan.

'How can you say that you have given me nothing, Colleen? You have allowed me to share in the joy that Rosa has brought to this house and that, my darling girl, is something that money can't buy. This is your home and it will be your home until there comes a day when you don't need it any more. So I'll have no more talk about money.'

'You're a saint, you are, you're a saint.'

'God forbid, Colleen, I'm no saint and I wouldn't want to be dragging that label around like a camel hanging off me shoulders.'

Colleen laughed. 'You do come out with the funniest things, Miss Ryan.'

'My grandfather used to say that I had funny bones.'

Colleen smiled. 'And kind ones.'

Once Colleen had taken Rosa upstairs to her room, Mary Kate sat by the window, looking out over the green. She thought back to the day that James Renson had told her about the money and the houses in London. She hadn't wanted the money and she had no use of the houses – what did she want with a load of houses? How foolish she had been. The money had scared her, she'd never had any before and had never expected to have any in her lifetime. It had felt like an unwanted burden, when in fact it turned out to be a blessing and a privilege. The money would change, not just her life, but the lives of people she cared for. Her mother's money wasn't just metal and bits of paper, it was a whole stack of red-letter days, to whoever had need of one.

CHAPTER 42

Orla and Polly had only been home a day but already Orla's brain was mashed.

'It's like the feckin Spanish Inquisition in there,' she moaned as they walked down to the quay. 'It's a wonder Mammy didn't ask us what colour knickers we were wearing.'

Polly laughed. 'Give her time, Orla, I'm sure she'll get round to it.'

'I wouldn't mind if it was just Mammy that was asking but half the bloody town have been in. You'd think we were prize bulls to be poked and looked over. Mrs Kenny had the cheek to tell me that I'd got terrible podgy round the ears since I'd been away. How would going to Dublin result in me getting podgy round the ears? Is it even possible to get podgy round the ears?'

'I'm not sure, Orla, I can't say I've ever heard of it.'

'The cheek of the woman. And her Bridgie, the size of a house.'

'Ahh, poor Bridgie.'

'You're very annoying, Polly, do you know that?'

'How am I annoying?'

'Because you never agree with me. It's hard to have a good old gossip when you're in the presence of a feckin' saint.'

'I'm sorry, Orla,' said Polly, grinning. 'I'll try and do better.'

'I'd be obliged.'

As they passed the Brennas' cottage, Polly stopped walking and stared up at Colleen's bedroom window. 'I can't believe she was locked up there for all those months and no one knew.'

'Thank God we found her.'

'Isn't it sad though, Orla? That they will never get to know their granddaughter.'

'Rosa deserves better grandparents than those two gobshites. From what Colleen said they didn't want anything to do with the baby, in fact they were all for giving it away.'

'And I'll bet you anything they still go to Mass on Sundays like good Catholics,' said Polly.

'I've half a mind to go up to the church and tell Father Benny.'

'And what good would that do?'

'It would make me feel better.'

'Colleen was very brave, wasn't she, Orla? To escape like that.'

'She was.'

'I don't think I could have been that brave.'

'You don't have to be, Polly, I'm brave enough for the two of us.'

Polly smiled at her sister. Orla had been born three minutes before her, so she was always known as the older twin. She had taken care of her; she had fought her wars. Those three minutes had pretty much shaped the people that they had become. If it had been the other way round, would she have been as brave as her sister? Somehow, she doubted that she would. But then she'd never had to be.

'I'm going to knock on the door, Polly.'

'And say what?'

'I don't know, you might have to help out.'

'I thought that might be coming.'

Polly stood back, as Orla knocked on the door but there was no answer. She was just about to knock again when the door opened and Mrs Brenna peered out at them.

'Hello, Mrs Brenna,' said Orla, smiling. 'We're off down the quay and wondered if Colleen would like to join us.'

'We're home for Christmas, Mrs Brenna,' said Polly. 'We thought it would be nice to catch up.'

Mrs Brenna shook her head. 'Colleen is in England, girls, staying with my sister. She'll be disappointed to have missed you.'

'That's an awful shame, we haven't seen her in ages. Could you let us have her address? At least then we can drop her a line.'

Mrs Brenna stared at them. She'd gone a sort of grey colour, like the poor fish that were caught up in the fishermen's nets. 'I've a cake in the oven,' she said, slamming the door in their faces.

Orla laughed and took hold of her sister's hand. 'Come on, let's leave her to her guilty conscience.'

As they turned the corner onto the quayside, the wind coming off the river nearly knocked them over. The water was grey and choppy, splashing against the old stone wall and spraying out over the quay.

'I've missed this, Orla,' said Polly.

'I suppose I have too, but it doesn't mean that I'd want to come back. Would you?'

Polly sighed and looked out over the water at the little white cottage standing on the shingle. 'When I was a child, I always thought that one day I would live in that cottage.'

'You never told me that.'

'Oh, it was just a silly daydream, you'd have laughed.'

'Well, you should have told me anyway and I wouldn't have laughed. Sure, aren't we all entitled to a bit of a daydream?'

'I used to imagine opening the curtains and seeing the River Blackwater flowing past my door. Wouldn't that be Heaven?'

'It might be your idea of Heaven, Polly, but it's not mine. It's the city for me, there's nothing going on in this place.'

'Do you know who lives there?'

'Lives where?'

'In that cottage.'

'No, but Mammy probably does. We'll ask her if it's that important to you.'

'Thanks, Orla.'

Orla smiled at her sister. 'You're very welcome. When you buy it, be sure to give me an invitation to take tea with you in the parlour.'

'Oh, I will and I'll get out the best bone-china tea set in your honour.'

'And I'll bring a cake especially for the occasion.'

'Have you ever baked a cake, Orla?'

'Now why would I do that when the shops are only full of them?'

'Do you have a dream, Orla?'

Orla looked across at the little white cottage. 'I'm not sure that I have.'

'Not even a little one?'

'Not even a little one, isn't that desperate? It makes me sound like an awful bore.'

'There's nothing boring about you. I think that your dream is so big, it's still growing.'

Orla smiled. 'Maybe you're right, maybe I'll surprise them all.'

'Oh, you will.'

They sat down on a wall and watched the little fishing boats bobbing up and down and tugging at their moorings, as if they were desperate to sail out of the harbour and across the sea for a life of adventure.

'Do you see those two fellers over there?' said Orla.

'Where?'

'Standing by the slipway.'

'What about them?'

'They look like tinkers to me.'

Polly looked across at the two young lads, pretending to push each other into the water. 'I'd say you're right, Orla.'

'Are you thinking what I'm thinking?'

'We're twins, aren't we? Of course I'm thinking what you're thinking.'

They hurried through the town and out towards the wood road, where the tinkers had been known to settle. The fields were empty, except for some muddy-looking cows, huddled together in the corner.

'Where else could they be, Orla?'

'I haven't a clue, maybe we were wrong about the two lads, maybe they aren't tinkers at all.'

Coming up the path towards them was an old man pushing a rusty bike.

Polly smiled at him. 'Good morning, sir.'

He nodded. ''Tis a soft day all right.'

'Um, would you know if there are any tinkers about?' said Orla.

The old man glared at them from under grey bushy eyebrows. 'And why would two young ones like yourselves be wanting to know about tinkers?'

'It's not so much the tinkers, sir,' said Polly, 'as the caravans. They're very interesting, don't you think?'

'Very pretty,' said Orla.

'It's just that we saw two lads down at the quay and we thought they looked like tinkers.'

'Well, you're right about that, they pitched up last night.

They're up on Connor's field and he's threatening to set the dogs on them.' As they walked away, the old man called to them. 'You are aware of what they say about tinkers?'

'Yes, sir,' shouted Polly. 'They ravage young girls and take the bread out of the mouths of babies.'

'That's right. So if you have a desperate need to be looking at the caravans, I suggest that you look at them from a distance.'

'Thank you for your sage advice, sir,' said Polly. 'We'll bear it in mind.'

Once the old man was out of sight, Orla started laughing.

'What's so funny?' said Polly.

'You are.'

'Am I indeed?'

'Thank you for your sage advice, indeed,' she said. 'Where in all that's holy did you get that from?'

'I must have picked it up at Clerys.'

'Well, you'd best put it down again.'

Connor's field was up behind the church, so they started walking back towards town. They made the sign of the cross as they passed St Mary's.

'What do we do if Colleen's feller *is* there?' said Polly. 'I mean, we can't just blurt out that he has a daughter in Dublin, can we?'

Orla stopped walking. 'You're right, we can't. It's not our story to tell, it's Colleen's. She might not want him to know about Rosa.'

'Not much point in trying to find him then, is there?'

'Something tells me that there is.'

'We could ask Father Benny,' said Polly.

'Good idea.'

'Should we be telling him about Colleen?' said Polly as she followed Orla around the side of the church to the presbytery.

'I'd say that there's not much goes on in this town that Father Benny doesn't know about.'

'And didn't Colleen's friend Theresa Mahon, may she die roaring, tell the nuns that Colleen was a fallen woman?'

'She did.'

'Then I don't think we're going to be telling Father Benny anything he doesn't already know.'

'OK, well, you knock.'

'Jesus, Polly. Would ya ever cop on to yerself.'

Father Benny's housekeeper set a tray of tea and apple cake on the table and smiled at them. 'You're looking grand,' she said. 'The big city must suit you.'

'It's great, Mrs Lacey, but it's nice to be home,' said Orla.

'Sure, there's no place like home,' said Mrs Lacey, stirring the tea. 'Your poor mammy must miss you.'

'We miss her,' said Polly.

'Well, it's lovely to see the pair of you looking so well, isn't it, Father?'

'It is indeed, Mrs Lacey, it is indeed.'

Mrs Lacey put another log on the fire, sending a blast of heat into the room. 'I'll leave you to it then, shout if you want the tea topping up.'

'So,' said Father Benny, 'what can I do for you, or have you just called in to say hello?'

'It's about Colleen Brenna, Father.'

'Isn't she in England?'

'No, Father, she's living with us in Dublin.'

Father Benny picked up his pipe, settled back into his chair and listened as they told their story.

PART FOUR

CHAPTER 43

Orla and Polly returned to Dublin after their Christmas break and although Orla had loved seeing her family, she was delighted to be heading back. Polly, on the other hand, spent the whole train journey crying her heart out.

'Jesus, Polly, will you give it a rest? You're no company, I might as well be on my own.'

'I'm sorry, Orla, but I can't get Mammy's face out of my head. I think she'd been up all night crying.'

'Of course she had, she's a mammy and that's what mammies do. She'll be grand as soon as she has a cup of tea. I'd say the neighbours would have swarmed in the minute our taxi went round the corner. There'll be weeping and gnashing of teeth and half of them won't know what they're weeping about, but they'll be having a great time.'

Polly sniffed. 'Oh, I do hope so, Orla.'

'You can be sure of it. Now buck up, we're nearly there. Once you've had a cuddle with Rosa and the face licked off ya by Guinness you'll be fine.'

Polly smiled. 'You're right.'

'Aren't I always?'

'You are, Orla.' Polly dried her eyes. 'Do you think we'll hear from Father Benny?'

'I'm sure we will, as soon as he has news of Roibin.'

'And if he does find him, are we going to tell Colleen?'

'That will need some thinking about. We can't just barge in with the news, we could give her a heart attack.'

'We could ask Miss Ryan or Miss Kent what they think,' said Polly.

'I was thinking the same meself, I trust the pair of them, and I'd welcome any advice they might give us on the matter.'

Polly sat back in her seat and sighed. Her sister always made things right and she thanked God that she had her. Orla was the leader and Polly was happy to follow her.

'Have you noticed that Colleen and Ashar spend a desperate amount of time with each other?'

'You'd have to be blind not to notice,' said Orla.

'Do you think they're in love?'

'How the feck would I know that?'

'It would be nice, though, wouldn't it?'

'What would be nice about it?'

'Well, they might get married.'

Orla rolled her eyes. 'You read too many romance novels.'

Polly grinned. 'I like happy endings.'

Two weeks had passed and there was no word from Father Benny.

'Maybe it wasn't to be,' said Polly as they walked home from work. 'Especially now Colleen is walking out with Ashar.'

'Maybe not,' said Orla, 'but we tried, we have no proof they're actually dating, do we?'

As they neared the house, the door burst open, and Eliza was standing there, smiling at them.

'I've been waiting for you,' she said.

'Well, that's nice,' said Polly.

'Do you want to know why?' said Eliza.

Polly nodded.

'You have a letter. It has your name on it. Mammy said I wasn't to touch it but I've been keeping an eye on it, in case someone takes it.'

'That was very kind of you, Eliza,' said Polly. 'But I'm sure that no one would want to take a letter that wasn't theirs to take.'

'Well, someone took the baby, and she wasn't theirs to take.'

Polly sighed. 'No, she wasn't.'

Just then Mrs Lamb came up the stairs from the kitchen. 'Jesus, Mary and Holy Saint Joseph, is she still guarding that bloody letter?'

'I can stop now, Mammy, Orla and Polly are home.'

Mrs Lamb shook her head. 'I can see that. Come on, Eliza, we have work to do.'

'Thank you, Eliza,' said Polly.

'Oh, you're very welcome.'

'Did I do the right thing?'

'You always do the right thing, Eliza,' said Orla, smiling at her.

'Did you hear that, Mammy? I always do the right thing.'

'Well, the jury's out on that one, girl.'

Orla picked up the letter and the sisters ran upstairs to their bedroom. 'What do you think it says?' said Polly.

'How would I know, ya eejit? I'm not psychic.' Orla sat on the bed and opened the letter, then started to read it out loud.

Dear Orla and Polly,

I hope this letter finds you safe and well. I have at last tracked down Roibin Carroll. I'm happy to say that he seems like a fine young man, who had nothing but good things to say about Colleen and was happy to hear that she was doing well.

I didn't give out her address in Dublin and I didn't mention the baby, I feel that is not my story to tell. I said that if he would like to get in touch with her, he could send his letter to me and I would make sure she got it. Now he might not want to make contact, so I would hold off letting her know for now.

I shall keep you all in my prayers.

May God bless you and watch over you.

Father Peter Benny

PS: I hope the pair of you are attending Mass.

Orla passed the letter to her sister.

'He has a lovely hand, doesn't he?' said Polly.

'Well, he's a priest and I'd say that he had a good education.'

'I suppose, now we must just wait and keep this to ourselves.'

'We can do that.'

'Do you think he'll write, Orla?'

'I'm not sure whether I want him to or not.'

'I feel the same. I don't want anything to upset Colleen.'

'That was what I was thinking, but it's out of our hands now, so let's leave it with Father Benny and Himself Upstairs.'

'You're right, Orla, but then you always are,' said Polly, grinning.

CHAPTER 44

Orla and Polly were at work and Jessie was at college but the rest of them were in the sitting room, waiting for Moira and Abby.

'Now, I hope you have all wrapped up,' said Mary Kate. 'It's arctic out there.'

'Do you think I should take Rosa out, Miss Ryan? Do you think that maybe it's too cold for her?'

Mary Kate knew that it had nothing to do with the cold. 'We'll wrap her up, Colleen, she'll be warmer than the rest of us.'

'Well, if you're sure.'

'She'll be grand.'

'I'd rather not be in charge of the pram, Colleen,' said Eliza quickly.

Colleen smiled at her. 'Dear Eliza, I'm sure Rosa would love you to wheel her out.'

Mrs Lamb nodded. 'Thank you, Colleen.'

'I might let go of the pram, Mammy, but I won't let go of the baby.'

'Of course you won't, love, of course you won't.'

'I'll let them have the pram, but I'll be sure to take the baby out first.'

'My darling girl,' said Mrs Lamb, 'what would I do without you?'

Just then, the door opened, and Moira and Abby came into the room.

'That's a gorgeous coat you have on you, Abby,' said Mary Kate.

'The missus bought it for me,' said Abby.

You could have heard a pin drop in the room as everyone stared at the little girl.

Mary Kate felt like crying; this was the first time she had heard Abby's sweet voice and she felt like scooping her up in her arms and dancing round the room with her. Instead she reacted as if it were no big deal. 'Well, now wasn't that kind of her?' she managed to say before quickly changing the subject. 'Are you coming with us, Mrs Lamb?'

Mrs Lamb shook her head. 'I'm going to prepare some food for when you get back.'

'I'd say that will be very much appreciated and something to look forward to. Now then, are we all ready to go?'

'We are,' they chorused.

Today was a very special day, as His Grace the Bishop was coming to bless the new houses in Tanners Row. It was cold but it was sunny and the sky was the deepest blue. It was the sort of day that made you feel glad to be alive.

Ahead of Mary Kate, Colleen was pushing Rosa in the pram, with Eliza and Abby on either side, like two little guards. God help anyone who went anywhere near that baby. Mary Kate was walking beside Moira.

'Did you know that Abby was going to speak?'

'I didn't, I was as surprised as the rest of you.'

'It was a wonderful surprise all right.'

'Well, you managed not to show it and that was the best thing you could have done. If everyone had leapt on the child, she might never have spoken again. You are a wise woman, Mary Kate Ryan.'

'As you are yourself, Moira Kent.'

Half the town were out to see the Bishop. It was mostly the women, standing in groups, sporting their Sunday hats and good handbags. It wasn't every day that the town had a visit from His Grace the Bishop and they were giving him the respect due to such a holy man.

As Mary Kate Looked down the lane it was hard to believe that this had once been a row of humble cottages. The dirt track where she had played ball and skipping with her friends, the gullies that had carried stinking waste in a stream down the hill, were no more. She shuddered as she remembered how they had sailed paper boats in the filthy water, running beside them to see whose boat got to the bottom of the lane first – it was a wonder they hadn't all died of some desperate disease. Now a smooth path ran in front of the new houses and the stench that no one seemed to have noticed was gone.

None of us knew that we were poor, so we didn't feel hard done by, we had nothing and yet we took pleasure in the smallest of things.

Erin, Gerry, Sean and herself had spent so many evenings poring over fabrics and paint colours, room sizes and ceiling heights. Oh, how she had loved those evenings, sitting in front of a grand fire in Sean's cosy house, laughing and drinking tea and making dreams come true.

'I think the houses should be a little different from each other,' said Sean. 'Rather than all the same.'

'I agree,' said Gerry. 'Each house should be unique.'

'They'll think they've landed in Paradise,' said Erin, 'after the way they've lived.'

Mary Kate smiled. 'What I want most is that they feel comfortable. I don't want them to be scared of making a mess or be frightened to touch anything. These houses are homes and I want them to be as proud of them as I am.'

'And they will be, Mary Kate,' said Sean. 'If I have anything to do with it, they will.'

The cottages had been so dark, the tiny windows letting in very little light, and so it was the light that was important to Mary Kate. It gave her such joy to see the large windows looking out onto neat front gardens. Each door had been painted a different colour and they looked so jolly they made her smile. She felt blessed that she had been able to make this happen. She hoped that her mother was looking down this day and feeling proud that, because of her, lives were being changed. She hoped that she was pleased with her daughter – it saddened her that they would never meet in this life.

There was a ribbon stretched across the top of the alley and two small boys were each holding onto an end as if their lives depended on it. That they were taking their task very seriously made Mary Kate smile. She saw James, Erin and Gerry amongst the crowd and waved at them. But it was Sean who she was looking for. Why wasn't he here? Surely today of all days should have been important to him. She'd been looking forward to seeing him and the day seemed a little duller without him there.

She looked at the house where her little cottage had once stood and where she had been so happy, but she didn't feel sad; all her memories were safely tucked away in her heart. The cottage had been nothing more than a pile of stones, it was her grandparents who had filled it with love.

She saw Mrs Finn standing behind the ribbon and walked across to her.

'Oh, Mary Kate, I keep thinking that I am going to wake up and find that it's all a dream.'

'Well, I'm happy to say that it isn't a dream, Mrs Finn, and I couldn't be happier for you.'

'And to think that the Bishop is going to bless my house.'

'And why wouldn't he? If anyone deserves to have their house blessed by the Bishop, it's yourself.'

Mrs Finn nodded her head towards a group of women. 'They're so green with envy, they look like a row of leprechauns.'

'Oh, Mrs Finn,' said Mary Kate, grinning. 'I'm sure they are pleased for you.'

'Pleased for me? They'd step over me dead body if they thought they could live in one of these houses.'

'Well, I'm pleased for you, Mrs Finn.'

'But don't you think it's a bit odd, Mary Kate?'

'What's odd about it?'

'Well, why should some feller in England decide to do this for a bunch of strangers that he has never met? Why would he take it upon himself to give us new houses and put us all up in a hotel while they're being built?'

'Maybe it's like the Holy Trinity, Mrs Finn?'

'What in God's name has the Holy Trinity got to do with it?'

'Well, the Catholic Church teaches us to have faith in what we don't always understand.'

'I suppose you're right. I don't have a clue who the Holy Ghost is, but if anyone questioned his existence, I'd eat the face off them.'

'There you are then. Just remember him in your prayers.' Mary Kate had her arm around Mrs Finn's shoulder as they stood together and watched the Bishop make the sign of the cross and cut the ribbon. One of the boys had been holding onto it so tightly that he fell backwards into the crowd; willing hands picked him up and comforted him.

'His mammy will murder him when he gets home,' said Mrs Finn. 'Making a show of himself in front of the Bishop.'

'I'm sure she won't,' said Mary Kate. 'I'd say she's as proud as punch that her boy was chosen to hold the ribbon.'

'Ah, you're probably right.'

'Let us pray,' said the Bishop and the crowd fell to their knees and bowed their heads.

'Dear God,' said Mrs Finn, 'I fear half of them will never manage to get up again.'

'I think you're being called over.'

Mrs Finn didn't move, she was staring at Mary Kate.

'What?'

'I don't know how you managed to do it, Mary Kate Ryan, but my heart is telling me that you are behind this miracle. You can deny it all you like but it's you who will be in my prayers this night, not some shite of a landlord in England.'

'Does it really matter who is behind this, my friend?'

Mrs Finn put her arms around her. 'God bless you, Mary Kate Ryan.'

Mary Kate could feel a lump in her throat as the families walked towards their new homes. Apart from the row of leprechauns, everyone seemed happy for them and began to clap and cheer. The day the Bishop came to their little street would be talked about for years to come.

Just then she saw Sean walking towards her and her heart lifted at the sight of him. 'I thought you weren't coming,' she said.

'I got caught up in a bit of business, but sure I wouldn't have missed this day for the world. Are you happy, Mary Kate?'

She looked at Sean's lovely face. 'I couldn't be happier.'

'That's grand then,' he said, smiling.

It seemed so natural when he reached across and held her hand. They were friends, why wouldn't they hold hands? But her heart was beating so loudly, she was afraid he could hear it.

Abby was standing beside Moira, watching the celebrations. 'The Bishop came to the convent once,' she said.

Moira didn't answer, so Abby tugged at her coat. 'Missus?'

Moira had been looking at a woman at the edge of the crowd. 'Sorry, darling, what did you say?'

'I said that the Bishop came to the convent once.'

'Did he now?'

'He did, and me and Jessie kissed his ring.'

'What an honour, was he nice?'

'He smelled of fags and he had a big belly, but I'd say there was no harm in the man.'

Moira laughed. 'You'll be the death of me, girl.'

Abby grinned. 'I bloody hope not,' she said.

Moira looked down at her, trying to keep a straight face. 'Abby Boniface and where did you learn language like that?'

'Off Eliza.'

'Eliza? You learned it off Eliza?'

'She learned it off her mammy. Her mammy says, "This bloody oven will be the death of me."'

'Well, it's a bad word, Abby, so I think it's best that you don't use it.'

'OK, missus, but don't you think it's a lovely word? I think it's a lovely word.'

'It has its uses, Abby, but you have to pick your moments, there are some people that would be shocked.'

Abby grinned. 'God love 'em,' she said.

Moira laughed; the child had an old head on young shoulders. She looked across at Mary Kate and Sean. *Now wouldn't that be lovely*, she thought. If only she could think of a way to hurry it along, because left to the two of them, it was never going to happen.

She glanced back to where the woman had been staring at Mary Kate, but she was gone.

CHAPTER 45

Orla and Polly were sitting on Colleen's bed. Rosa was asleep in her cot so they were talking quietly.

'Would you like to see Roibin again, Colleen?' said Polly.

'Where in God's name did that come from?'

'Just wondering.'

'Well, the answer is, I don't know. I've thought about it and I don't know.'

'You loved him, though?'

'I suppose I did, Polly.' Colleen frowned. 'Maybe I was too young to know what love really was.'

'Well, there's no good asking Polly,' said Orla.

'Thanks a lot.'

'Well, it's true, you'd run a mile if a boy asked you the time of day.'

'And *you* wouldn't?' said Colleen.

Orla grinned. 'I've kissed a few frogs all right, if that's what you mean.'

Colleen stood up and walked across to the cot. She smiled down at her little girl, who was looking more like her daddy every day. She only had to look into those beautiful blue eyes to see Roibin looking back at her, so how was she supposed to forget him? The truth was she never would.

Rosa started to make sniffling noises.

'We'll let you get on,' said Polly.

After the girls had gone, Colleen picked up her writing book. She turned the pages until she got to the poem that she was going to give to Roibin.

It had been a beautiful spring morning as she'd hurried towards the gypsy camp with the poem in her pocket. It was dark in the woods but she knew them so well that she could have found her way blindfolded. A thin strand of sunlight suddenly made its way through the thick branches of the trees and lit the path in front of her. She had never been happier. Is this what first love felt like? Is this why people sang songs about it and wrote poems and made movies? Is this what her parents had felt when they'd first met? She doubted it somehow, as she had never seen any signs of real affection between them. Maybe this was the best bit, maybe this was as good as it was ever going to be. But even that didn't make her sad because she had felt it and whatever happened she would have known what it felt like to love someone more than she loved herself and she knew that this beautiful morning would come back to her every spring day down the lanes and roads of her life.

She read the last few verses.

> I'll leave this house that was my home
> No, love, I am not sad
> The only home I need is you,
> My own dear gypsy lad.
> Your people I shall make my own
> Their ways shall be as mine
> I'll take the water from the stream
> And envy not their wine.
> The stars shall be my blanket,

My bed the earth below
And whither thou stayest I'll stay my love
And whither thou goest I'll go.

What would Roibin have thought of it? Would it have scared him? Would it have had him running for the hills? She looked at it again; it was no more than the ramblings of a silly lovesick girl. It wasn't even a good poem, it was a load of romantic shite; he would probably have laughed and shown it to his friends. Well, she would never know, would she? Because when she came out into the sunshine the field in front of her was empty. Roibin had gone and he had left her with a child in her belly.

Would she have gone with him if he'd asked? Maybe she would have. Maybe back then, but not now. She wanted more for Rosa than a life on the road, a life of little education, where they would be hated wherever they settled. She had loved Roibin for that short magical time but her heart belonged to Rosa and it always would.

'Well, that didn't work, did it?' said Orla, plonking herself down on the bed.

'Perhaps we should have told her straight out that Roibin had written her a letter.'

Orla sighed. 'That's what comes of trying to be clever.'

'We weren't trying to be clever, Orla, we were trying to be kind. If she'd said right out that she loved the lad and thought about him every day and she was only dying to see him again, we could have given her the letter and she would have been only delighted with us. As it is she'll probably think that we are a pair of interfering baggages, who have no right to be meddling in her love life.'

'Well, it's not our fault, is it?' said Orla.

'Whose fault is it then?'

'OK, it's ours, but we did it for the right reasons.'

'I'm sure hundreds of passengers got on the *Titanic* for the right reasons and look how that turned out.'

'Well, we can't just ignore it, can we? We have the letter, it has Colleen's name on the envelope, and that's who it belongs to. We need help with this, Polly. I think it's time to ask Miss Ryan's advice.'

Mary Kate had just received a phone call from the convent, asking her to come in. She couldn't for the life of her imagine what they wanted to see her about. She was just about to set off when there was a knock on the door.

'Come in,' she said, picking up her handbag.

'Oh, you're going out,' said Polly, stepping into the room.

'I'm wanted at the convent.'

'We won't hold you up, we can come back another time,' said Orla.

Mary Kate could sense that something was bothering them. 'No, come in, I've no particular time to get there,' she said, taking off her coat.

The girls sat down and told their story.

'So you see, we don't know what to do now, Miss Ryan, and we were hoping for a bit of advice.'

'You have the letter?'

Orla took the letter out of her pocket and handed it to Mary Kate.

'Does Roibin know about the baby?'

'Oh no, Miss Ryan, Father Benny said it wasn't his story to tell,' said Orla.

'And does Roibin know where Colleen is living?'

'Father Benny didn't tell him that either.'

'Your Father Benny sounds like a wise man.'

'Oh, he is, Miss Ryan, and he's awful kind as well.'

'You could tell him you'd murdered your mammy and he wouldn't tell a soul,' said Polly.

'Jesus, Polly,' said Orla. 'That's an awful odd thing to say. Why would you murder yer mammy?'

'I was just trying to say...' She stopped. 'Oh, I don't know what I was trying to say.'

Mary Kate smiled. 'That you trust him?'

'That's it.'

'Well, next time you're trying to explain something, don't bring the mammy into it,' said Orla.

Polly had gone red in the face. 'I won't.'

'Back to Colleen,' said Mary Kate, smiling at the pair of them. 'I agree with what you're saying, the letter is addressed to her and, for good or bad, it's up to her whether she wants to open it.'

'I know it's a lot to ask, Miss Ryan, but I think it would be better coming from yourself. I think you'd know how to put it without bringing murdered mammies into it,' said Orla.

Polly glared at her. 'Will ya stop going on about murdered mammies.'

'Away with the pair of you and don't worry, I'll speak to Colleen when I get back from the convent.'

'Thanks, Miss Ryan.'

'You're an eejit, Polly Dooley,' said Orla as she ran up the stairs.

'And you're a baggage,' shouted Polly running after her.

Orla stopped running and looked down at Polly. 'But I still love ya.'

Polly grinned. 'And I love *you*.'

CHAPTER 46

'And he wants to see Jessie?' said Mary Kate.

Sister Luke nodded. '"I'm her father," he said. "'I have a right.'"

Mary Kate frowned. 'And where has he been these last ten years? I'd say he lost any right to her when he abandoned the child and never came back.'

'I agree, but she's not yet sixteen and he might well be able to lay claim to her.'

'Over my dead body,' said Mary Kate. 'Jessie is happy, she's doing well at college and she has friends, she certainly doesn't need a father this late in the day. Why does he suddenly want her?'

'Reading between the lines, I think he's looking for someone to take care of him and, to be honest, he doesn't look as if he's much longer for this world.'

'Did he seem nice?'

'It was hard to tell. The man was plastered. I was nearly comatose from the fumes coming off him. But sure, he's one of God's children, so who I am I to judge?'

'Is he intending to come back?'

'He said he'll be back on Sunday week at three o'clock.'

'Well, if Jessie wants to meet him, that will be her decision, not his.'

'So you'll tell her?'

'I don't think I have a choice, Sister. He's her father, after all, and she has a right to know. What she does with that knowledge is entirely up to her.'

Sister Luke smiled. 'I thought that is how you'd see it.'

'But whether or not she wants to see him, I shall be here on Sunday and we'll tackle this together.'

'Thank you and may Almighty God find the time to pop in as well.'

'What proof do we have that he is indeed Jessie's father?'

'Fair point, but you see, I was there the day he left Jessie with us and although life had not been kind to him, it's the same man all right.'

Mary Kate frowned. 'What I don't understand is why he hasn't come looking for her sooner?'

'Well, there's the rub. The man has been in prison.'

'In prison?'

Sister Luke nodded.

'Well, he must have done something pretty desperate, to have been in prison all this time.'

Sister Luke gave a half smile. 'He said that he accidentally killed someone.'

'How can you accidentally kill someone?'

'Well now, I humoured him and asked that very question. His answer was that the man got in the way of his fist, and he didn't mean to do him any harm at all. He said that he might have had a bit of drink in him at the time.'

'I've heard everything now,' said Mary Kate.

'Well, that's the story he gave me.'

'Do you think there was any truth in it?'

'I've been struggling with that ever since meeting him.'

'And what do you think now?'

'Well, he's a pitiful old slob of a man and I'd say there hasn't been an abundance of luck in his life. But it's a stretch of the imagination to think that out of the whole of Dublin, his fist managed to find yer man's face, causing him to fall backwards, hit his head and die, but, sure, stranger things have happened this side of Heaven.'

'It will be a lot for Jessie to take in.'

'It will, so let us pray,' said Sister Luke.

Mary Kate closed her eyes and bowed her head.

'There now,' said Sister Luke. 'There's no harm giving Himself upstairs a bit of a nudge, to remind Him that we are still here.'

'Oh, Sister, you have a great way with words.'

Sister Luke grinned. 'I was saucy as a child and I still have a bit of sauciness left in me. Now, God willing, I'll see you on Sunday. And, Mary Kate, before you go, we have orphans coming out of our ears at the moment, you wouldn't consider relieving us of a few of them?'

'I have a lot going on at the moment, Sister Luke.'

'But you wouldn't rule it out?'

Mary Kate grinned. 'I wouldn't rule it out.'

'May God go with you, child.'

As Mary Kate walked home, she wasn't only worried about Jessie's reaction to her father's return, she was also worrying about Colleen's thoughts on the letter from Roibin. Jesus, she was turning into a counsellor. When she had imagined her boarding house, her only thought had been for the comfort of those who came through its doors. She knew what it felt like to live in a place where there wasn't a scrap of comfort. Her boarding house would be clean and warm and welcoming. She had never imagined getting so involved in the lives of her guests and yet, surprisingly, their need of her only matched her need of them, and oh, how wonderful it felt to be needed after years of being needed by no one.

As she neared home, she took a deep breath. Jessie was at college, so it was Colleen who she would speak to first. Mary Kate straightened her shoulders and ran up the steps.

CHAPTER 47

Diane Mason sat in the garden at the back of the hospital – oh, it was lovely to be outside. She lifted her face to the sun and gloried in the warm air as it touched her skin like the gentle hand of a lover. She breathed in the sweet fragrance of purple and white crocuses, bright-yellow daffodils and the white snow-drops that gathered around the base of the trees like little ballerinas.

She'd just come from a meeting with her doctors. She felt sorry for them, really, it couldn't be easy telling someone that the treatment wasn't working and she had to have more. It hadn't come as a shock; she'd always known there had been very little hope and she'd made her peace with it.

But how terrible sad that she should die now, when trees were green and everything around her was bursting with new life. Wouldn't it be easier if the branches were bare and the sky hung heavy and grey above her head? She'd been to a fair number of funerals in her time and, to be honest, she liked the black-umbrella kind the most; the renting of garments kind of funeral, they were the most satisfying, you felt like you'd really sent them off in style.

This was not the season to be buried, this was not the season to be lowered into a black hole. This was a time of new beginnings and hope and second chances, but not for her, not for good old Dolly Mason – she'd used up all her chances. There were no miracles for her and she didn't expect any. If Almighty God Himself had poked His head through a cloud at this moment and offered her more time, would she take Him up on the offer? Somehow, she doubted it. The best was behind her and the future held nothing that would make her want to stay.

She'd had one hell of a life, though, and probably broken every rule in the Bible, but she didn't regret one second of it, not one second, and she had hurt no one. She'd never been a great fan of the Ten Commandments, she had never liked to be told what to do, especially by a man, and as for penance, Purgatory and Limbo – well, she'd never really got her head around that. But once a Catholic, always a Catholic, and she'd take the head off anyone who was stupid enough to mock it in her presence. She was born a Catholic and she'd die a Catholic with a full Requiem Mass and candles and hymns. There wouldn't be a soul there to appreciate it, but sure, it wasn't for anyone else's entertainment but hers.

She smiled as she thought of how different her funeral would have been if she'd died in London. They would all have been there: the drag queens in their feather boas and stiletto heels that defied gravity, the pimps, the con artists, the spivs and, of course, her girls. She could see them now, those people of the night, staggering from their beds into the daylight, shielding their eyes against the glare of the sun like a motley crew of vampires. The police would have had a field day with most of the criminal fraternity of London in the one place.

Oh, yes, they would all have been there to see Dolly Mason on her way and then they would have partied until the sun rose over the rooftops of Soho, but she had chosen to come home. She was born here, she would die here, and she would be buried beneath Irish soil. Until then, she would come back to the pain clinic – no reason to be rolling round the floor if she didn't need to. She had one thing left to do before she gave up the ghost, and time was running out.

CHAPTER 48

Mary Kate was sitting in her chair, looking out over the square. The trees were heavy with spring blossoms that were lifted from the branches into the air before settling on the ground, turning the grass into a carpet of pink petals. She wished she could capture the scene in front of her, but she could neither paint nor write, – in fact, she had no talents to speak of. Maybe that was why her grandfather had encouraged her to put down her thoughts in a diary, so she would remember them. She was blessed and she thanked God every day for bringing her to this place in her life.

It puzzled her why people came to her for advice, as if she was some wise woman who had all the answers. She was probably the most unworldly person in the house. Hers had been a narrow life, with no expectations of it ever getting any better. Rotten boarding houses and rotten jobs, mean landladies and fat old men with wandering hands had taught her just one thing, that the only person she could rely on was herself. The money hadn't made her any wiser but because of the people it had brought into her life, she was gradually learning to trust again.

Just then she saw Colleen and Eliza walking across the square, pushing the pram. It seemed Eliza had taken it upon herself to be Rosa's minder. Mary Kate went outside to help.

'She's just nodded off,' said Colleen as, between them, they pulled the pram up the steps.

Eliza sighed like an old one. 'We thought she'd never go to sleep.'

Mary Kate looked into the pram. 'She's a little dote, Colleen.'

Colleen smiled. 'She'll do.'

'We've been visiting the Indian people, haven't we, Colleen?'

'We have, Eliza. Oh, Miss Ryan, you should see the place now, it's only gorgeous.'

'It's like a palace,' said Eliza.

'Come into the sitting room and tell me all about it, Colleen. Eliza, be a pet and mind Rosa.'

'On my own?'

'We'll be on the other side of the door if you're worried.'

'Shall I sing to her, Colleen?'

'Best not, Eliza, she's asleep.'

Mary Kate closed the door and Colleen sat on the couch.

'So, Mr and Mrs Patel are happy?'

'They're over the moon, Miss Ryan. Ashar says it has given them a new lease of life and they pray for their new landlord every night before they go to sleep. He says it's a miracle.'

Mary Kate smiled. 'I couldn't be happier for them. They are lovely people and they deserve all the miracles going.' She joined Colleen on the couch. 'I was wanting to speak to you,' she said.

'About moving out?'

'Now where did you get that idea, child?'

'I just thought, you know, with me not paying you any rent.'

Mary Kate shook her head. 'Have I ever asked you for any rent, Colleen?'

'No, Miss Ryan, you haven't.'

'And why do you think that is?'

'I haven't a clue.'

'When you came to my boarding house, I felt as responsible for you as if you were mine and it was never a burden, nor has it ever been a burden. This is yours and Rosa's home for as long as you need it to be, so we'll have no more talk of rent, but we *do* need to talk.'

'That sounds serious.'

'Well, no one has died, thank God, but you *do* have a decision to make, Colleen.'

Colleen frowned. 'All right.'

Mary Kate took a deep breath and told Orla and Polly's story, as gently as she could.

Colleen's eyes filled with tears. 'Does Roibin know about Rosa?'

Mary Kate shook her head. 'No, he doesn't, love, that is yours to tell and only if you want to.'

'I don't know what I want, Miss Ryan.'

Mary Kate went over to her desk and took the letter out of the drawer. 'Roibin has written you a letter,' she said, handing it to Colleen.

That's when the girl broke down and Mary Kate took her into her arms and let her cry. 'There now, my love, there now. It's been a bit a bit of a shock, hasn't it?'

Colleen nodded and sat up. 'Oh, Miss Ryan, I've made your good blouse all wet with me snivelling.'

'Sometimes a good snivel is just what's needed and the blouse will wash.'

'How does he know where I live?'

'He doesn't. When Orla and Polly went home for Christmas, there were gypsies in the town and they wondered if your

Roibin might be with them. They weren't sure what to do, so asked Father Benny for his advice and it was him that found Roibin. The letter was sent to Father Benny, who sent it on here.'

'I don't know how to feel or what to do.'

'Well, as I see it, you have a few options. You can read it here, now, with me beside you, or you can take it upstairs and read it in your room. You might want to give yourself some time to mull it over, or you can decide you don't want to hear from him and we'll put it back in the drawer, in case you change your mind at a later date.'

'What would you do, Miss Ryan?'

'I'm the last person you should be asking about affairs of the heart. Why don't you talk to the girls about it? I think it would help them too, as they are worried you might think they were meddling in your affairs.'

'I'd never think that, they're my friends.'

Mary Kate smiled at her. 'I didn't think for one moment that you would.'

'Sure, if it wasn't for them I would never have ended up here and I thank God every day that they found me.'

'So, you'll speak to them?'

Colleen nodded. 'I'll speak to them.'

After she'd gone, Mary Kate went back to the window. The nights were lighter now and it was lovely after the dark evenings of winter. She had no idea what Colleen was going to do about the letter but she was sure that between the three girls they'd work something out.

She'd had friends when she was child but as her grandparents grew older and their need of her became greater, those friends had moved on without her. She hadn't the time to go to the dances at the town hall like other girls of her age. There was no one to chat with or just be silly with, in fact she'd never felt young. She seemed to have gone from being a child to being a middle-aged woman, with nothing in between. She didn't regret looking after her grandparents, of course she didn't, but she wondered what her life would have been like if her mother hadn't abandoned her. It would have been her mother taking care of the old ones and Mary Kate would have been able to, well, just to be young and carefree, even make mistakes and learn from them. Sometimes she felt like a child in the body of a woman. It was only when she looked at Sean that her feelings were anything but childlike.

CHAPTER 49

Rosa had a big grin on her face when Colleen came out of the sitting room.

'She woke up,' said Eliza. 'But not because I was singing to her, she just woke up.'

Colleen smiled at her. 'Babies have a habit of doing that.'

'I propped her up a bit,' said Eliza. 'She likes looking around.'

The baby reached out towards Colleen, who picked her up. 'You're getting awful heavy, Miss Rosa,' she said, kissing her warm little cheek.

At six months, Rosa was beginning to notice the world around her. She would go to anyone in the house and she rarely cried. She had been loved by so many people since the moment she was born, she had no need to. Mrs Patel was besotted with the child and as soon as Colleen walked into the café, she whisked her away. Those were the times when herself and Ashar would go for a walk in the spring sunshine. The more time she spent with him, the more she grew to like this gentle boy. She felt safe in his company, and she found herself thinking about him when they were apart. Had she felt safe with Roibin? Maybe not, maybe safe was as far from her mind as it could have been. When she was in his arms she forgot everything, her parents, her friends, even the teachings of the Church, nothing mattered except him; he had become her Heaven and she didn't care that Hell was waiting around the corner.

Just then, Orla and Polly came in the front door. 'Jesus, me feet are only killing me,' said Orla.

'I'm not surprised,' said Polly. 'Those shoes are so pointed, it's a wonder your poor toes aren't screaming out for help.'

'Sometimes you have to put beauty before comfort. Isn't that right, Rosa?' Orla said, smiling at the baby. Rosa gave a gummy grin. 'See, she agrees. You're a girl after me own heart, so you are.'

As the girls started up the stairs, Colleen stopped them.

'I know you've only just come in from work,' said Colleen, 'and you're only dying to lie down, but I need to talk to you. Is that OK?'

'Of course it is, come up when you're ready,' said Polly.

'I'll just take Rosa downstairs to Mrs Lamb and I'll be with you.'

'Shall I carry her down?' said Eliza.

'Best not, those stairs are a bit steep.'

'You're right, they are. I nearly broke me bloody neck on them last week.'

'Eliza, would you mind not swearing around Rosa?'

'What, the bloody word?'

'Yes,' said Colleen, grinning.

'I'll try, Colleen, but it's Mammy who does all the swearing in this house. I could ask her to stop but I don't think she can, she loves the word.'

Once Rosa was sitting in her highchair, happily munching

away on a biscuit, Colleen ran upstairs to the girls' bedroom. She went in and sat down on Polly's bed. The girls clearly knew what Colleen wanted to talk to them about and seemed anxious.

'You're not cross with us then?' said Orla, sitting next to her.

Colleen smiled. 'Now why would I be cross with you?'

'We thought you might think we were meddling in your affairs.'

'You're my friends, for God's sake, and there's a big difference between meddling and having my best interests at heart and I know which one I believe.'

'Well, that's a relief,' said Orla.

'Have you read it yet?' said Polly. 'The letter?'

'I wanted to open it with you two.'

'Are you nervous?'

'I am a bit, because I can't imagine what he has to say.'

'Well, Father Benny says that he's a lovely lad and he only spoke well of you.'

Colleen looked at the letter in her hand. 'If he was just another boy that I'd had a bit of a fling with, I wouldn't care what he had to say, but he's the father of my child.'

'We bought cake on the way home,' said Orla. 'I think we should have some. I always think that however bad things might be, they are easier with a slab of cake in your hand.'

Colleen laughed. 'I think I should read the letter first. I might be in need of the cake afterwards.'

'Good decision,' said Polly.

As she sat on the bed, with Orla on one side of her and Polly on the other, Colleen was glad that she had them there. She started to read out loud.

Dear Colleen,

I was surprised to hear from your Father Benny, surprised but pleased.

First, I need to apologise for leaving without saying good-bye. At the time I thought it was for the best, and I still do, but I am glad that I now have the opportunity to explain why I did that. I am aware that gypsy lads have a reputation for kissing the girls and running and I'm ashamed to admit that I may be guilty on that score but that was not the case with you, Colleen. I fell in love with you, girl, and that was a first for me, but I had nothing to offer you. No real home, no steady job, it wouldn't have been fair on you and I fear it wouldn't have worked.

I always knew that I would marry one of my kind and that is what I am about to do. Her name is Natalia and we have known each other since we were young ones. She's a lovely girl who has been brought up in our ways and will be content with a life on the road. I hope that you can find it in your heart to be happy for me.

I wish you only good things in your life and I hope that you find the happiness that you deserve. You will always hold a special place in my heart, Colleen, and I hope that I can lie gently in yours and that there are no regrets.

With love,

Roibin

She had tears in her eyes as she put the letter back in the envelope.

'Oh, Colleen,' said Polly, putting her arms around her. 'Are you desperate sad?'

'I'd say it's a mixture of relief and sadness. I now know why he left and I understand his reasons.'

'I thought it was a lovely letter,' said Orla.

'And very sincere,' said Polly. 'I mean, he didn't have to write to you at all but he wanted to.'

'And he said he loved you, Colleen,' said Orla, 'and that was lovely. No one has ever said that they loved me.'

'*I* love you, Orla,' said Polly.

'I'm talking about a feller, ya eejit,' said Orla.

'What will you do?' said Polly.

'When the day comes that Rosa asks about her daddy, I'll show her this letter, so that she can see he's a good man. If she wants to go running around the countryside looking for him, I'll be right there, running by her side.'

'You're a great mammy, Colleen. Rosa's lucky to have you.'

'I hope she sees it that way.'

'Of course she will and if she doesn't, she'll have meself and Orla to remind her.'

'Do you think we'll still know each other when she's grown up?'

'Of course we will, won't we, Orla?'

'Friends forever, Colleen, whether you want us to be or not.'

'I can't imagine ever leaving this house,' said Polly. 'I could cry me eyes out, just thinking about it.'

'I feel the same,' said Orla. 'How the feck did that happen?'

'I know it sounds daft – in fact, I don't know how to explain it,' said Colleen. 'But I've never felt so, um, so...'

'Jesus, Colleen,' said Orla. 'You never felt so what?'

'Leave her be, Orla, the girl's thinking,' said Polly.

'I can see that, but what's she thinking about?'

Colleen grinned; these two were like a double act and she loved the pair of them. 'I think I've got it.'

'Well, thank the lord for that,' said Orla. 'I'm ageing here.'

'I've never felt such a part of something, not a big part, and that's the best bit. I can be myself, I'm accepted, warts and all. At home, I felt I was being judged. I was forever trying to make my parents proud of me, but they never were, unless it was on their terms. I had to be seen to be a good girl, that was the most important bit.'

'Well, you failed miserably there,' said Orla. Which had the three of them rolling around in fits of laughter. 'Anyone for cake?'

Colleen dried her eyes and smiled. 'You bet.'

CHAPTER 50

Moira was standing at her bedroom window looking out over the garden, watching Abby running around with Guinness. She loved this child, and she knew that her love was returned. Moira had given up on love the day Katherine died and hadn't expected or wanted to love again. Yet here was this sweet little girl, who, without her noticing, had crept into her cold empty heart, filling it with warmth and something else – hope, yes, hope. She opened the window, letting a blast of cold air into the room, she shivered and pulled her cardigan around her, but she left the window open so that she could hear Abby's laughter echoing around the spring garden. Abby looked up and waved and Moira waved back.

She walked over to the dressing table and sat down in front of the mirror. What she saw was the same face that she had been looking at all her life. A face that had lived in the shadow of her sister's beauty throughout her childhood. She put her head to one side and looked again; OK, it was an unremarkable face, but ugly? She had two eyes that were a pale grey, quite pretty really, they weren't crossed or anything. She had two ears that sat nice and flat against both sides of her head, her teeth were straight and her lips were full. Everything was exactly where it was meant to be and, if that was the case, why was she so ugly?

She heard Abby calling to Guinness and smiled. She was shocked at the face that was staring back at her; this was a face that was still getting used to smiling. Was it just her imagination or were the contours softer? She smiled at her reflection again. Perhaps beauty was about who you were on the inside, the outside was just the wrapping paper, it was the inside that counted. She had let her father's bullying define who she was. He'd told her that she was worthless, and she had believed him; she hadn't given anyone the chance to be her friend, she hadn't given anyone the chance to see that she was quite nice really. She had pushed everyone away – the girls hadn't passed their exams because she was such a good teacher, they had passed their exams because they were terrified of her. What a terrible waste of her talents and what a grave disservice she had done those young girls.

She had walked away from Clifton College, carrying everything she owned in two small cases. Not much to show for the forty-eight years that she had inhabited this planet. Not much for a life, was it? The driveway had seemed to go on forever, she hadn't remembered it being so long. She didn't look back for there was no one waving her off and no one interested in where she was going. She had spent thirty years within those walls and yet she knew that not one person would miss her.

She had been a good teacher, the best teacher they had ever had, but it hadn't been enough. She didn't exactly dislike the girls she taught, she just didn't understand them and, to be fair, she had never tried to. And as for her colleagues... well, she had never let them close enough to share the intimacies that might have resulted in friendship. She had watched them come and go – young, enthusiastic women with modern ideas on education and scorn for the old ways. They weren't rude to her, but they didn't include her in their little tête-à-têtes in the staffroom, which suited her fine, she couldn't think of anything worse. They hadn't asked for her advice and she rather wished that they had, she could have imparted a little wisdom as the more mature member of staff. To them she was a dinosaur, unwilling to embrace the new ways, unwilling to change. Sometimes she would watch them, in a detached way, trying to figure out how they were able to make friends so easily.

Men had the least trouble fitting in, all they needed was a modicum of knowledge about football and to be able to navigate a cricket pitch. They would come in on Monday morning and say things like, 'We slaughtered them on Saturday, lads,' as if they themselves had actually scored the goals when in fact they had been in the stands, wearing woolly hats and clutching Thermos flasks.

The day she had walked away from the school, she had felt so lost and hopeless, all she could see ahead of her was loneliness, stretching away down the days and years, until she breathed her last. She looked across the field at the little cottage, that she had thought would one day be hers. It was the cottage that had kept her going. In her head she had decorated every room; she would have pale-lemon walls, cream curtains and comfortable sofas. Miss Williams had favoured maroons and browns and heavy brocade at the small windows, turning the room into a sort of gloomy cave. Moira's cottage would be filled with light and comfort, it would be her private piece of Heaven. Losing it had been a kind of bereavement.

When she had got to the end of the drive she had stopped and put her cases down and then, with a glimmer of hope in her heart, she had picked them up again and strode purposely towards a future filled with meaning and friendship and love. In this house she had good friends and for the first time in her life she felt valued, maybe even liked.

It was a house she knew. As the years passed she had

watched it fall into disrepair and it had broken her heart. The beautiful pillars that formed a portico around the stout double doors became broken and cracked, yellowing with age and neglect, while bits of broken glass littered the steps. Most weekends she would bring her lunch and sit on a bench in the square, opposite the house. It had become a kind of pilgrimage, but not the kind that brought her any spiritual peace, or personal enlightenment. She was drawn back time after time, hoping to feel some of the happiness that the house had once held within its walls – but there was only sadness, and as the house lost all hope so did she and she stopped going there.

Last year, when she had been sure that the little headmistress's cottage was hers, she came back one last time. She didn't know why, maybe she just felt the need to say goodbye and move on. What she had seen when she walked across the square that day had filled her heart with such joy. In front of her was a beautiful house. She walked closer and discovered that it was now a boarding house. It gave her hope, for if the house could rise out of the ashes, then maybe she could as well.

She walked back to the window. Abby and Guinness were gone, the garden was silent, but she had been silent long enough – it was time.

Mary Kate was sitting by the fire reading a book. She looked up as Moira tapped on the door and walked in. 'Is everything all right?'

'I have something to tell you, Mary Kate.'

'That sounds serious, Moira.'

'It's something I should have told you when I first arrived and I'm sorry I haven't felt able to.'

'Sure haven't we all got things that we are unable to share? You have nothing to be sorry for, Moira. Sit yourself down and stop looking so worried, I'm not easily shocked and I hope I'm right in thinking that we are friends and sorry has no place between friends. Now tell me what it is and shame the Devil.'

Moira smiled. 'Yes, I do think of you as my friend.'

'There you are then, aren't we the lucky ones?'

'We are,' said Moira.

'Shall I get us some tea? I find that most things are better with a cup of tea in your hand.'

'Thank you but not just now. Would you mind coming up to my room? It will be easier to explain up there.'

Mary Kate followed Moira up the two flights of stairs. Moira walked across to the window and Mary Kate stood beside her.

'Do you see that tree?' said Moira.

'I do and I've always thought it was beautiful.'

Moira paused and Mary Kate waited.

'My little sister, Katherine, fell out of that tree when she was seven years old. Those roses growing against the wall, they might well be the roses my mother tended when I was a child. Katherine and I would spend all our time in this garden playing with our little dog. In the summer we would sit on the grass making daisy chains and, in the winter when the snow arrived, we would build a snowman and...' She couldn't go on.

Tears ran down Mary Kate's cheeks as she reached out and held Moira in her arms.

'Oh, my dear, dear friend, you came home.'

'Yes, Mary Kate, I came home.'

CHAPTER 51

Mary Kate was writing in her diary, with Guinness at her feet – in fact, he was *on* her feet. Every so often she'd stroke his head. He was the most loving and loyal companion anyone could wish for and was adored by everyone in the house. She had no idea how old he was but, like herself, she guessed he was getting on a bit.

Mary Kate thought back to the day her grandfather had made her promise to buy a diary at the start of each new year. She'd thought that being so close to death, he was losing his mind, but she had kept her promise. She'd asked him why she needed one and she had never forgotten his answer.

'To keep account of your life, Mary Kate,' he'd said. 'To mark your red-letter days, to gain wisdom from your failures and pride in your successes. Never throw them away but read them now and again, for they will remind you of how far you have come.'

These words, from a man who had little in the way of an education and yet was as wise as Solomon, and oh, how she missed his wisdom. She had written his words on the first page of the first diary she had bought.

She smiled as she thought about Moira. It made her happy to think that this beautiful house had once been her home, the house where she had grown up, the garden where she had played with Katherine, her beloved sister. It was strange to think Moira knew the house better than she did.

A car pulled up outside and Sean got out. Her heart skipped a beat as she opened the door to him.

He grinned at her. 'I hope you don't mind me popping in, unannounced.'

'You don't have to announce yourself, Sean Barry,' said Mary Kate, smiling at him.

'I wondered if you would like to see inside the new houses. I bumped into Mrs Finn and she said she would love to show the place off to you.'

'Oh, I'd love to, Sean.'

'I thought you might, I think you'll be pleased.'

'Sit yourself down while I get changed.'

'You look fine as you are, Mary Kate.'

She ignored the comment. 'I won't be a minute.' She ran upstairs to her bedroom and opened the wardrobe door. She wanted to look nice and she wasn't kidding herself that she was doing it with Mrs Finn in mind. She had intended to go to see the houses, she couldn't wait to see the beautiful fabrics and paint colours that had been decided on.

It was a lovely day, so Mary Kate chose a blue cotton dress, with a pattern of little white daisies around the hem. Jenny had persuaded her to buy it, she'd said it brought out the blue of her eyes. She knew she was no beauty, but she thought her eyes were nice, the one redeeming feature in an unremarkable face. Mary Kate wondered if her mother had had blue eyes. She picked out a white cardigan, put it round her shoulders and ran downstairs.

Sean looked up as she walked into the sitting room. 'You look lovely,' he said, smiling.

Oh, how she loved that smile. She could feel the blood rushing to her face and she felt like the old fool that she was. *Cop on to yourself, Mary Kate Ryan*, she thought, *this isn't a date, it's just a kind gesture and you'd be daft to read anything more into it than that.*

They drove in comfortable silence towards Tanners Row. Sean parked the car at the bottom of the lane and they got out.

'Excited?' said Sean.

'Funnily enough, I feel a bit nervous.'

'This is your vision and I wish I could shout it out to the whole of Tanners Row.'

'Please don't,' she said, laughing. 'I'd be only mortified.'

'You should be proud of what you have achieved here, Mary Kate, and I for one couldn't be prouder of you.'

Sean knocked on Mrs Finn's blue door and she opened it with a big smile on her face.

'Well, aren't you a sight for sore eyes, Mary Kate? Come in, girl, and welcome.'

The room they entered was lovely. Sunshine streamed through the long windows, filling the once-dark little cottage with light, which was exactly what she had wanted.

'It's beautiful, Mrs Finn.'

'I keep thinking that it's all a big mistake and at any minute the bailiffs will be hammering on the door and hauling me out into the lane.'

Mary Kate suddenly wondered if this was all too much for her friend. After all, it hadn't been her choice to pull down her home. 'Do you miss the cottage, Mrs Finn?'

'Well, I suppose you'd miss a spot on the end of your nose if it was there long enough.'

Sean laughed. 'I suppose you would.'

'But would I swap this house to have the cottage back? Not in a million years. I've had nothing all my life and never expected anything. I thought that I would end my days in those damp little rooms but instead I shall end them here, in this beautiful house. This was never on the cards for me and I'm not even sure that I deserve it.'

Mary Kate smiled at her. 'Oh, Mrs Finn.'

'Look at this,' she said, turning on the tap and letting the water gush into the sink. 'And we have a proper toilet. You pull a chain and the whole lot flushes away. Did you ever see the like of it? Oh, I wish your grandmother had lived to see this. She was a very private woman and a clean one, but then you'd know that. She hated throwing the slops into the gully, but there, we had no choice. The cottages in Riley's Terrace throw theirs over the back wall into the graveyard. I don't know which is worse, except that I wouldn't want to be buried under a pile of shite.'

Mary Kate was laughing. 'You're a tonic, Mrs Finn,' she said.

After being shown the rest of the house, they had tea in the garden. 'A bit of a change from the old yard, eh, Mary Kate?'

'It's wonderful.'

As they were leaving, Sean said, 'I'll be round in the week with some shrubs.'

'That's good of you.'

'Not at all,' he said.

'I'll come back again soon,' said Mary Kate.

'You will always be welcome. And, Mary Kate?'

'Yes?'

'Am I right in thinking that you have a wall of your own now?'

Mary Kate smiled. 'I do indeed, Mrs Finn.'

'Then I'd say it's time to take back your grandmother's picture of the Sacred Heart.'

'Yes, it is and I know exactly where to hang it.'

Mrs Finn went upstairs and came back with the picture, which she handed to Sean.

'Thank you for looking after it for me, Mrs Finn.'

'You have nothing to thank me for, girl. It's myself and the rest of the street that should be thanking you.'

Mary Kate didn't answer, she just smiled and nodded.

'She knows, doesn't she?' said Sean as they started to walk away.

'She thinks she does,' said Mary Kate, grinning. It was then that she noticed the front door of her old home was painted bright red. 'Whose idea was that?'

'All of us,' said Sean. 'There had to be some part of you in Tanners Row and a red door seemed fitting.'

They arrived back at the boarding house and as Mary Kate got out of the car, she said, 'What would I do without you, Sean Barry?'

'Well, unless you decide to up and move to pastures green, I will always be here for you, Mary Kate.'

She was smiling as she ran up the steps and opened the red door. *He will always be here for me, that's what he said. Now isn't that the nicest thing?* She picked up a letter that was lying on the mat. There was no stamp on it, so it must have been delivered by hand. She was just about to open it when she heard someone calling her name. She turned around to see Jessie, running across the square. There was a young girl with her and they were holding hands as they ran. She had been hoping to catch Jessie on her own, as she needed to talk to her about her father, but maybe it wasn't such a bad thing, for she would have a friend to speak to afterwards.

The pair of them were laughing as they ran up the steps. Mary Kate met them in the hallway.

'Miss Ryan, this is my best friend, Aishling. Is it OK if she stays for her dinner?'

'Of course it's OK, Jessie.'

Jessie smiled at her friend. 'See, I told you she wouldn't mind.'

'Thank you, Miss Ryan,' said Aishling.

'You're very welcome, love. Now, Jessie, I need to talk to you on a very important matter.'

'Have I done something wrong?'

'Not at all, girl.'

'Can Aishling stay with me? We tell each other everything.'

'If you're happy with that, then of course she can stay with you. Come into the sitting room and we'll have a chat.'

The girls sat down on the couch. Mary Kate was glad now that Jessie had her friend with her.

'Now, Jessie, what I have to say might shake you up a bit, but it's really nothing that you need to be worried about.'

'Jesus, Miss Ryan, if I wasn't worried before, I am now.'

'Oh dear, I'm making a dog's dinner of this, aren't I? So, I'll just say it how it is. It's about your father, Jessie.'

'My father?'

'He turned up at the convent, wanting to see you.'

'He took long enough.'

'Indeed he did.'

'So where has he been all this time?'

This was the one thing that Mary Kate had been hoping Jessie wouldn't ask. But she had and now she had no option but to tell her the truth; she was going to find out anyway.

'Your father has been in prison, Jessie.'

Aishling moved closer to Jessie and held her hand. 'Are you OK?' she said gently.

'I suppose I am, but it's a lot to take in.'

'It is,' said Aishling. 'How well do you remember your father, Jessie?'

'He was sad after my mother died, and just so lost. He seemed unable to reach out to me in his grief. I wanted him to cuddle me but he never did.'

'But was he kind to you?'

'I don't remember him being unkind. In fact, the day he left me at the convent he brought me a bar of chocolate. He said he would come back for me but he never did, he never did come back.'

'Did that make you sad?' said Aishling gently.

'Whenever there was a knock on the convent door I would run to answer it, in case it was him, but it never was. There must have been a day when I realised that he was never coming back, because I stopped answering it.'

'I'm so sorry, Jessie,' said Aishling. 'I'm so sorry you had to go through that.'

'Sure it was a long time ago, I grew up and I got over it. So, he wants to see me, Miss Ryan?'

Mary Kate nodded. 'On Sunday, at the convent, but you don't have to go if you don't want to. There is no law that says you have to meet him.'

'Won't he be cross if I don't turn up?'

'Did he turn up for you? No, he didn't, so I wouldn't worry about that.'

'Can I think it over?'

'Of course you can. Now pop downstairs and tell Mrs Lamb that there will be an extra guest for dinner.'

As the girls walked out the door, Moira walked in with a tray of tea. 'I thought you might like some company.'

Mary Kate smiled at her. 'No Abby?'

'She's cooking up a storm in the kitchen with Eliza.'

'The pair of them seem to get on great.'

'They do. Shall I pour the tea?'

'I certainly need one, I've had quite a day.'

'Anything exciting?'

'Sean took me to see Mrs Finn's new house. Oh, Moira, it's lovely and she's so proud of it.'

'She must be. It's not every day you get a new house handed to you on a plate. I'm pleased for her.'

Mary Kate went across to the desk and picked up the letter. 'This was on the mat when I came home. It must have been delivered by hand, there's no stamp on it.'

'Perhaps you have an admirer.'

'And pigs might fly.'

'Aren't you going to open it?'

Mary Kate took the letter out of the envelope and read through it quickly. 'We have a new guest.'

Moira frowned. 'That will feel strange, don't you think?'

Mary Kate thought for a minute and then nodded. 'I think it will, and I can't explain why.'

'When I came here,' said Moira, 'I never expected or hoped that I would become part of something more than just a guest. We are all very different in age and background, aren't we? But between us it feels as if we have become a kind of family.'

Mary Kate smiled. 'That's it exactly, and now we must be open-minded enough to welcome another member into the fold.'

'And does this interloper have a name?' said Moira, laughing.

Mary Kate looked at the letter. 'Diane Mason,' she said, smiling.

CHAPTER 52

Mary Kate, Jessie and Aishling had been sitting in Sister Luke's office for more than an hour, waiting for Jessie's father to arrive.

'He's not coming, is he?' said Jessie. 'I don't know why I was stupid enough to think he would. I believed him when I was a child but I don't believe him now and I'll never believe him again.'

'He may have been held up,' said Mary Kate gently.

'We'll wait a bit longer,' said Sister Luke.

'I waited years, thinking he would come back for me, but he never did. Why should I wait any longer now?'

Sister Luke shook her head. 'Ah, Jessie, I'm so sorry. I feel to blame here, for I trusted the man, he seemed sincere.'

'I expect he seemed sincere all those years ago as well.'

'I'd say he did, Jessie, I'd say he did.'

They sat in silence watching the hands on the clock, ticking away the minutes. No one knew what to say.

Jessie stood up. 'I want to go home,' she said.

'Then we'll go home, love,' said Mary Kate just as there was a tap on the door.

'Come in,' called Sister Luke.

An elderly nun came into the room. 'I think we have Jessie's father at the door, Sister.'

'Is he drunk, Sister Ruth?'

'I don't think he is. He seems pretty steady on his feet and he was very polite and humble.'

'Then please show him in, Sister.'

Jessie remained standing.

The man who stepped into the room was a pitiful sight. He was wearing a suit that was too big for him, the sleeves hung down over his hands, and he was pulling at the tie around his neck.

Jessie stared at him, silent tears running down her cheeks.

'Daddy?' she said. 'My daddy?'

Her father nodded, his tears matching hers. He held out his arms and Jessie walked into them.

Sister Luke stood up and beckoned to the others, who followed her out of the room.

They held each other for a long time. Jessie closed her eyes and leaned into him. The wall she had built around her heart began to crumble, brick by brick, like sand, taking all the years of pain and sadness with it. Had she really refused to leave the convent because of Abby? Or had she still been that abandoned child, waiting for the knock on the door? Jessie wiped away her father's tears. There was no bitterness left now, only love, for the father she thought would never come back to her.

He held her away from him and gently cradled her face in his hands. 'I don't deserve this, Jessie, I don't deserve your forgiveness.'

'Don't we all deserve forgiveness?'

'I never expected it, it's not why I came here.'

'I don't care why you came, it doesn't matter any more. All

that matters is you are here and I have my daddy back and I will never let you leave me again.'

Jessie led him towards Sister Luke's special chairs by the window and they sat down opposite each other.

'I'm sorry I'm late, Jessie,' he said.

Jessie smiled. 'Are you talking about the last ten years or the last hour?'

'Ah, Jessie, I have no excuses for my behaviour. I meant to come back but I lost myself in self-pity and drink. I'm ashamed of the man I became but I never forgot you. I carried you with me, like the cross of Jesus, it was my penance for walking away. In the end I told myself that you were better off with the nuns than with a drunken father.'

'And what about today?'

'I had no decent clothes; I didn't want to arrive here looking and smelling like a gutter rat. I went to the Sally Army, who kitted me out and let me have a bath. I wanted to look nice for you, I didn't want you to feel ashamed of your old dad.'

'I wouldn't be ashamed of you, whatever you were wearing.'

'Has the world been kind to you, my Jessie?'

She nodded. 'I was taken in by Miss Ryan, Daddy. I live in her beautiful boarding house, I go to college, I have a special friend and I am happy.'

'That is why I wanted to see you, to make sure that I hadn't ruined your life completely. To let you know that I never stopped loving you and that I'm desperate sorry for what I did. Now, this special friend of yours, do I need to be giving him the once over, to make sure that he's good enough for my girl?'

Jessie laughed. 'It's not a lad, Daddy. Her name is Aishling, I met her at college.'

'And is she enough for you?'

'She's enough for me, Daddy.'

'Then I am happy for you, my Jessie.'

There was a tap on the door and Sister Luke came in,

carrying a tray of tea and sandwiches. 'You look as if you could do with a feed, Mr Logan.'

'I can always do with a feed, Sister, and it's good of you.'

'You're very welcome. Can I ask where you are living at the moment? You don't have to tell me if you don't want to.'

'It's no secret. I think it's called a squat and it's full of no-hopers like myself but it's better than the streets. I nearly froze to death last winter. I'm looking for somewhere else but I've no money, so I guess I'll be staying there for now.'

'I may be able to help you.'

'I could do with any help going.'

'There is a condition, though: you'd have to want to be off the drink.'

'I've been sober since I last saw you, Sister, and as God is my witness, I'm determined to stay that way.'

'We have a hostel just outside Dublin, it's comfortable and warm. We also provide counselling that will hopefully help to keep you off the drink. I'm not saying it works for everyone, some are just too far gone, they prefer the streets to a warm bed, but if you think you can do it, then I can offer you a safe place to live.'

Jessie stood up and knelt at his feet. 'Will you do it, Daddy? Will you do it for me?'

Her father stroked her hair. 'Yes, my love, I'll do it for you.'

'And Daddy?'

'Yes.'

'Take the bloody tie off before you choke to death.'

CHAPTER 53

Diane Mason had been with them for almost a month and Mary Kate couldn't make the woman out. It wasn't that she didn't like her, she was friendly enough, she fitted in nicely with the rest of them, she paid her rent on time and she was no bother, but she wasn't giving much away. Mary Kate knew nothing about her, where she had come from, or what had brought her to the boarding house. She was very sure of herself – she was no shrinking violet – so why did Mary Kate have the feeling that there was something more going on? She reminded herself that it had taken her some time to warm to Moira and they were now the best of friends. Perhaps Miss Mason just needed a bit more time.

'What is it you find unsettling about the woman?' asked Moira.

Mary Kate thought about it. 'Her clothes,' she said.

'Her clothes?'

'Yes, her clothes.'

'She has some lovely clothes, a bit plain but good-quality, there's nothing offensive about them.'

'But they're not hers.'

'Are you telling me she stole them?'

'No, but she certainly didn't choose them.'

Moira stared at her. 'You've lost me now, Mary Kate. What in God's name are you talking about, woman?'

'It's as if she's trying to be someone she's not.'

'Or maybe she's trying to get back to who she *was*,' said Moira.

'I hadn't thought of that.'

'Well, I could be wrong and I probably am,' Moira said, laughing. 'I mean, what do I know?'

Mary Kate smiled at her. 'I think you know more than you're letting on, Moira Kent.'

'Ah, you've found me out – a woman of mystery, that's me.'

Mary Kate frowned. What was it about the woman that fascinated her so much? Because that was exactly it, Diane Mason fascinated her. OK, she didn't know her story but she hadn't known Moira's story when she'd first arrived and had felt no need to know. People had a right to their privacy without someone poking their noses into their business.

'I have noticed one thing, though, Mary Kate.'

'You have?'

Moira nodded. 'Every Wednesday morning, dead on eleven, she goes somewhere. Abby and myself have seen her on our walks.'

'Ah, so there *is* a mystery.'

'There might be.'

'We shouldn't follow her though, should we?'

'Absolutely not. I can't believe you even said that.' Moira paused. 'Next Wednesday, then?'

'Next Wednesday it is,' said Mary Kate, grinning.

The dreaded day came round quicker than Mary Kate had wanted it to. She'd been talking herself in and out of it all week.

What right did she have to be following someone? The woman had done nothing wrong and yet Mary Kate knew that she was still going to do it.

Moira came into the room and the pair of them watched from the window until they saw Diane Mason leave the house and walk down the steps.

'Now, before we set off, are you sure you want to do this?' asked Moira.

'Of course I don't want to do it. I think what we are doing is awful but there is something about Diane Mason that's doing my head in. When we discover that she's off to buy apples, you can tell me that I'm an awful eejit and that I need to go to confession and have my sins forgiven for being such a suspicious baggage.'

'Mary Kate?'

'Yes?'

'Will you take off that red coat, we're trying to be inconspicuous.'

'Oh dear, I don't think that I'm cut out for this.'

'And you think I am?'

'Of course not.'

Mary Kate ran upstairs and swapped the red coat for a black one.

'Let's go then,' said Moira. 'Before we lose sight of her.'

As they got to the bottom of the steps, they could see Diane Mason leaving the square.

'We need to stay well back,' said Moira, 'or we'll have some explaining to do.'

'Well, let's hope she's not catching a bus.'

Diane Mason walked quickly, as if she was late for an appointment. She was a good deal older than Mary Kate and Moira, and yet they were having a job keeping up with her.

'Jesus,' said Moira, 'O'Connell Street must be the longest fecking street in the whole of Ireland. Will she ever slow down?'

'Moira Kent, I don't think I've ever heard you swear before.'

Moira grinned. 'I get it from Abby, who got it from Eliza, who got it from her mother.'

'We've been a bad influence on you, my friend.'

'Far from it,' said Moira. 'I needed to loosen up a bit.'

Mary Kate smiled fondly at her. 'You're fine as you are.'

They hurried along beside the Liffey. The water looked grey and oily, and Mary Kate shivered as she thought of what she had been going to do.

'Are you cold?' said Moira.

'Not exactly. I'll tell you about it one day.'

'Ah, so there's a story?'

'There is, but it's not a nice one.'

'I think she's headed for the Mater,' said Moira.

'The hospital?'

Moira nodded. 'I'd say so.'

After about five minutes, they watched Diane Mason walk through the doors of the Mater Misericordiae hospital.

'Well, there's the mystery solved,' said Moira.

'But we don't know what she's doing here, do we?'

'We'll wait until she comes out and then we'll go in and ask. We'll say we're picking her up.'

They found a bench and sat down. 'I'm exhausted,' said Moira. 'I hope you don't expect me to do this every week.'

The sun was warm on Mary Kate's back as she sat beside Moira. It had been a lovely spring, given that this was Ireland and it never stopped raining; it hadn't earned the title of the Emerald Isle for nothing. The last of the daffodils were saying goodbye, their yellow petals tinged with brown, their long stems collapsing onto the grass like soggy seaweed, their job done. Summer was waiting around the corner and Mary Kate felt blessed.

They sat there for at least half an hour before Diane Mason eventually came out of the hospital. Mary Kate was beginning to feel guilty – what right did she have to follow an innocent woman through the streets of Dublin? This obsession with Diane was going to have to stop.

'Shall we go in?' said Moira.

Mary Kate shook her head. 'I think we've done enough, don't you?'

'Sure?'

'Sure.'

Diane Mason smiled as she walked back to the boarding house. Did they really think they could get one over on her? She knew every trick in the book, they'd have to get up a lot earlier to catch out Dolly Mason.

PART FIVE

CHAPTER 54

James Renson paced up and down the lounge, driving Erin mad.

'For God's sake, James, will you stop marching back and forth? Wearing the carpet out isn't going to solve anything.'

'I can't keep it from her, Erin. She's our friend, I must tell her. Wouldn't you want to know if the mother you thought was dead is very much alive?'

'Then tell her, James, you owe that woman nothing. It would be different if she was your client but she's not and for God's sake sit down.'

James stopped pacing and sat in the nearest chair. 'But she told me in confidence, Erin.'

'You're not a priest, James, you won't have the wrath of the Catholic Church down on your head if you divulge the truth.'

'But I'm a solicitor, surely that must count for something?'

'Well, I think that Mary Kate is more important than Agnes Ryan; we don't even know where the woman is. You've been avoiding Mary Kate, haven't you?'

'You noticed, then?'

'You wear your heart on your sleeve, my darling, of course I noticed.'

'I have to deliver this letter from England. I'm pretty sure it's from Ronald Devlin. I don't know how I'm going to face her, knowing what I know.'

'Well, in this instance, I think you should follow your heart and not your head. Tell our dear friend the truth and shame the Devil, James.'

'Who taught you to be so wise, Mrs Renson?'

'A certain, rather handsome man called Mr Renson. Now go see Mary Kate.'

James grinned. 'Handsome, eh?'

'Don't let it go to your head. Do you want me to come with you?'

'You don't mind?'

'Of course I don't mind and, anyway, you're less likely to bottle out if I'm there.'

'That's what I was thinking.'

'Let's get this over with. Maybe then you'll start eating the good food I cook for you, instead of pushing it around your plate. It's a wonder you haven't faded away.'

James patted his belly. 'No fear of that,' he said, laughing.

They were still laughing as they left the house and headed towards Merrion Square.

It felt as if Diane Mason had been with them for years, instead of months. She would often be found in the kitchen chatting with Mrs Lamb and drinking tea, their laughter drifting up the stairs. She babysat Rosa so that Colleen could spend some time alone with Ashar and often joined Moira and Abby on their walks. Mary Kate found herself warming to her, although there were still times when she sensed that something was not quite right. *Cop on to yourself, Mary Kate Ryan. Give the woman a chance and stop being so bloody dramatic.*

There was a tap on the door and Diane Mason came into the room.

'I was just thinking about you,' said Mary Kate.

'Good thoughts, I hope,' Diane said, smiling.

There it was again, that feeling she couldn't put a name to.

'I'm off to the shops. Can I get you anything?'

'You can, actually,' said Mary Kate. 'Could you get a box of rusks? Rosa's teeth are having trouble coming through.'

'And how about a couple of apple cakes? Hogan's do a lovely apple cake.'

'Are you trying to make me fat?' said Mary Kate, laughing and handing her some money.

'You're like me, Miss Ryan, you and I will never get fat.'

'Is that so?' said Mary Kate.

Diane Mason smiled at her. 'I think I'll treat everyone to cakes, the girls will be delighted when they get home from work.'

'I'm sure that they will. Would you mind getting one for Aishling as well? She seems to be a fixture here these days.'

Diane Mason nodded. 'I won't be long.'

After she'd left the room, Mary Kate stood at the window and watched her walk across the square. You got the feeling that nothing would faze Diane. She knew who she was and didn't feel the need to explain herself. Mary Kate would like to know her better. Moira certainly got on well with her, in fact everyone in the house did, including Guinness. The problem wasn't Diane Mason, it was *her*.

She opened her desk drawer and took out her diary. Maybe by writing down her thoughts she could make some sense of it all. The sun was streaming through the long windows as she wrote; she loved this room, it never ceased to give her pleasure. She thought back to those early months, seeing Sean every day, laughing with him, enjoying his company, and watching as he turned a sad neglected house into this beautiful home.

She had only written a couple of lines when there was a knock on the front door. She looked out the widow to see James and Erin standing on the steps. She hadn't seen James in a long while and was delighted they were paying her a visit.

'How lovely to see you both,' she said, opening the door.

'I hope you don't mind us dropping by unannounced,' said Erin.

Mary Kate smiled. 'Not a bit of it, you are always welcome. There is no need to herald your arrival. Sit yourselves down while I ask Mrs Lamb to bring us up some tea.'

When Mary Kate returned to the sitting room James was standing by the window and Erin was sitting on the couch. They weren't speaking. In fact, Mary Kate could feel tension in the room. She sensed that something was wrong but couldn't imagine what it could be.

James turned around. 'There's something I need to tell you, Mary Kate.'

Mary Kate frowned. 'That sounds serious.'

'Come and sit beside me,' said Erin.

Just then there was a tap on the door. 'That will be Miss Mason,' said Mary Kate, smiling. 'My newest lodger, you haven't met her yet.'

Diane Mason opened the door and walked into the room. 'Cakes for every—' She stopped dead and stared at James.

'Do you know each other?' Mary Kate said.

'Oh yes,' said Diane, 'we know each other.'

Erin stood up and went to her husband, who looked as if he'd seen a ghost.

'Is this who I think it is, James?'

He nodded. 'Oh, Mary Kate,' he said. 'I'm sorry, I am so very sorry.'

Mary Kate looked at her friend. 'Why are you sorry?'

'I came here today to tell you something, something I have been keeping from you and wish I hadn't.'

Erin walked across to her. 'Come and sit down, love.'

'I don't want to sit down, Erin, I want to know what is going on here.'

'For God's sake tell her, James,' said Erin. 'Or I will.'

Diane Mason took a deep breath. 'No, if she is to hear this from anyone, then she should hear it from me.'

'Hear what?'

'My name isn't Diane Mason and I'm sorry that I have lied to you.'

Mary Kate stared at her. 'I don't understand.'

'My name is Agnes Ryan.'

Mary Kate looked across at James and Erin, who stood there saying nothing. 'What in God's name is she talking about, James?'

'Tell her,' said Erin.

'Mary Kate,' he said gently, 'she is speaking the truth. This is your mother.'

Mary Kate felt as if she'd been punched in the stomach. 'My mother's dead. You know that, James, it was you who told me.'

Agnes Ryan wanted to be anywhere but in this room. She didn't do emotion. As far as she was concerned emotion was for losers and she was not a loser. She was fond of her girls in London, she cared about them, she listened to all their dramas, but she hadn't loved them, in fact she had never truly loved anyone in her entire life except her baby. She had learned early on that love made you weak, it made you needy and, in the end, it broke you. If she had given in to weakness, she would never have survived London, and Soho would have eaten her up and spat her out. She looked at the daughter she had walked away from all those years ago and knew what she had to do. She could sense them waiting, she knew something was expected of her. Well, if they wanted her to prostrate herself on the ground, wailing like a banshee and begging forgiveness, they were going to be sorely disappointed.

James glared at her. 'Do you feel nothing, woman? Do you feel nothing for the daughter you abandoned?'

'I don't know her.'

'And I don't know you,' shouted Mary Kate. 'And I don't want to know you. I want you out of my house and if I never see you again in this lifetime, it will be too soon.'

'Oh, Mary Kate,' said Erin.

'Don't Mary Kate me. You knew, you both knew and you kept it from me. I thought you were my friends.'

'We are your friends,' said James. 'I made a bad judgement keeping this from you and I wish to God I had told you right away but at the time I thought it was for the best. I was wrong, I wouldn't hurt you for the world, but I have and I couldn't be sorrier.'

Mary Kate felt as if she was suffocating, she had to get away from them. She walked out of the room, opened the front door, slammed it behind her and ran down the steps.

After she had gone, you could have heard a pin drop. Mr Renson shook his head.

'What have I done, Erin?'

'You made a mistake, James, and don't we all make mistakes? She'll come round, she's not one to bear a grudge. She knows the core of you, James, and she knows you wouldn't hurt her deliberately. Sometimes you just need someone to be angry with and I'm afraid you happened to be standing in the eye of that storm. All we can do is give her time.'

'Well,' said Diane, 'I suppose I might as well go and pack.'

'Oh, no you won't,' said James, glaring at her. 'You will stay right where you are until Mary Kate comes back.'

'But she doesn't want me here. She doesn't want to know me at all.'

'Then fight for her. Fight for her like you've never fought for anything before. Be a mother, or at least try to be one.'

Agnes looked calmly at James. 'I'm not the motherly kind, Mr Renson.'

'Then it's time you learned to be.'

'I gave her the money, didn't I?'

'You can't buy forgiveness, Miss Ryan, and you can't buy love. You owe Mary Kate much more than money. God knows how it happened but despite having you as a mother she turned out to be a wonderful human being, one of the best women I have had the privilege to know.'

Agnes stared at him. 'So what would you have me do, pretend?'

'If that's what it takes, then yes, I would have you pretend.'

What none of them realised was that she was already giving the performance of her life. How she had longed to take Mary Kate in her arms, to beg her forgiveness and to tell her that she had never stopped loving her. She was going to leave her again and this time she wouldn't be coming back. It was better this way because her leaving wouldn't cause her daughter any more pain than she had already caused her, in fact she would be glad to see the back of her and that is precisely what Agnes Ryan wanted.

She looked across the room at James. 'Have you finished lecturing me on my terrible mothering skills?'

'You disgust me,' he said.

'Well, feck you Mr High and Mighty Solicitor.'

'And feck you right back, Agnes Ryan.'

CHAPTER 55

Sean

Sean Barry knew exactly who he was – laid-back, was most people's opinion of him. He was loyal to the people he cared about and he was trustworthy. But according to Lorna's best friend, Linda, he'd turned into a bit of a cold fish. It wasn't that he didn't care, he just didn't care *enough*. The worst had happened to him when he lost Lorna and since then he couldn't summon up the energy to bother about the small stuff. Did that make him a cold fish? Maybe it did. Did that bother him? Not one bit.

When Lorna died, the women in the town decided that he must be lonely, and he became a bit of a project. He became Poor Sean Barry; voices were lowered in his presence, as if he'd suddenly turned into a saint, he wouldn't have been surprised if they'd genuflected in front of him. Mass cards were posted through the door, then piled up on the dresser. He could have fed the whole of Ireland with the amount of food that was delivered. Stews and cakes and home-made bread, apple pies and jars of jam piled up on the side until they went bad and had to be thrown away. He survived on fags and whiskey instead, and the weight fell off him, which resulted in more food being thrust into his hands. There were invites to Sunday lunches, quizzes down the pub and all sorts of other shindigs. Worst of all were the family weddings. Why did they think that for one minute he'd want to sit in a church and listen to two young people promising to love and cherish each other till death do us part? He turned them all down and the invitations eventually stopped coming.

The thing was, he wasn't lonely – in fact, he preferred his own company – it was only when he was around people that he felt alone.

For months after Lorna died he hadn't washed the sheets on his bed, but it didn't matter because every night he drank himself into a stupor and crashed out on the couch or the floor, whichever was closest.

One morning Linda came round. 'Jesus, Sean, it smells as if something died in here and you smell like a feckin' brewery. What would Lorna think?'

'Haven't you heard, Linda? Lorna died.'

'I know she did but you didn't. You don't have the monopoly on grief, Sean Barry,' she'd said. 'You're not the only one grieving. Her parents have lost their daughter, I have lost my best friend, but none of us are wallowing in self-pity, and do you know why? Because it is not what Lorna would have wanted. I'm not telling you to snap out of it, because none of us can, but I am asking you, for Lorna's sake, to at least try.' Her parting shot was, 'You make a shite drunk, Sean Barry.'

After she'd gone, he'd walked across to the mirror. The gaunt, unshaven face that stared back at him looked like a man who had given up on life. He went into the kitchen and emptied every bottle of whiskey down the sink. He'd cried as he watched the golden liquid disappear down the plug hole, because he didn't know how to live without it. But he did, somehow, he did.

Over the years, Linda had set him up on blind dates, nice enough girls but not for him. There had only ever been one girl for him and he'd thought that was how it would always be.

Linda was losing her patience. 'You don't give them a chance, Sean,' she'd said after another disastrous date. 'What was wrong with Maeve Butler, for God's sake? She might not be Marilyn Monroe but there isn't a bad bone in her body.'

'There isn't a bad bone in your body either, Linda, but forgive me if I don't get down on one knee and propose to you.'

'I bloody hope you don't.'

Sean smiled at her. 'She wasn't Lorna,' he'd said.

'Oh, Sean,' she'd said gently. 'I just want you to be happy.'

He walked across to the dresser and picked up the framed photograph of Lorna. He remembered the day he'd taken it. They were on the beach, Lorna's favourite place in the world. She would collect things – stones, bits of wood and long slippery strands of seaweed – that she'd chase him with, then carry them home like pieces of treasure, and place them on the windowsills around the house. She was smiling into the camera, her hair blowing across her beautiful face. How young they had been back then and how happy, their future stretching ahead of them like the ocean she loved so much. Nothing bad could touch them, they were the golden couple, and he would kill any monster that came to their door. How could he have known that even then, as she smiled her beautiful smile, that monster had already crept silently into her brain like a thief in the night and would take his precious girl away from him.

He rubbed the glass on the sleeve of his jumper, he could almost hear her giving out to him. 'Would it kill you to give the place a bit of a clean now and then, Sean Barry?'

'Isn't that your job?' he said, grinning. Jesus, he was talking to himself again. He looked back at the photograph. 'I've something to tell you, my love, and I hope you can be happy for me. You see, I have grown very fond of someone, someone who is not you. You'd like her, Lorna, she's kind and sweet and the most caring person I know. I'd say the two of you would have been great pals, for you are very alike. I will never forget you, my darling, but perhaps it's time for me to move on. Perhaps, God willing, I get to have a second chance at happiness.'

He put the photograph back on the dresser and left the house. He needed to talk to someone.

'Now, what I have I done to deserve a visit from the elusive Sean Barry?' said Gerry, answering the door.

'I am in need of some advice, Gerry, and if I don't talk to someone soon my head will explode.'

'Jesus, Sean, that sounds a bit desperate.'

'It is a bit.'

'Then I'm glad you came to me. Come in and if I can help, I will.'

Sean followed her into the cosy sitting room. There were swatches of material on every surface. Gerry scooped a pile of them off the couch and he sat down.

'Am I holding you up, Gerry?' he said.

'Not at all. I'm a good listener, Sean, and whatever you tell me will stay within these four walls.'

Sean ran his hands through his hair and stared at the carpet.

'I think I recognise a man who needs something stronger than tea,' said Gerry, leaving the room.

Sean walked across to the window and looked out over the park. A black-and-white dog was running around, it reminded him of Guinness and the first time he'd met Mary Kate. It hadn't been love at first sight but he had liked her, even then, he had liked her.

Gerry came back into the room and put two glasses of wine on the coffee table. 'Aren't we the daring ones, drinking alcohol in the middle of the day?'

'Ah sure, no one's looking,' said Sean, sitting back down.

'Except Him Upstairs,' said Gerry. 'And I'm sure He has more Important things on His mind.'

Sean smiled. 'I'd say He has.'

Gerry took a sip of the wine and stared at her friend. 'Put me right if I'm wrong, lad, but is this about Mary Kate?'

'Jesus, Gerry, how did you work that out?'

'It didn't take much working out, Sean. You'd have to be blind not to notice the way you look at each other.'

'You think that maybe she likes me then?'

Gerry smiled at him. 'Yes, Sean, and I don't *think* she likes you, I *know* she does.'

'So, what do I do now? I mean, how do I go about it?'

'Well, first you have to find the right location, that's very important. You don't want people walking in on you when you're down on one knee.'

'Jesus, Gerry, who said anything about going down on one knee?'

'Well, you might as well get it over with in one go. It's more than a liking you have for the girl, isn't it?'

Sean nodded.

'Well then?'

He shook his head. 'That's a big step, Gerry.'

'For God's sake, Sean Barry, neither of you are young chickens, you don't have time to be dithering about like a couple of lovesick eejits. If you love her, say it out loud.'

Sean stared at Gerry. 'What, now? Right now?'

'Well, if you can't say it now, how are you going to say it

when she's standing in front of you? Go on, say it and shame the Devil.'

'I'll feel daft.'

Gerry laughed. 'I'm waiting.'

'I love her,' he mumbled.

'I don't believe you.'

'What do you mean?'

'You can't plough a field by turning it over in your mind, lad. Say it like you mean it. Pretend I'm Mary Kate.'

Sean thought about all the things he loved about Mary Kate. Her gentleness, her kindness, her empathy for others. The way she laughed with her head thrown back, the way she took care of everyone in the house and the softness of her in his arms. He looked into Gerry's eyes. 'I love you, Mary Kate. I really love you.'

'Now that's more like it. You'll have me falling for you meself.'

Sean grinned. 'So where is the right location?'

'Glendalough, up in the Wicklow Mountains.'

Sean stood up. 'I'll leave you in peace then and thank you for your advice.'

'Well, don't leave it too long, Sean, or you'll go off the boil.'

They hugged at the front door. 'I'll see you around, Gerry.'

She smiled at him. 'Well, if you don't, I'll be banging on your door. Now go and get on your white charger.'

Sean was smiling as he waved goodbye. He'd done the right thing coming to Gerry, she was easy to talk to and a grand girl. He didn't have to weigh his words with her, she didn't judge, she just sort of nudged the truth out of you. He felt lighter as he walked down the street in the direction of the boarding house.

He hadn't gone far when he saw someone running towards him. Whoever it was, they were in a desperate hurry. As the woman got closer, he could see it was Mary Kate. He ran towards her and she almost collapsed into his arms.

'Dear God, Mary Kate, what's wrong?'

She was crying so hard that she couldn't speak.

'Do you want to go to Gerry's house?'

Mary Kate shook her head.

Sean held her hand as they crossed the road and went into the park. He found a bench under a shady tree and they sat down. He put his arm around her shoulder and she leaned into him. Neither of them spoke, they just held each other and that was enough. There was a warm breeze rustling the leaves above them and Sean felt Mary Kate relaxing in his arms.

'That dog looks like Guinness,' she said softly.

'I thought the same myself.'

Mary Kate sat up and looked at him.

'Do you want to tell me what's wrong?' said Sean. 'You don't have to, but it might help.'

And so, bit by bit she told him about Diane Mason. 'James and Erin knew she was my mother, Sean, and they kept it from me.'

'Knowing the pair of them as I do, I'd say they had their reasons, but I can see that you feel let down.'

'I don't know what I feel, Sean. My mother has been living in my house and I didn't know.'

'But you know now, Mary Kate, so you have to decide what you want to do about it.'

'I told her to get out, I told her that I never wanted to see her again.'

'You thought your mother was dead, anyone would have reacted as you did.'

'I was beginning to warm to Diane Mason. I even thought that, in time, we might become friends, but I felt nothing for Agnes Ryan.'

'They are the same person, Mary Kate,' said Sean gently. 'Whatever good you saw in Diane Mason is also in your mother.'

'I don't even think that she wanted to know me.'

'Then why did she come to the boarding house?'

'What do you mean?'

'Well, if she didn't want to know you, why did she come to the boarding house?'

'You have my brain mashed, Sean.'

'Then let us put our mashed brains together and work this out.'

'I wouldn't know where to start.'

'We'll start with what we know and go from there.'

'OK.'

'Well, somehow she found you, yes?'

Mary Kate nodded.

'And the only reason she found you and moved into the house has to be because she wanted to get to know you.'

'Then why do her damnedest to make sure that I didn't get to know *her*?'

'Look, I'm no philosopher, and I'm not saying I have all the answers, but the only thing that makes any sense is that she didn't *want* you to like her.'

'But why?'

'Perhaps because she knew that she would let you down again.'

'Do you really think so?'

'It's the only thing that makes any sense.'

Mary Kate sighed. 'It feels strange to suddenly have a mother.'

'Good strange, or bad strange?'

Mary Kate frowned. 'I'm not sure.'

'So, not all bad?'

'Not all bad.'

'So, are you ready to face them?'

'You won't leave me, will you?'

Sean took her hands in his. 'I shall never leave you, my love, and if it's OK with you, I'd like to never leave you for the rest of our lives.'

Mary Kate touched his face. 'It's OK with me.'

'I was supposed to do this at Glendalough. Gerry said location was important.'

Mary Kate was laughing now. 'To do what?'

'To tell you that I love you and to ask you to marry me. I don't even have a ring.'

'I love you, Sean Barry,' she said. 'And I don't need Glendalough and I don't need a ring. I only need you. I think that I have only ever needed you.'

Sean stood up and reached out his hand. 'Let's go and meet your mother, shall we?'

CHAPTER 56

Agnes had had a belly full of James bloody Renson and his wife glaring at her as if she was the Devil incarnate, so she left the room and went upstairs to start packing. She had taken a chance coming to the boarding house; these were her daughter's friends and it was inevitable that one day they would bump into each other.

Did she regret coming here? No, not for one minute. She had wanted to see her daughter, the baby she had walked away from. The night before she'd left the cottage in Tanners Row, she had stayed awake, holding her child in her arms, whispering words of love, so that maybe one day, in the distant corners of her mind, there might be a memory of being held in the arms of a mother who had loved her.

In the early hours of the morning, she'd crept downstairs, left a letter on the table and turned her back on everyone she loved. She'd taken the train to Dun Laoghaire, where she boarded the Innisfallen. She'd walked up the gangplank as Agnes Ryan and stepped onto British soil as Diane Mason.

She hadn't been surprised at Mary Kate's reaction, how could she have expected anything else? She hadn't come to try to win her daughter's love, she had lost all rights to that the day she left. But she was dying and she had to know that her child was OK and that growing up without a mother hadn't harmed her in any way or made her bitter. Well, nothing could have been further from the truth, for her daughter turned out to be everything she wasn't. Mary Kate was kind and generous, without a selfish bone in her body. She hadn't squandered Freddie's money, she had used it for the benefit of those who needed a bit of a hand up and she had done it without the need of praise or recognition. She was as proud of her as a mother could be but Mary Kate would never know.

Agnes put the last of her clothes into the case and walked across to the window. She was smiling as she thought of darling Freddie. He was one of life's gentlemen, who wanted nothing more than the company of another human being and that is what he had paid for. He was just a lonely old man who'd wanted someone to talk to.

Over the years they had become friends and Agnes found herself looking forward to his visits. Freddie never arrived empty-handed, he would bring flowers for herself and boxes of chocolates for the girls. They all grew very fond of this lovely, gentle man who treated them with a respect they weren't used to.

The funny thing was that he knew more about her life than she knew about his. He never judged her, he just let her talk. They were like two ould ones, sitting by the fire, drinking cups of tea and putting the world to rights. When a couple of months passed with no sign of him, Agnes feared the worst. Her fears were confirmed when she had a letter from her solicitor, informing her that Freddie or, as it turned out, the Honourable Frederick Cashel Fitzgerald, had passed away and left his entire estate to his dear friend Agnes Ryan, known to all who loved her as Dolly Mason.

Agnes left her case on the bed and walked downstairs but

she didn't return to the sitting room. Instead, she went into the garden and sat on a bench. A warm breeze touched her cheek and lifted the hair on the back of her neck. The scent of the roses that trailed over the stone wall reminded her of the little cottage in Tanners Row. Oh, to go back, to be a better version of herself than the selfish girl she had been. To start again, to make her parents proud. But she'd left it too late, she'd left everything too late. Then she noticed the gate, partly hidden beside a large tree. Maybe it would be better if she just slipped through that gate and disappeared into the streets of Dublin. No one would care, in fact they would probably be relieved. She was going to be thrown out anyway, at least this way she would have a bit of dignity left.

She had achieved what she had set out to do. Her daughter was happy and she was loved, what could she give her that she didn't already have? But then she remembered Freddie's words.

'It's never too late to put things right, my friend. Make your peace with your daughter.'

'But what can I offer her, Freddie?' she'd said.

'Yourself, Dolly Mason. Yourself is enough.'

'OK, Freddie,' she said out loud. 'But if it all goes wrong, I shall be giving you an earful when we meet again.'

Mary Kate had left Erin in floods of tears after they had all hugged and said sorry and hugged some more. It was going to be all right, they were her dear friends and nothing was ever going to change that. Whatever they had done had been with her best interests at heart. She knew the core of them and the core of them was pure gold.

Now she was standing at the back door, staring across the garden at her mother. *Mother*. She tried to get her head around the word. Had she been a child she would have been calling her

Mammy. But she wasn't a child and the woman sitting on the bench had hardly been a mother, let alone a mammy.

Mary Kate walked across and sat beside her. Neither of them spoke but somehow it didn't feel awkward; there was so much to say but it would take a lifetime to say it in and so they sat with their thoughts that were louder than any words could be.

Mary Kate wasn't angry any more, she felt at peace. There was a tiny space between them on the bench and yet to cross that space was going to be the longest journey she would ever take.

Mary Kate reached across and took her mother's hand in hers. It felt familiar, as if she had held this hand before. They smiled at each other and there was so much hope in that smile, then together, they walked across the lawn and into the boarding house with the red door.

EPILOGUE

SOME YEARS LATER

Mary Kate

I stood in our little cottage garden, watching the last of the sun slowly sinking behind the Wicklow hills. The sky was awash with colour, pinks and oranges, reds and golds, as if the hand of God had taken a paintbrush and smeared it across the heavens, setting it on fire with colour. I felt blessed to be standing here amid such beauty and I had no right to be asking for more, but oh, how I wished my mother was beside me, to share just one more memory.

My mother was funny and more worldly than I would ever be. We laughed together about silly things. She told me about Freddie and her life in Soho and I shared with her my memories of growing up in Tanners Row and how her parents had never forgotten her or blamed her for leaving, they had spoken only of her beauty and of how much they loved her.

We had grown to like each other and out of liking had come respect and out of respect had grown love. A love that reached into the very corners of my heart, healing the broken bits as if they had never existed.

Our most precious moments were at night, when the house was silent and there was just the two of us. I would lie beside her and read to her until she fell asleep. In her last days I would just hold her. My mother slipped peacefully away in my arms as dawn broke over Merrion Square and a light went out of my life.

We buried her in the grounds of Saint Kevin's church in Glendalough and on a perfect spring day that is also where Sean and I said our vows and became husband and wife. We were surrounded by our friends and I thought myself the luckiest, happiest girl in the world.

Three years ago I said goodbye to my beautiful boarding house and gave Moira her home back. It was now children who ran through the red door as Moira had turned it into a school. She adopted Abby but only on the condition that Abby kept her name. 'I'm Abby Boniface,' she'd said, 'and that is my name and I don't want another.' Moira, bless her, changed her name to Boniface to please the little girl. We held a party on the day of the adoption and Mrs Lamb spent the whole afternoon crying.

Our little family was moving on. Orla was happily working behind the glass counter at Clerys and in love with a fine boy called Donal. Polly had grown tired of Dublin and so I bought her the little white cottage on the ferry point that she had always dreamed of. As for Jessie, her and Aishling owned a bookshop and they took care of Jessie's father until he died. Mrs Lamb and Eliza were cooking school meals and loving it, and Colleen and Ashar were planning their wedding.

Darling Guinness remained with Abby and although that was hard, I felt it was where he belonged.

If success was judged by the people I loved and who loved me, then my life had indeed been a success.

As I stood there in the garden, watching the last of the sun disappearing behind the hills, I heard Sean calling my name. I turned around and walked back to the cottage and into the arms of the man I loved.

A LETTER FROM SANDY

Dear reader,

I want to say a huge thank you for choosing to read *The Irish Boarding House*. If you did enjoy it, and want to keep up-to-date with all my latest releases, just sign up at the following link. Your email address will never be shared and you can unsubscribe at any time.

www.bookouture.com/sandy-taylor

Thank you so much for choosing to read my new book. I do hope that you enjoyed Mary Kate's story. I really enjoyed writing it. I would like to thank all my readers, bloggers and reviewers, including Linda Fetzer Boyer, Lola Ostrofsky, Jenny Nelson and Patti, to name but a few. Thank you all for your continued loyalty, it means so much. I love hearing from you and I will always respond to your lovely messages, you really are the best and I appreciate you all.

I hope you loved *The Irish Boarding House* and if you did, I would be very grateful if you could write a review. I'd love to hear what you think, and it makes such a difference helping new readers to discover one of my books for the first time.

Thank you again,

Sandy x

KEEP IN TOUCH WITH SANDY

facebook.com/SandyTaylorAuthor

twitter.com/SandyTaylorAuth

ACKNOWLEDGEMENTS

There have been so many people who have walked beside me on this writing journey of mine. There have been times when the path I travelled got a bit overgrown and I nearly lost my way but you were always there, urging me on and supporting me.

I would like to thank my beautiful, slightly bonkers family. Kate, Iain, Millie, Archie and Emma, and not forgetting our special little dogs, Peppa and Beau. I love you all so much and I don't know what I would do without you.

Thank you to the wonderful team that is Bookouture, who have always gone the extra mile and always been there if I have needed you with your encouragement and kindness. You are more than just a publisher, you have become a family. My thanks to Claire Bord, Natasha Harding, Kim Nash, Alexandra Holmes and Lauren Finger. It has truly been a joy working with you all.

Thanks to my brothers and sisters. Mag, Paddy, Marge and John and my extended family in Ireland, and a special hello to Clive with lots of love.

The Beatles were spot on in their song 'With a Little Help from My Friends'. Thank you, Sue, Miranda, Becky, Phil, Julie B., Maggie, Wenny, Louie, Lis, Angela, Izzy and Lesley. To the cabana girls, Jan, Julie, Irene, Jane, Sue B. and Suechenie, what fun we have had over the years and what wonderful friends you have always been. I am indeed a lucky girl. (Well, 'girl' is pushing it a bit!)

Emily, my beautiful and amazing editor, thank you for everything you have done for me.

And last but not least, Kate Hordern, my beautiful friend and agent. The sun was shining the day I met you. You are one special lady. Thank you so much.

Remembering my darling son Bo and my dear friend Linda, you are missed every day.